Status of Women
in
Islam

Status of Women

in

Islam

by

Dr. Muniruddin Qureshi

Reference Press

4831/24, Ansari Road,
Darya Ganj,
New Delhi -110002.
Phone:23 26 0807
Fax:23 27 4173
E-mail: essess@del3.vsnl.net.in

First Published, 2003

ISBN : 81-88583-19-7

Price Rs.750/-

Published by:
Reference Press
4831/24, Ansari Road,
Darya Ganj,
New Delhi -110002.
Phone:23 26 0807
Fax:23 27 4173
E-mail: essess@del3.vsnl.net.in

Printed in India at:
Printline, New Delhi.

Contents

Part Five - Practical Life

Preface

Islam, as a faith and philosophy and way of life, was the first religion in the world to grant a respectable status to women, at par with men. It bestowed equal property rights to women — again a first. It issued clear instructions for women to obtain education and create a niche for them in society.

Under Islam, there is no discrimination for women in any area, be it household matters, social affairs, academic disciplines or even inheritance of property and the marital affairs. Under Islam, a woman enjoys the right to solicit, reject and even abandon her husband as per her choice — a hard fact, which is lesser known.

Islam is not a rigid framework of laws and institutions, but a set of principles, capable of fresh applications in changing social conditions. The Western orientalists have projected the faith in a bad light. In particular, the position of women under Islam has been the subject of repeated controversy among educated Muslims — not to talk of non-Muslims — ever since, they came under the impact of Western civilization. It is still a live issue, capable of generating much heat and passion In fact, the rights of women versus those of men spring from sexual, biological and social realities, not from romantic idealism but in accordance with scientific facts. Similarly, the attitude of any civilization towards women is largely determined by its total pattern of life and particularly by the view, it takes of sex-life in all its manifold manifestations. As far as family life and the marital life is concerned, Islam had anticipated centuries ago, much of what the modern scholars have learnt only recently.

Today, women lib and gender equality are very much in vogue. Needless to say that these are new concepts in the West — hardly a century old. But, a few people may know that Islam had pioneered in putting gender equality and gender justice in practice and it had accorded equal rights to women, fifteen centuries back, when Europe was still living in a dark age; not even accepting the womenfolk as human beings.

The dearth of good books on the subject inspired and motivated the undersigned to work on the subject: 'Status of Women in Islam'; one of the most controversial issues, inviting heated debates. Hence, this modest effort, in order to produce a comprehensive exhaustive, authentic and exclusive study on the subject, in an objective and unbiased manner.

This humble study is a step in the direction of eradicating misunderstanding and correcting the wrongs in prevalence. Hopefully, this effort would be successful in filling the vacuum for an authentic work, with an academic, scholarly and highly empirical approach. This work has taken a toll of years and a lot of energy, as it involved painstaking research and thoughtful analysis. The Author would feel pride and take it as an honour, if this effort is received warmly in academic circles and acknowledged as a genuine work.

Author

Part - One

General

One

Introduction

Islamic attitude towards life has been defined by the Holy Qur'an in the following verses:

> Blessed is He in Whose hands is the kingdom and He has power over all things, Who created Death and Life-that He may try you-which of you is best in conduct.
>
> And He it is Who created the heavens and the earth in six days and His throne was on water that He may try you - which of you is best in conduct.
>
> Lo! He produceth creation, then reproduceth it that He may with justice recompense those who believe and do good works.

Life, for the individual, according to the above verses is an opportunity, provided by nature, to bring out the best and most spiritual in him by being placed within a network of human relationships which constantly put him on trial in respect of his social sympathies and sense of justice towards his fellow-men. The purpose of life, therefore, is the spiritual betterment of man. Nature secures this cud by placing individuals in a social situation where they may develop their altruistic self and restrain their egoistic desires. The response of the individual to the requirements of this situation is a measure of his spiritual progress and an index of his success or failure in the trial spoken of by the Holy Qur'an.

It is clear from the verses quoted above that Islam does not judge civilisation by its mechanical efficiency, technical progress or productive capacity. A society may achieve phenomenal success in any or all of these aspects and still remain spiritually bankrupt, if in the distribution of material wealth and the products of technical development, it betrays an insufficient regard for social justice and human equality. On the other hand, there may be civilisations lacking in material productivity, yet marked by a high sense of fellow-feeling and greater regard for human values. The test of a civilisation, from the Quranic viewpoint, lies in the harmony of relations between its component parts, whether horizontally as affecting the different national groups which inhabit its sphere of influence or vertically as, reflected in the mutual attitude of the different economic classes whose total productive efforts sustain its material existence. That is the meaning of the Quranic statement that 'God created Death and Life in order to try which, of you is best in conduct.' The primary value of civilisation, according to this attitude, lies in the moral conduct of its individuals as reflected in their beliefs, institutions and class and sex relations, etc. Here, and not in its mechanical development and technical efficiency, should be sought the criterion of its success or failure.

That social conduct in its various manifestations is the main concern of the religious spirit, has been further emphasised by the Holy Qur'an in the following verses:

> The love of desires, of women and sons and hoarded treasures of gold and silver and well-bred horses and cattle and tilth is made to seem fair to men: this is the, provision of the life of the lower level, and Allah is He with Whom is the higher goal (of life).
>
> Say: Shall I tell you of what, is better than these? For those who guard (against evil) are Gardens with their Lord, beneath which rivers flow, to abide in them, and pure mates and Allah's pleasure: add Allah sees His servants.

> Those who say: Our Lord! surely we believe, therefore forgive us our faults and keep us from the chastisement of fire.
>
> The patient and the truthful, and the obedient, and those who spend (benevolently) - and those who ask for forgiveness in the morning times (iii. 13-16).

Here the Holy Qur'an presents two alternative ways of life. First, the-lower way, which is distinguished by the predominance of acquisitive desires, the love of sexual pleasure, the pride of family, wealth and other kinds of material acquisitions and, secondly, the life of creative social sympathies marked by the pursuit of higher ideals which call forth our powers of patience, philanthropy, and remind us of our duties to our fellow-men. The Holy Qur'an declares its preference for this latter way of life and holds out the prospect of a rich reward for those who follow it. Here again Islam emphasises, social values other than those which lead merely to greater abundance; of material goods without in any way ennobling and harmonising human relations.

Further evidence of this attitude towards human social existence is provided by the following statement:

> Permission (to fight) is given to those upon whom war is made, because they are oppressed ... those who have been expelled from their homes without a just cause ... those who, should We establish them in the land, will keep up prayer and pay the poor-due and enjoin good and forbid evil. (xxii. 39-40)

The Holy Qur'an describes here the distinctive qualities of a, party which comes into power as the result of a successful struggle against the forces of evil. What is significant is that we miss here any emphasis on purely physical valour, military preparedness, technical efficiency and mechanical skill — qualities which, by any test of fitness, are necessary for those who wish to come out successful in a military struggle. Instead, the virtues recommended by the Holy Qur'an are those which tend to, harmonise and ennoble human relations-deference to the claims of the downtrodden, humility in a state of power and success manifested in efforts to establish prayers, and an active desire to stamp out evil and injustice in all forms, at reforming zeal to encourage virtuous behaviour leading towards improved human relations. For a group engaged in a life-and-death struggle for survival, these qualities seem rather inappropriate, since a state of struggle calls for just the opposite qualities of physical valour, mechanical efficiency and technical superiority. The only explanation for this seeming paradox is that, according to the Holy Qur'an, the latter virtues are the necessary but secondary products of a struggle whose inspiration comes exclusively from a spiritual vision of life. The main object of human existence is the continuing improvement of human relationships. But this object requires for its successful accomplishment the secondary qualities of material strength and mechanical efficiency, etc. A civilisation which inverts this natural order and sets up material progress and technical skill, etc., as ends in themselves runs the grave risk of disintegration from within by social conflicts arising from the deteriorating relations of its component parts.

In passing judgment on Islamic teachings with regard to sex relations and the ideal of sex equality, it is necessary to keep in mind this aspect of the matter. As against Western civilisation which regards the abundance of material wealth, technical skill and mechanical efficiency as of primary importance and which subordinates, as of instrumental value and secondary importance, the ideal of social justice and other spiritual values. Islam puts primary emphasis on just those qualities of the soul which lead to greater social harmony and prevent class conflicts. Material wealth and the human qualities which tend to increase it are not belittled by Islam. They are allowed only a rank of secondary importance. This difference in the two systems of values alters the perspective in which human and social problems are tackled respectively by Islam and Western civilisation. Islamic civilisation stands midway between ancient ascetic cultures, which negated life and matter and looked upon the things of this world as having a soul-degrading effect, and the materialistic culture of the modern West, which has turned material wealth and economic prosperity into objects of idolatrous worship. From the Islamic viewpoint, economic wealth and the qualities which help its furtherance are good only in so far as they subserve spiritual interests and make for greater social harmony. When raised to the level of primary importance, they become the agents of the devil.

Equal Rights

As far as legal and property rights and facilities for divorce are concerned, Islam has given equal rights to the members of the female sex. Many of the rights conferred on women by the Prophet of Islam fourteen hundred years ago have only partially and grudgingly been given to them in Western and Eastern countries during the course of the last two centuries. Similarly, with respect to sex equality, the mental human dignity and fundamental equality of women, Islam is at one with the leaders of the feminist movement. But as the application of an abstract principle is qualified and conditioned by social realities and concrete situations, Islam has modified its stand on sex equality in consonance with social, biological and sex realities. What the modern women and particularly those of Pakistan, who are trying to ape foreign customs and manners, are likely to find objectionable in Islam are not the legal, economic and social rights it has conferred on them, for on this score they can hardly have any genuine grievance, but the few social and family duties and some slight restrictions on dress, speech and movement which have been prescribed for them in order to regulate sex and social behaviour. Untrammelled freedom amounting to license is self-stultifying and soon negates itself. Many of the checks devised by Islam to limit male and female freedom in regard to dress, speech and movement spring from biological and sexual facts which can be ignored only at a peril. Sexual misconduct is justly abhorred and condemned by Islam as the source of innumerable social evils. It is to prevent such misconduct that a few restrictions have been placed both on men and women. If men have been more easily let off and fewer restrictions have been placed on them, it is because they have to bear the main burden of economic responsibility and their economic activities demand greater freedom of movement. Even in advanced countries where women have come forward to earn their own living, legal responsibility for the maintenance of the family still rests with men. No doubt, a social system may be developed in which the husband and the wife equally share the responsibility of providing economic sustenance to the family. But this is still a remote possibility. Apart from this, any arrangement whereby women are forced to share in an equal measure the economic responsibility of winning the bread for the family is really an infringement of the principle of equality, because men cannot equally share with them the responsibility of motherhood. So under a system which places equal economic burden on women, the latter will be at a serious disadvantage. They will have to shoulder heavier burdens without the accession of additional rights. This will not lead to equality but to gross and palpable inequality. Even if it is maintained that the female sex is capable of shouldering the additional economic burden side by side with the responsibilities of motherhood, which is not at all true, there is a strong probability that the interests of children, under such a social system, will suffer to such a degree as to make them materially and spiritually ill-equipped and ill-fitted for the duties of life. Besides, a vast army of female competitors will be thrown into the economic field with all its attendant social consequences, many of them undesirable. Indiscriminate intermixture of men and women is sure to provide greater opportunities for sexual irregularities resulting in the weakening of family ties and a further deterioration in the social and educational condition of children arising from diminished interest in domestic life and its everyday affairs.

There are people who maintain that sexual misconduct is not of much consequence in social existence and the sexual immorality need not necessarily lead to all-round moral deterioration. This is not the view of Islam which attaches great importance to sexual purity. People who hold the former view overlook the interpenetration of habits in social life and the constant interaction between different aspects of social morality. It is not true, as many people imagine, that there is a separate sex morality, a separate trade morality and another political morality. All morality is a single, unified whole with its manifold aspects which interact with and interpenetrate each other. A man of loose conduct may not be initially dishonest in politics or commerce. But his habits and mode of life as shaped by his sexual conduct are bound, sooner or later, to affect his outlook and behaviour in other spheres of activity. Morality is really the product of one's way of life. If you adopt a wrong way of life, if you fall a victim to sexual lust, economic greed or love of political power, you cannot but trespass, in one way or the other, on the rights of others in order to satisfy your inordinate desires. It is just possible, that a man who is guilty of sexual misconduct, once or twice in his early life, or without deliberately planning sexual enjoyment, falls off and is a victim to sexual temptation, may otherwise maintain his moral purity. But there is no guarantee that he who succumbs to temptation once will not be dragged by his weakness on the road to repeated and permanent misbehaviour. One act of sin leads easily to another just as one act of virtue prepares the way for further virtuous behaviour. It is the peculiar nature of moral acts that they set in a train of reactions on the agent which makes it easier for him to repeat his conduct and predispose him towards similar acts. Those who desire to condone sexual irregularities have really no idea of the wide ramifications of sex in everyday life. A man of loose sexual morality cannot be expected to devote the same care and attention to his wife and children as another whose sex morality remains unvitiated. He has to spend more and more on his pleasures and the ever-increasing demands of his paramours. To that extent he is likely to injure the economic rights of his wife and children. If he still remains just to his family and attempts to give his wife and children their due, he will be forced to adopt undesirable and unlawful methods for adding to his income in order to meet the growing expenditure caused by his extra-marital sexual relations. This means that he has avoided injustice to his family by doing injustice to society. This is particularly true of men with limited incomes who form the vast majority of population in every country. It may be said that the rich can afford to indulge in sexual irregularities without causing economic injustice. But this is not true. All moral diseases are contagious. People in the lower strata of society often follow the social pattern set by the upper classes. If the higher classes in a nation are morally corrupt and sexually immoral, the whole nation becomes corrupted sooner or later. All these facts are overlooked by people who look upon sexual misconduct as a mere foible which should not call forth more than ordinary condemnation. Islam is right in unreservedly and severely condemning sexual misbehaviour and taking precautionary measures against its general prevalence. These measures certainly entail a few restrictions on men and women but they are necessary for the moral, sexual and physical health of the community. It is true, of course, that when once the moral outlook of an individual, male or female, has become spoiled, no amount of restrictions can prevent him or her from committing sexual immorality. But this is a matter which concerns moral and religious education and the moulding of beliefs. Islam has not ignored this vital aspect of the matter. It lays greater emphasis on moral and spiritual reformation than on legal or preventive measures. But this does not mean that the legal and social aspects of the matter are of no consequence and the preventive measures taken by Islam are necessary. A government does not abolish its laws about theft, robbery, forgery or black marketing on the ground that, unless the moral outlook of the community improves, these laws by themselves are insufficient to hold in check the miscreants. A healthy society makes simultaneous use of moral and legal sanctions to maintain its standards of integrity. Both are equally necessary, but the primary importance must be attached to moral sanctions. It is the moral and spiritual outlook of individuals that determines their social conduct and this, again, is the product of their educational environment. Without maintaining that the preventive and precautionary measures taken by Islam to regulate sex morality are necessary, we do hold that the task of moral and spiritual reformation is more primary and fundamental.

What the Muslim women in several Muslim countries lack is not any rights but the consciousness of their rights. They are depressed, they are ignorant and they have been placed under many fetters. of custom and artificial tradition not sanctioned by Islam. If they receive proper Islamic education, become conscious of their rights as well as their duties, they can easily break their chains. At present being ignorant of Islamic teachings, they think that the traditions and customs they have been forced to observe are the art of Islamic teachings. Education (proper education) is their dire and essential need. But education for the majority of women involves economic considerations. The common women cannot be educated unless there is a general economic uplift and every woman is made secure against the daily cares and anxieties of life. Muslim women who have come forward as champions of sex equality and demand equal rights with men would do well to bear this aspect of the matter in mind. To imagine that you can raise the social status of women and release them from the fetters of artificial customs and traditions without making education so cheap as to enable every member of the female sex to enjoy access to educational institutions is to live in a dreamland. Unless the champions of female liberty undertake an organised effort to make female education cheaper and more widespread so as to bring its benefits within easy reach of the poorest woman, the common people will continue to doubt their sincerity. What the common mind feels at present is that the women's movement does not spring from genuine altruistic motives or from a real desire for social and national reformation but from a desire to throw off all restraints, some of which are necessary and salutary, in order that a few fortunate women may be able to enjoy a life of luxurious self-indulgence without inviting social opprobrium. More and more of fashion, more and more of luxury, distinguishes those of our women who have stepped out into the threshold of public life and demand equality of rights with men. Material acquisitiveness and pleasure-seeking, not service and social work, seem to be their motto. Their insistence on teaching fashionable arts like music and dancing to the exclusion of useful domestic arts and religious or political instruction is disliked by the people in general. As leaders of the feminine movement, it was their duty to teach by instruction and example the virtues of plain living, economy, frugality, and national self-sacrifice for wider social objectives. Proper and scientific education of children and observance of hygienic principles in domestic life, not dancing and fashionable arts, should have been the object of their attention. If they are really sincere in their desire to raise the social status of women, let them devote themselves to those fundamental requirements. Let them demand and press for social security measures for women designed to ensure free education for the poorest members of their sex; then and then alone shall they be held in true respect and become truly representative of the common urge for social and educational uplift and their empowerment.

Two

Reforms First

In a soceity, there are certain principles which are to be followed by the individuals. No society can allow the opposition or rejection of the principles, because the non-compliance amounts to rebellion against the society. If any society gives up these principles or fails to enforce them, it will disintegrate.

The Islamic society has its own principles which must be followed by the Muslims. The requirements of these principles are explained by the Holy Quran at various places. At one place it says :

> "O mankind ! Be careful of your duty to your Lord who created you from a single soul and from it created its mate and from them twain hath spread abroad a multitude of men and women. Be careful of your duty toward Allah in Whom ye claim (your rights) of one another, and toward the wombs (that base you).
>
> Lo ! Allah hath been a Watcher over you." (4 : 1)
>
> "O Prophet, when believing women come to thee to take oath of fidelity, that they will not associate in worship any other thing whatever, with Allah, that they will not resort to stealing, that they will not commit fornication, that they will not kill their children, that they will

> not utter slanders intentionally forging falsehood, and that they will not disobey thee in any Just matter, then -do thou receive their fidelity, and pray to Allah for the forgiveness (of their sins) for Allah is Oft-forgiving, Most Merciful."
>
> (60 : 12)

The principles are meant for the women because, when the Islamic society was developing in Madina, the Islamic State had entered into a treaty with the people of Mecca, on account of certain diplomatic considerations, undertaking not to give shelter to any of the Quraish against their wish. The Muslims could afford asylum to only such women who wanted it. In this background, the Holy Quran has explained the conditions to be followed by a woman in order to become a part of the Islamic society. However, the Muslim men are no exception to these rules. Hazrat Ubada-bin-Samit (R.A.A.) says:

> "The Holy Prophet (S.A.W.) had taken oath from us similar to those of women, that we must not believe in plurality of God, nor steal, nor commit adultery, nor commit infanticide, nor blame each other."
>
> (Muslim)

This statement of oath clearly explains the concept of Islamic society. It also explains the aims and objects of Islam in respect of the human society. There is no place for the people other than those who are good and virtuous. It is but natural that a good society cannot permit unhealthy environment within itself.

The Quran says:

> "We also sent Lot. He said to His people; Do ye commit lewdness such as no people have so far committed before you? For ye practise your lusts on men in preference to women :

> Ye are indeed a people transgressing beyond bounds. And his people gave no answer but this : They said, -Drive them out of your city : These are indeed men who want to be clean and pure." (7 : 80-82)

If a man thinks that evil practices are destructive to the mankind, he has to change the present criminal environment and make the society free from evil.

One of the most important facts is that though there are rules in all societies for the prevention of evil, the failure of implementation is seen everywhere. It is not possible to have a good society unless the laws are strictly implemented and followed.

The distinct characteristics of Islam is that it creates a refined society. It becomes incumbent upon every Muslim to follow the principles of Islam strictly in order to make his own life safe and respectable. It is not possible to lead a peaceful and respectable life without adhering to the principles prescribed by the Shariah.

Force of Ideology

For the enforcement of an ideology, a society must have three powers : The force of ideology, the force of collective thinking and feeling and the force of law. The force of Islamic ideology is the only capable force to wipe out the evil from the surface of the earth and establish a pious society all over the world. The other ideologies have failed because they are man-made and devoid of Natural laws. The world has tried all possible laws made by man and achieved nothing. On the contrary there prevails disturbance and uneasiness. Therefore, the world has no other alternative but to adopt Islamic laws for the peace and good of mankind.

The man-made laws demand the obedience to the man in authority. Therefore, the people easily ignore these laws and indulge in evil practices. Besides, these laws fail to punish and change the offenders. Whereas, the laws of Islam demand the obedience to Allah, the Creator of all. It is the fear of Allah that keeps man away from the evil practices. The man, who loves Allah, would never like to displease Almighty Allah. The Holy Quran says:

> "Eschew all sins, open or secret : Those who earn sin will get due recompense for their Earnings." (6 : 120)

At other place, the Holy Quran says :

> "Say : the things that my Lord hath indeed forbidden are shameful deeds, whether open or secret." (7 : 33)

Islam does not permit any kind of evil under any circumstances. Moreover, the Islamic law cannot be changed by man because he has no authority to do so. Islam disbands the jungle law and enforces the law of Islamic Shariah for the establishment of good and refined society. Islam makes the man and the woman morally high and cultured.

It is a fact that woman can live honourably and peacefully only if the society is good, and good society is possible only- if its members are good. Suleman bin Baridah (R.A.A.) relates from his father that the Holy Prophet (S.A.W.) has said

> "Those men who do not go to the battlefield for Jihad and remain at home, for them the wives of the Mujahideen are as respectable as their own mothers. If a man from amongst the people who have stayed at home happens to be the custodian of a Mujahid and if he misappropriates, he shall be brought before the Mujahideen on the Day of Judgment and he would take away as much good deeds from him as he would like. Just imagine, what would be the condition of that culprit."
> (Muslim, Abu Dawood)

Zaid-bin-Khalid (R.A.A.) relates that the Holy Prophet (S.A.W.) said

> "A man who provided arms to a Mujahid, he got the reward of Jihad. And the man who looked after the family of the Mujahid, too earned the reward of Jihad." (Bukhari, Muslim)

Moral Values

Undoubtedly, the society which is based on such lofty ideals and piety, gives prime importance to moral values. Such a society is the noblest in the world. The men and the women of such a society bear high moral character, and such is the Muslim society. The moral values help men and women to ward off evil and lead virtuous life. In this Islamic society, the individuals respect each other and never become hurdle in any way. The man, who possesses high moral character, is an asset for the society because he not only himself remains good but also helps in the prevention of evils in the society. He has great regard, specially, for the women. The moral values also make the human conscience strong.

> "Who so obeyeth Allah and His Messenger, He will make him enter gardens underneath which rivers flow, where such will dwell for ever. That will be the great success."(4: 13)

> "And who so disobeyeth Allah and His Messenger, and transgresseth His limits, He will make him enter Fire, where such will dwell for ever; his will be a shameful doom." (4 : 14)

Imam Ibne Taimiyah (R.A.) says:

> "If a person is forced to commit fornication, It is incumbent upon him or her to resist. If the attacker runs away, then it is well and good. If not, then the attacker's life can be taken which is in accordance with the

> unanimous view of the jurists."(Mukhtarat-e-Islamiyah)

Islam considers it a human right to protect one's honour. Therefore, it gives no authority to any person to violate the chastity of any woman or dishonour her. It also forbids false accusation against a woman. The Holy Quran says:

> "And those who level false allegation of adultery against a chaste woman and fail to produce four witnesses (to support their allegation), flog them with eighty stripes and reject their evidence for ever, for such men are wicked transgressors." (24 : 4)

On the one hand, Islam considers it unlawful to falsely defame an innocent woman; this is done in order to enable her to live honourably. On the other hand, Islam condemns the wicked people specially bad characters. Such bad characters are not accorded a decent position in Islamic society as that of virtuous men and women. They always lead disgraceful life. Only the western society harbours such ruffians but there is no place for them in the Islamic society. In fact, a bad character cannot survive in Islamic society. As the Holy Quran says:

> "Let no man guilty of, adultery or fornication marry any but a woman similarly guilty, or an unbeliever. Nor let any but such a man or an unbeliever marry such a woman. To the believers such a thing is forbidden." (24 : 3)

> Hazrat Abu Hurairah and Zaid-bin-Khalid (R.A.A.) relate that the Holy Prophet (S.A.W.) was asked what should be done with an unmarried slave-girl who commits adultery? The Holy Prophet (S.A.W.) replied, "If she commits adultery, she must be lashed, if she commits adultery again, then lash her again;

and if she still commits adultery then lash her and then sell her off even at the cost of a rope." (Bukhari)

Celibacy Forbidden

In Islam there is no place for celibacy. If a person is poor, it is the duty of the other well-to-do Muslims to help that person to get married. This is the only way to save that person from immorality and enable him or her to lead a respectable life in the society. According to the Holy Quran it is the natural right of the person.

> "Marry those among you who are single, or the virtuous ones among your slaves, male or female." (24: 32)

The demand of this verse is that no one should remain unmarried in the Islamic society so that the sexual desire may not lead one to unlawful means. This command applies to all Muslim men and women whether free or slave. The Islamic Society of the early era made all necessary arrangements for the marriage of deserving persons to fulfil the conditions of the Shariah.

> A well-known 'Tabie or companion of the companions, Ahnaf (R.A.) says that there are three matters which cannot be delayed. When he was asked to name those matters, he said, "The performance of good deed, the burial of the dead and the marriage of a virgin." He has also said, "He would prefer to have the presence of a python in a corner of his house than to refuse the proposal of marriage from a man of equal age for an unmarried girl."
> (Al Bayan Wat Tibiyan)

> Shaddad bin Aus (R.A.A.) said to his relatives, "Make the arrangement for my marriage because the Holy Prophet (S.A.W.) has advised

me not to meet my Allah without marriage."
(Al Ahkam-ul-Quran)

Mujahid (R.A.) relates that Abdullah bin Abbas (R.A.A.) used to tell his slaves, "If Any one of you wants to marry, I can arrange. Remember, there is a possibility of indulgence in adultery if you remain celibate. And Allah takes away the faith (Iman) from the man who commits adultery. Then it is left to Allah whether to return the faith to him or not."
(Al Muhalla Ibn Haim)

Imam Nakhayee says, "The masters used to force their slaves to marry and if they refused, they were locked in the houses."
(Tafseer Qurtubi)

They were locked up so that they may not be the cause of evil in the society. It is not only an individual who is responsible in the society but it is also the duty of the state to make the necessary arrangement for marriage of the people who cannot afford.

The Holy Prophet (S.A.W.) has said

"The ruler of the time is the guardian of the woman who is helpless." (Tirmizi, Abu Dammed)

The Holy Prophet (S.A.W.) had asked Hazrat Ali to remember three things:

"Offer the prayers in time; if somebody dies, do not delay the burial; and if an unmarried person finds a suitable match then arrange the marriage immediately." (Tirmizi)

In reply to the Governor of Koofa Zaid-bin-Abdur Rehman, Hazrat 'Umar-bin-Abdul Aziz (R.A.) says, "You have written that there is surplus money even after paying the salaries to the army.

Then pay the debts of the debtors and the amount of the dower of those who are unable to pay. (Seerat Umar bin Abdul Aziz)

Sexual feelings exist in a man upto a certain period of the age but the life of woman repeatedly passes through such stages when her emotions become weak and sometimes this state continues for a long period; therefore she cannot adequately fulfil the sexual demands of her husband. It is for this reason, Islam has allowed man to marry four wives. Thus, Islam prevents him from going astray. However, if he has four wives at a time, he has to do justice and treat them equally because the Holy Quran says:

> "Marry women of your choice, two or three or four, but if ye fear that ye shall not be able to deal justly (with them), then only one, or a captive." (4 : 3)
>
> "Ye will not be able to deal equally between (your) wives, however much ye wish (to do so). But turn not altogether away (from one), leaving her as in suspense." (4 : 129)

Thus it is crystal clear that Islam grants a conditional permission to marry upto four wives and not a licence. Islam is the natural religion hence the Quranic injunctions are also based on human nature.

The Holy Quran claims:

> "O ye who believe ! Be ye staunch in justice, witnesses for Allah, even though it be against yourselves or (your) parents or (your) kindred, whether (the case be of) a rich man or a poor man, for Allah is nearer unto both (than ye are). So follow not passion lest ye lapse (from truth) and if he lapse or fall away, then to Allah is ever informed of what ye do."
>
> (4 : 135)

The Holy Prophet (S.A.W.) remarks,

> "When a man has two wives and he does not observe equality and deal unjustly with them, he will come before the Throne of Justice of Allah with only half of his body." (Bukhari)

Allama Ibn Ilham Hanafi has explained the legality of this verse in these words :

> "This proves that a man can marry four wives only if there is no fear of injustice to them and if there is a fear, then no more than one wife is allowed. It is clear that in case of more than one wife, justice is essential."
>
> (Fathul Qadeer)

Allama Badruddin Kashani remarks :

> "If a husband has two wives or two captives, then it is essential for him to maintain equality and justice between them as regards clothes, house and passing of the nights."
>
> (Al Badae-was-Sanai)

The physical conditions of the woman are different from those of the man. Therefore, Islam also enjoins strictly the marriage of the woman. And the stress is the same as that of the man. However, Islam does not permit the plurality of husbands for the woman, but has made the provision for the continuity of her conjugal life. It never deprives her of her legitimate right of sexual satisfaction. In case she is separated from her husband owing to his death or divorce, Islam lays stress upon her second marriage after the passage of the requisite period of 'iddat'. The History of Islam shows that the second marriage of the women was performed very easily during the period of the Holy Prophet (S.A.W.) and the Khulafa-i-Rashideen (R.A.A.).

'Aatika-bint-Zaid was married to Hazrat Abu Bakr's (R.A.A.)

son, Abdullah. Due to some reasons, Hazrat Abu Bakr (R.A.A.) advised his son to divorce his wife. Though, Abdullah divorced his wife to please his father but he was very sad because he loved her very much. When Hazrat Abu Bakr came to know of this fact, he gave his son permission to re-marry her. After the second marriage, Abdullah was martyred in the battle of Taif. It is related that Zaid-bin-Khattab married 'Aatika after the martyrdom of her husband. When he was also martyred in the battle of Yamama, Hazrat Umar (R.A.A.) married her. And after Hazrat 'Umar (R.A.A.), Hazrat Zubair (R.A.A.) married her. After his martyrdom, Hazrat Ali (R.A.A.) offered her to marry but she herself refused.

Sohaila-bint-Sohail married four companions of the Holy Prophet (S.A.W.) one after the other. Similarly, Jamila, the daughter of Abdullah-bin-Ubai was married to Hazrat Hanzla (R.A.A.). When he was martyred in the battle of Uhud, Sabit-bin-Qais married her. After him, Malik-bin-Wakhsham married her and after him she was married to Habib-bin-Liaf.

Asma bint Umais's first marriage was solemnized with Jafar (R.A.A.), the brother of Hazrat Ali (R.A.A.). After his death, Hazrat Abu Bakr (R.A.A.) married her. And after the death of Hazrat Abu Bakr (R.A.A.), Hazrat Ali (R.A.A.) married her.

Umme Kulsoom daughter of Hazrat Ali (R.A.A.) was married to Hazrat 'Umar (R.A.A.). When Hazrat 'Umar (R.A.A.) was martyred, Aun-bin-Jafer (R.A.A.) married her. After the death of Aun, his brother Abdullah married her. (Tabaqat, Al Istiyab).

These examples prove that the second marriage of the woman is not a matter of disgrace in Islam. It is done with respect and honour to keep the society clean and good,

Islam permits divorce but not just like that. Not only that it is discouraged but also considered as the most abhorrent act. It is allowed in a situation when it becomes inevitable owing to the danger of violation of the limits prescribed by Allah.

When the lives of the husband and the wife turn into a hell, the

Islamic law would not compel them to bind themselves together for ever. When the confidence between them is shaken, it is better for them to separate.

In case of an extremely difficult situation, the Holy Quran says:

> "As for those who accuse their wives but have no witnesses except themselves; let the testimony of one of them be four testimonies, (swearing) by Allah that he is of those who speak the truth; And yet a fifth, invoking the curse of Allah on him if he is of those who lie. And it shall avert the punishment from her if she bear witness before Allah four times that the things he saith is indeed false. And fifth (time) that the wrath of Allah be upon her if he speaketh truth." (24 : 6-9)

The Holy Quran is the complete code of life. It deals with every aspect of human, life. And divorce is one of the aspects. The law of divorce provides protection to human modesty and chastity.

The aim of marriage in Islam is to enable a person to lead virtuous life and to create healthy environments in the society. The marriage can be successful only if there is harmony between husband and wife. It is also essential that they must be capable to satisfy the sexual need of each other. Islam gives the full right to the spouses to divorce each other in case the other party lacks the capability for proper discharge of sexual functions. Hazrat 'Urnar (R.A.A.), Hazrat Ali (R.A.A.') and other Companions opine that not only the sexual incapability but also the diseases like blindness, leprosy and lunacy are the valid grounds for divorce. However Imam Ibn Qayyim (R.A.) says:

> "It is not enough to rely on Two, Six, Seven or Eight defects and neglect the other major or equal defects. The separation can take place on any ground that creates hatred

> between the spouses and the love is lost which is the sole aim of the marriage."
>
> (Zad-ul-Muad)

On the one hand, Islam emphasises the discontinuation of the conjugal relation, which fails to fulfil the requirement of the marriage and on the other hand, it encourages the spouses to adhere to the bonds of marriage which help in leading a virtuous life. Unless there is love between the spouses and they satisfy the sexual wants of each other, the marriage cannot be successful. Besides, the strained relation leads to evil practices.

The marriage is considered a firm bond in the Islamic society. It is based on the natural wants of a man and a woman. Hence the sanctity of the Nikah cannot be violated under any circumstances. Though, Islam allows divorce but only on solid grounds. The marriage cannot be dissolved on trivial matters. The Holy Prophet (S.A.W.) has said :

> '""The women who seek divorce from their husbands without valid reasons are the hypocrites." (Nasai)

He (S.A.W.) has said on another occasion :

> "The woman who seeks divorce from her husband without any solid ground, even the smell of Heaven is forbidden for her."
>
> (Tirmizi)

Yet on another occasion, the Holy Prophet (S.A.W.) has said:

"He is the greatest sinner before Allah who marries a woman and leaves her after satisfying his sexual desire and also swallows her dower." (Mustadrak Hakim)

It is the duty of an individual and also of the society to respect the lawful marriage.' When the illegitimate relation is condemnable in Islam, the legitimate and lawful relation is respected. It is the duty of the whole society to respect the sanctity of solemn marriage. In

Islam no one is permitted to violate the sanctity of marriage. According to the Holy Quran the married women are forbidden for the other men. The Holy Prophet (S.A.W.) has said :

> "That man is not from amongst us who turns a woman rebellious against her husband or the slave against the master." (Abu Dawood)

Imam Ibn Taimiya (R.A.) has remarked :

> If a man with an intention to marry someone's wife himself or get her married to another man, kills her husband, the law of Islam says that such a man must be deprived of the rights to marry her and it is immaterial whether she herself was involved in the conspiracy or not." (Iqama-tul-Daleel)

Social Responsibility

It is but natural that an individual leaves his or her impressions on the society as a whole. The person of a good moral character leaves good impressions on the society and if the person happens to be of bad character he or she leaves bad influence on the society. Thus, a good person helps in the establishment of a good society and a person of bad character spoils the good society. Therefore, it is not possible to have healthy environment and good society in the world unless every individual realises that it is his or her duty to protect the good character of the society.

Islam creates a sense of duty in an individual and reminds that he or she is the real architect of the good society. Moreover, it is not enough for an individual just to be good but it is also his or her duty to correct and improve others. An individual bearing good moral character plays an important role in the building of a good and healthy environment. Such an individual saves others from the moral degeneration. The Holy Prophet (S.A.W.) says:

> "Listen, everyone of you is a guardian and

> everyone of you shall be questioned about the people. The Caliph who is the ruler of the people is a guardian and he shall be questioned about his subjects. The man is the guardian of the members of his family and he shall be questioned about them. The wife is the guardian of her children and the members of her husband's family, and she shall be questioned about them. The slave is the guardian of his master's wealth and he shall be questioned about it. Listen again; Every one of you is a guardian and everyone of you shall be questioned about the (concerned) people." (Bukhari)

The pressure of the society is always strong. And if it remains strong, no one would dare to disobey its set principles. If overall environment of the society is bad then all sorts of evils would creep in and the situation would go beyond control and the moral values would die.

Islam keeps the sense of morality alive in the society, hence it would not tolerate any kind of immoral act of an individual. Once a woman, who had scented her clothes, was passing through a road. Hazrat Abu Hurairah (R.A.A.) saw her and asked, "Are you coming from the mosque?" She replied "Yes". He further asked, "Have you applied this perfume for going to the mosque?" She replied in affirmation. Then Hazrat Abu Hurairah (R.A.A.) scolded her and said that he has heard his beloved friend the Holy Prophet (S.A.W.) saying:

> "A woman who applies perfume and goes to the mosque, Allah accepts not her prayers unless she takes bath as in case of dirtiness."
> (Abu Dawood)

The Holy Prophet (S.A.W.) saw Umme Darda (R.A.A.) coming from the bath and directed her not to go again. He (S.A.W.) told her:

> "The woman who removes her clothes at the place other than her house, tears the curtain that exists between her and Allah."
>
> (Musnad Ahmad)

According to Islam, it is the duty of man to protect moral values of the people who are socially related to him. This responsibility becomes vital if relation is closer. The chastity of the relative and the woman-neighbour must be protected. Any violation in this respect would amount to unpardonable sin.

> Hazrat Abdullah bin Masood (R.A.A.) says that a man asked the Holy Prophet (S.A.W.), "Which is the greatest sin?" The Holy Prophet (S.A.W.) replied, "The greatest sin is to associate someone with Allah, Who alone created you." He asked, "Which is the lesser sin than this?" The Holy Prophet (S.A.W.) replied, "After that, the greatest sin is to take the life of your baby thinking that it will take away the part of livelihood (and you would starve)." He again asked, "Which is the greatest sin after these two." The Holy Prophet (S.A.W.) replied." The adultery with your neighbour woman (Bukhari, Muslim and Mishkat).

Once the Holy Prophet (S.A.W.) asked one of his companions, "What is your opinion about adultery?" The companion replied, "Allah and his Messenger (S.A.W.) have forbidden adultery and it shall remain forbidden until the Day of Judgment." The Holy Prophet (S.A.W.) said, "The adultery with ten women is lesser sin than the adultery committed with his neighbour's wife." A greater sin is dead.

Three

Preferential Treatment

Islam advocates justice. It has not only determined the rightful position of women, put an end to female infanticide and removed the unfounded fear of poverty by restoring confidence in Allah; but whenever he found an opportunity the Holy Prophet (peace and blessings of Allah be upon him) persuaded the people to show better treatment to their women folk.

The Holy Prophet (peace and blessings of Allah be upon him) said: "He who brought up his girls properly till they grew up, he and I would come (together) very closely on the Day of Resurrection." And he interlinked his fingers (for explaining the point of nearness between him and that person).

'A'isha (Allah be pleased with her) reported:

> "A poor woman came to me with her daughters. She gave a date to each of them and then she took up one date and brought that to her mouth in order to eat that; but her daughters expressed desire to eat it. She divided that date, which she intended to eat, between them. This (kind) treatment of hers impressed me. I mentioned that which she did to Allah's Messenger (peace and blessings of Allah be Upon him). Thereupon he said, 'Verily Allah has assured Paradise for her, because of this act of hers, or He has rescued her from Hell-fire."

Just go through the beautiful piece of literature above. It should be quite easy to understand how much Islam insists on the proper upbringing and training of daughters. In the above Hadith, the need for the proper upbringing of daughters has been impressed upon us in a beautiful style.

How humane Allah's Prophet (peace and blessings of Allah be upon him) was, and what respect and honour Islam gave to women! Allah's Prophet (peace and blessings of Allah be upon him) warned the people not to be forgetful of the rights of the two downtrodden creatures, women and orphans. All this was done to safeguard female modesty and chastity and to give them that position and status in society which they deserved, so that the people may not consider a woman only a worthless, fallen thing.

The Holy Prophet (peace and blessings of Allah be upon him) said: 'A person came to me and told that he himself buried alive ten daughters.' Another person said: 'I called my daughter who came with me laughing and playing. When she reached a well, I caught hold of her arm and flung her into the well. She cried, "O my father! O my father!"

Hearing this Allah's Prophet (peace and blessings of Allah be upon him) wept so profusely that his sacred beard became wet with tears.

The above events affirm the fact that Muhammad (peace and blessings of Allah be upon him) was not only the Prophet of men but also that of women. His heart was moved alike to see any man or woman in distress.

Share in Inheritance

The Holy Quran ordains:

> Allah chargeth you concerning (the provision for) your children: to the male the equivalent of the portion of two females, and if there be women more than two, then theirs is two-

> thirds of the inheritance, and if there be one (only) then the half. (4:11)

Woman was perhaps for the first time given the right to own personal property whereby she could spend her life with ease and comfort without depending upon man.

Hitherto women had no share in inheritance. When Islam gave the woman the rights to possess her share of inheritance, it surprised a lot of people as to how the poor, weak creature who could not fight, would get her share in inheritance.

But Islam has come to give the rights to their rightful owners, to put an end to injustice, aggression and oppression and it aims at giving due share to men and women in power and property.

This has been explained in the Holy Qur'an:

> Unto the men (of a family) belongeth a share of that which parents and near kindred leave and unto the women a share of that which parents and near kindred leave, whether it be little or much-a legal share. (4:7)

As a Mother

A woman, may she be mother, daughter or wife, cannot be disowned from legacy. As regards the share of a mother, it has been said in the Holy Qur'an:

> And to his parents a sixth of the inheritance, if he have a son; and if he have no son and his parents are his heirs, then to his mother appertaineth the third, and if he have brethren, then to his mother appertaineth the sixth. (4:11)

Whereas the father is the inheritor of legacy, the mother too is the legal inheritor; in some cases she gets one-third and in others one-sixth of the inheritance. She has not been deprived of legacy merely on the grounds of being a woman.

As a Wife

A woman gets her share and legacy as a daughter and as a mother. She is also not deprived of a legal share as a wife.

> And unto you belongeth a half of that which your wives leave, if they have no child; but if they have a child then unto you the fourth of that which they leave, after any legacy they may have bequeathed or debt (they may have contracted, hath been paid). And unto them belongeth the fourth of that which ye leave if ye have no child, but if ye have a child then the eighth of that which ye leave, after any legacy ye may have bequeathed or debt (ye may have contracted, hath been paid).
> (4:12)

You have seen that just as a husband is the legal heir of his wife, the wife is also his legal heir and no one can deprive her of her legal share.

Not a Loser

As regards the extent of shares, a probe into the matter would reveal that in the existing conditions, the woman is in a better position. What I mean to say is that a woman might have received a big dowry, or she might be possessing a large property, yet all the household expenses are borne by the husband and it is his legal and religious responsibility to bear the expenses of his wife and those of his children. So whatever the woman gets is sufficient to meet the exigencies if God forbid, she is deprived of her husband's help.

Prestige as a Mother

Another way in which Allah has enhanced the prestige and honour of woman is that He has enjoined respect and regard for mothers and made mention of motherly love and affection so frequently. He has forbidden the use of harsh words: "Say not 'fie' unto them and speak unto them a gracious word."

We should respect our mothers from the core of our hearts and our attitude towards them should be very polite and courteous.

The Holy Prophet (peace and blessings of Allah be upon him), used to explain the meanings of the verses of the Holy Qur'an. He said: 'It is your mother who deserves your respect the most. Paradise is under the feet of your mother. You will not enter the gate of Paradise without having earned the good wishes and pleasure of your mother.'

The above and scores of other traditions lay stress on treating mothers with utmost respect and regard.

In short woman was given her rightful place in society, and instead of the erroneous views it was impressed upon the people that woman was not born only for serving man and multiplication of the race, but that she deserves to be treated with the same respect and honour as man. The details of this can be read in the books on Fiqah (Islamic jurisprudence). I have only dealt here with some introductory points. The real aim and object of this book is to discuss the rules and regulations enforced by Islam for safeguarding feminine morality and chastity, which every Muslim is legally bound to observe.

Protection of Modesty

There is no denying the fact that female modesty and chastity is such a precious thing that all the wealth of the world put together cannot take its place. So we must protect it, even at the cost of wealth and it should not be sold for the sake of money. Only one who is devoid of any respect and honour can disgrace his women-folk by making them whores and prostitutes.

The customs of the Days of Ignorance, the sending of his wife by the husband to a stranger for sexual union to get a child of noble descent, and copulation of nine men with one woman at a time; all such derogatory and detestable customs were put to an end by Islam for ever, You have already read that Hadrat 'A'isha (Allah be pleased with her) reported: 'When the Holy Prophet (peace and blessings of Allah be upon him) came with the True Faith, he put an end to all the customs of marriage of the Days of Ignorance except the one which is in vogue today.'

He not only banned all such marriages but he also declared all practices illegal which led to immodesty and immorality and created discord among families, hatred among near relatives and confusion in the matter of inheritance. He prohibited all such evil practices, declaring them to be adultery and warned the people against this sin as has been given in the Holy Qur'an:

> And come not near adultery/fornication Lo! it is an abomination and an evil way. (17:32)

It has not been said: "Do not commit adultery"; but it has been said; "And come not near adultery." This means that it is not only adultery, but it is ordained that all such ways and means which directly or ultimately lead to this sinful act should be avoided. A further probe would reveal some points of special significance. The word' ' which has been used to denote the inherent feeling of abhorrence and contempt attached to the word adultery is also due to the reason that it disturbs the purity of race, creates confusion in matters of inheritance, strikes at the roots of morality and decency and tramples upon the rights of others. Counting the evils of this act, Imam Razi (May Allah have mercy on him), writes:

1. Adultery disturbs the purity of race, making the lineage doubtful. No one can be sure about the father of a child which an adulteress has delivered, with the result that no one undertakes the responsibility of bringing up this child. The child dies (or the mother herself kills such a child and throws it away), or it is spoiled in the absence of any guardian. This is nothing short of infanticide, of the cutting down of the human race, a means of creating chaos and wilderness in the world.

2. According to the Shari'ah an adulteress is not under anyone's charge, as she is not the legal wife of any person. Everyone would try to possess this woman,

without any question of preference. The destruction which this way of life brings in, can be read in the histories of love, flirtation and scandals etc.

3. An adulteress is addicted to adultery. A decent man hates such a woman and is not inclined to marry her, not to speak of having feelings of love and affection for her. An adulteress is generally looked down upon and held in contempt and disgrace in society.

4. If adultery becomes a common feature and there are no rules and regulations imposing restrictions on sexual behaviour, no man will have special regard and love for any one woman. He will be free to call any woman at any place and do this evil act. There would remain little difference between man and animal.

5. A woman is not meant for satisfaction of lust only; but the purpose of marriage is that both husband and wife should participate in their household activities and share the responsibilities of bringing up their children and providing their needs. They should also share their joys and sorrows. This purpose can be achieved only through a legal marriage in which case a woman would remain legal to one man. The only way to achieve this end is that adultery should be strictly prohibited and the relation between the two sexes should not transgress lawful limits.

6. Sexual intercourse is a hidden act. A mention of this act is, therefore, made through a hint. This act is done in privacy, and is hidden from the eyes of the public. So this act should be done rarely and the proper way is that the woman should be the legal wife of the man, otherwise privacy is not possible.

(Tafsir-e- Kabir: 394)

The above six are apparent vices.

Advice of the Prophet

Imam Ahmad (may Allah have mercy on him) mentioned a Hadith in his Maunad on the authority of Hadrat Abu Imama, who said: 'A young man came to the Holy Prophet (peace and blessings of Allah be upon him), and said: "O Allah's Messenger! Allow me to commit adultery." The Companions of the Holy Prophet (PBUH) were very much enraged at this impudence and rebuked him and expressed their contempt at this request.

The Holy Prophet (peace and blessings of Allah be upon him), said to him: "Come near". When he came near, he asked him to sit. Then he (the Holy Prophet), questioned him in order to reform him:

The Prophet — "Do you like this act (of adultery), for your mother?"

Young Man — "No, Allah's Messenger!"

The Prophet — "Other people also do not like this evil act with their mothers. Do you like the commitment of this act with your daughter?"

Young Man — "No, O Allah's Messenger!"

The Prophet — "Other people also do not like this indecent act to be committed with their daughters. Would you tolerate this evil act with your sisters?"

Young Man — "No, not at all'."

The Prophet — "Other people also do not tolerate this abominable act with their sisters. Well, would you like this sinful act with your father's sister?"

Young Man — "No, Allah's Messenger!"

The Prophet — "Other people also do not like this detestable act with their father's sister. Would you tolerate the commission of adultery with your mother's sister?"

Young Man — "No".

The Prophet — "Other people also do not like this adulterous act with their mother's sister."

When the evil consequences of this sinful act were fully understood by the young man, the Holy Prophet (peace and blessings of Allah be upon him), put his sacred hand on him and prayed:

> "O Allah! Forgive his sin, purify his heart and protect his private parts." (Ibn Kathir)

The narrator says that the above speech and prayer of the Holy Prophet (peace and blessings of Allah be upon him), impressed the man so much that thereafter he never thought of committing adultery. It, is a plain fact that a woman is either someone's mother or daughter or sister or father's sister or mother's sister, and no one can tolerate illicit sexual union with her.

The Holy Qur'an has mentioned the evil consequences of adultery in the following words:

> And marry not those women whom your fathers married, except what hath already happened (of that nature), in the past. Lo! It was ever lewdness and abomination, and an evil way. (4:22)

In the above verse extra-marital sex has been called .... and .... (abomination and an evil way). The one word ....

which has been added to the verse implies that it, saps the roots of central power. We can judge the extent to which the Holy Qur'an has stressed the evils of unlawful sex, the bad consequences of which can be seen every now and then.

Bai'at (Pledge)

The significance of female morality and chastity in the eyes of the Holy Prophet (peace and blessings of Allah be upon him) can be judged from the fact that he used to take Bai'at (pledge), from women in this matter in the words which have been laid down in the Holy Qur'an:

> O Prophet' If believing women come unto thee taking oath of allegiance unto thee that they will ascribe nothing as partner unto Allah, and will neither steal nor commit adultery nor kill children nor produce any lie that they have devised between their hands and feet.
> (60:12)

The evil consequences of adultery know no end. The commission of this act gives rise to hatred and enmity, bloodshed and murder.

The society becomes demoralized and no weight is attached to manners and morals. Corruption is the order of the day and an adulterous nation loses all its prestige and honour. With the degeneration of moral force, the peace and tranquillity of people is lost, and the poor people suffer the most. The general health and vitality of the people is shattered and they, especially young men, contract all sorts of chronic diseases and infections.

Illegal Sex, a Great Sin

Due to the evil consequences of illegal sex, it is a major sin and its mention has been made after murder in the Holy Qur'an. Although it is not murder, so far as its evil consequences are concerned, it is not less than murder. Whereas, the Holy Qur'an mentions the qualities of Allah's virtuous people, it also mentions:

> And those who cry not unto any other god along with Allah, nor take the life which Allah hath forbidden save in (course of), justice, nor commit adultery/fornication, and whose death this shall pay the penalty. (25:68)

The import of the above verse is that like polytheism, atheism and unlawful killing of man, unlawful sex is also a major sin and it cannot be pardoned except through Tauba (repentance), and virtuous deeds. It has been mentioned in the adjoining verse:

> The doom will be doubled for him on the Day of Resurrection, and he will abide therein disdained forever. (25:69)

Just ponder over the above verse. Adultery is one among the major sins which are liable to severe punishment in the Hereafter.

The Holy Prophet (peace and blessings of Allah be upon him) has observed:

> "The greatest sin after polytheism is that a man commits fornication with a woman who is not his legal wife." (Ibn Kathir)

In another Hadith, Allah's Messenger (peace and blessings of Allah be -upon him) said about adultery/fornication:

> So long as a person commits adultery/fornication there goes out of him the faith. (Mishkat)

The above Hadith affirms the fact that the faith leaves the person as long as he commits the evil act.

In other words, a believer, being a believer, should not indulge in this abominal act.

In another Hadith, the Holy Prophet (peace and blessings of Allah be upon him) observed:

> 'When a person commits fornication there goes out of him the faith and hover like an awning over his head and when he quits this act the faith reverts to him again. (Mishkat)

It is clear from the above Hadith that adultery is such a heinous crime and detestable act, that the faith forsakes a person during this act, it leaves his body, as a sacred thing like faith cannot stay with him in such a state. When he quits this act and his conscience pricks him and he repents, his faith reverts to him, taking pity on him. When the Almighty Allah shows His wrath at this act, why should the faith of a person not leave him during this loathsome act? This is why all sorts of acts of indecency are prohibited. It has been said in the Holy Qur'an:

> Say! My Lord forbiddeth indecencies, such of them as are apparent and such as are within, and sin and wrongful oppression. (7:33)

God's Wrath

It has been said in a Hadith that a person questioned the Holy Prophet (peace and blessings of Allah be upon him) 'If any one sees his wife engaged (in sexual intercourse), with another person what should he do?'

He said: He should produce four witnesses. But Sa'ad bin 'Ubada (Allah be pleased with him) who was, by nature, a very self respecting man said: 'If I happen to see my wife in such a state, I would never tolerate it and holding my sword would cut asunder that man.' When this news reached the Holy Prophet (peace and blessings of Allah be upon him) he said: 'Verily, by Allah! I am even more self respecting than him and Allah is most Honourable. This is the reason why Allah has declared all sorts of evil acts manifest or hidden as illegal.'

There was an eclipse of the sun in the Prophet's (peace and blessings of Allah be upon him) time and on that occasion he delivered an eloquent speech called Kusuf sermon:

> "Oh Unimah of Muhammad By Allah! He (Allah), is not so much enraged at any sinful act as He is enraged when a man and woman commit unlawful sex. And, by Allah, if you happen to know what I know, you would weep more and laugh less."

And in order to stress this point, he said: 'O Allah! Have I not conveyed?' In other words, he has conveyed this special commandment to the people.

Go through the above Hadith and think over the evil consequences of unlawful sex with a special reference to the previous Hadith according to which the faith of a person leaves him so long as he commits this evil act. In another verse Allah has prohibited all sorts of abominations. It has been said in the Holy Qur'an:

> Lo! Allah enjoineth justice and kindness, and giving to kinsfolk, and forbiddeth lewdness and abomination and wickedness. He exhorteth you in order that ye may take heed.(16:90)

This verse is generally recited in every Juma sermon in order to impress upon the people the significance of these commandments. The reason for the prohibition of adultery is that it is a heinous crime and it has disastrous consequences in this world and in the Hereafter.

Hazrat Yousuf's Story

The story of Hazrat Yousuf (peace be upon him) which has been narrated in the Holy Qur'an also exposes the evil consequences of adultery. Aziz of Egypt purchased Yousuf (peace be upon him) and entrusted him to the charge of his wife and asked her to look after this slave properly. The wife acted upon the order of her husband; but when Yousuf (peace be upon him) grew up and was in the bloom of youth, she fell in love with him and used all her feminine tactics and coquetry to allure Yousuf (peace be upon him) into this evil act, as her heart suggested. There were all sorts of comforts and luxuries, youth in full bloom, the company of the opposite sex, charming and captivating, and perfect solitude. All the doors and windows were bolted with no apparent danger of being exposed; a great ordeal for an unmarried man.

> And she in whose house he was, asked of him an evil act. She bolted the doors and said: "Come." (12:23)

The heaven, the earth and the angels were witnessing this scene as to what would Yousuf (peace be upon him) do. Nothing was left undone by evil to allure him. If he desired, he could do this evil act with the wife of Aziz but it has been said in the Holy Qur'an that Yousuf's (peace be upon him) conduct was unwavering. He said:

> Lo! He is my Lord, who has treated me honourably. Wrong does never prosper. (12:23)

Root of Tyranny and Oppression

1. It is not surprising that in one of the above verses, adultery has been called oppression. A probe into the matter would reveal that adultery is the root cause of all oppression and all evils. There is no denying the fact that an adultery/ fornication is a tyrant and an aggressor. By committing this act a person is guilty of self-persecution. His actions and moral conduct are perverted and his wealth and vitality is wasted. His semen which is for the perpetuation of the human race goes waste. It shatters the health and brings on insult and disgrace. An adulterer remains always gloomy, panic sticken and depressed. He contracts venereal diseases. He is characterless, immodest, deceitful, a liar, selfish, the slave of his passions, lacking self-control and mentally weak and perturbed. These and many other physical and mental diseases overcome him.

2. An adulterer/fornication brings ignominy and disgrace to his

family and sets a bad example for them by paving the way to fornication.

3. Fornication is the looting of female chastity. The doer of this act is a dacoit who plunders and loots the weaker sex and spoils her inherent modesty and chastity. Thereafter the woman becomes a flirt and loses all sense of shame and becomes arrogant towards her brothers and sisters. All the brothels in the cities owe their existence to these corrupt people.

4. A woman is after all, a member of some family, she either remains a daughter, or someone's wife or sister. Just imagine the stigma which a person who has unlawful sex attaches to the family of that woman. The members of the family often commit suicide to escape disgrace.

5. If the woman is already the legal wife of some one, it is a shameful aggression and direct attack on the prestige and honour of that man.

6. It is an oppression on the child, as either he will be destroyed by abortion or killed, or will be spoiled in the absence of any protecting hand of a guardian. Even if he grows up, who will wash the stigma which his illegal father has attached to his face? He will always be held in contempt in society. Sometimes the illegal children suffer from chronic diseases.

As a matter of fact the proper development of a race depends upon the sentiment of discharging our duties in respect of this sacred trust honestly, and slight negligence on our part may prove disastrous for the physical and mental health of families and nation.

Whatever might happen, Hadrat Yousuf (peace be upon him) preferred the dungeon to the commitment of this sinful act. He prayed:

> O my Lord! Prison is more dear than that unto which they urge me, and if thou fend not off their wiles from me, I shall incline unto them and become of the foolish. (12:33)

The evil consequences of this guilty act mentioned in the Ahadith are a lesson and warning for a thoughtful reader. A few Ahadith are given below:

Sayings of Holy Prophet on Adultery

Once the representatives of the Jews came to the Holy Prophet (peace and blessings of Allah be upon him) and enquired; 'What are .... plain or clear verses?' He observed:

> Do not associate anything with Allah and do not commit theft and unlawful sex nor slander chaste women. (Mishkat)

It is clear that adultery is one of the major manifest evils.

Once a person asked the Holy Prophet (peace and blessings of Allah be upon him): 'Which is the greatest of sins in the sight of Allah?'

He said: 'Associating anything with Allah, the Creator.'

He asked: 'Which act after this?'

He said: 'To kill one's own child for fear of feeding him along with him.'

He again asked: "Which sin comes next?'

He said: 'Having sex with the wife of your neighbour.'

The Holy Prophet (peace and blessings of Allah be upon him) warned against adultery/fornication in such a way that the people might become fully aware of its evil consequences and avoid this abomination. Once he (the Holy Prophet) observed: 'Mostly the people would be thrown into the Hellfire because of their mouths and sexual organs.'

Once the Holy Prophet (peace and blessings of Allah be upon him) said: 'The following are the signs of the approaching of the Doomsday:

(1) Want of Knowledge (2) Spread of ignorance (3) Drinking wine (4) Adultery (5) Reduction in the number of men to such extent that fifty women are under the charge of one man.

Destruction by Promiscuity

Hadrat Abdullah bin Masud, a Companion (Allah be pleased with him) said: 'Where usury and Promiscuity are rife, Allah ordains that habitation to be wiped out of existence.'

(Aljawab al-Kafi).

Promiscuity sometimes leads to the destruction of a habitation and sometimes it so happens the whole population is wiped out of existence. The wrath of Allah descends upon the adulterous nation.

When Hadrat Abu Bakr Siddiq, the Great, assumed the charge of Khalifatul Muslimin (Caliph of the believers), and took Bai'at (pledge), from all the Muslims, he ascended the pulpit and delivered his first sermon as Caliph during the course of which he said: 'Allah degrades a nation who forsakes Jihad (fighting in the cause of Islam), and inflicts punishment upon a nation among whom adultery is rife.'
(Tarikh-i-Millat)

The outlook of Islam regarding the significance of chastity can be easily understood from the above speech of our first Caliph. Sins and vices are definite signs of the decline of a nation. The first Caliph alluded to these signs in his first speech.

The Holy Prophet (peace and blessings of Allah be upon him) said: 'When promiscuity is rife among a people, there are frequent deaths.'

The Holy Prophet (peace and blessings of Allah be upon him) pointed out in a lengthy Hadith five sins and their evil consequences. In addition to other things he observed that Allah inflicts upon people among whom promiscuity is rampant, the scourge of plague and gives them such an exemplary punishment as was not known before.

There is another Hadith in which the Holy Prophet (peace and blessings of Allah be upon him) said: 'Whenever adultery spreads among a people, they are struck with famine and when the evil of bribery spreads among a people they are panic stricken.' (Mishkat)

When a person loses decency and modesty and transgresses the laws and restrictions imposed by religion and the Shariah and makes no distinction between good and bad, the whole nation is put to trial. In Bani Israel which is a unique Ummah of historical importance, this evil of adultery also penetrated through the women and it caused havoc among the whole nation.

The Holy Prophet (peace and blessings of Allah be upon him) said: 'Fear world and women. Verily the first evil of Bani Israel was of women.'

Institution of Marriage

After pointing out the evil consequences of sexual immorality, Allah enjoined every man and woman in need of marriage to marry; it is the only means of protecting chastity and satisfying the sexual instinct. Allah the Almighty ordains:

> And marry such of you as are single and the
> pious of your slaves and maidservants.
> (24:32)

Maulana Ashraf Ali Thanvi writes in his interpretation of the Holy Qur'an:

'Out of free people, those who are single, male or female, if they are still unmarried or rendered solitary due to death or divorce, you should get married. And in the same way, marry those of your slaves and maidservants who have attained the age of competency, and do not sacrifice their interests for your own interest, if they are in need of marriage.'

It is clear that Allah has enjoined marriage for all men and women in need of marriage. It is necessary even for helpless servants who cannot afford to marry. Almighty Allah has put this responsibility on the people which shows the significance attached by Islam to this institution, so that everyone can derive benefit therefrom. The trend of leading an unmarried life is harmful for the whole nation. There is no denying the fact that if legal marriages are banned, the whole nation would be in the grip of moral turpitude. Allah, the Almighty has said in the next verse; 'If they be poor, Allah will enrich them out of His bounty.' That is to say, unfounded fears should in no case be a plea for not marrying.

This verse, however, affirms the fact that one who is competent to marry must get married and its responsibility also devolves on the parents, guardians and the nation. No one can avoid this responsibility.

Views of Experts

Some Ulama consider marriage as an incumbent duty and this view is also supported by Ahadith. The worthy scholars of Islamic Jurisprudence have said that if the sexual urge is unbearable to such an extent that there is risk or fear of transgressing the limits imposed by Shariah, marriage becomes necessary for a believer; but if the sexual urge is under control, marriage is delayed. The Holy Prophet (peace and blessings of Allah be upon him), has stressed upon marriage). If a person is sure that he is impotent (lacking of sexual strength to satisfy his wife), it is unbecoming to bind him in wedlock, rather it is unlawful to marry.

A Means of Protecting Chastity

In addition to the above verses of the Holy Qur'an, there are a large number of Ahadith which exhort and lay stress on marriage. It is amply clear that one who is in need of marriage should marry. The Holy Prophet (peace and blessings of Allah be upon him) said: 'O party of young men! He who has power of sexual intercourse, must marry as it safeguards stray looks and protects chastity.'

Not only in the above Hadith, has stress been laid on marriage, but its merits have also been pointed out. Marriage is a great protector of chastity and morality. It is a safeguard against adultery, rape and fornication. This Hadith is also applicable to aged persons whose sexual power has not declined.

The Holy Prophet (peace and blessings of Allah be upon him) said: 'Marry a fertile woman and produce children, so that I may feel pride over other Unimahs because of your number on the Day of Resurrection.'
(Ibn Kathir)

According to the above Hadith marriage has been made incumbent. The purpose of marriage is the reproduction and perpetuation of the human race. There is a narrative in the Mishkat:

'Marry a very loving and fertile woman so that I may feel pride over other people because of your number on the Day of Resurrection.'

Besides the perpetuation of the race, stress has been laid on the amicable nature of a woman which lends beauty and charm to married life. The happiness and well being of the family lies in love and cooperation between the couple.

In another Hadith the Holy Prophet (peace and blessings of Allah be upon him) said: 'Marriage wards off many evils.' If anyone desires to meet his Lord in a stage of purity and chastity he should act upon the Hadith mentioned below:

> 'Whosoever desires to meet his Lord in a stage of cleanliness and purity should marry a pious woman. (Mishkat)

According to the above Hadith, marriage is a means of attaining purity and chastity. The style is very eloquent. The words which have been used impress upon the mind the advantages of marriage as a means of protection against sins and vices and other indecencies, ultimately providing for the deliverance and salvation of man on the Day of Resurrection. Unmarried and sexually starved people are generally more liable to commit sins deliberately or unintentionally but a married person possesses the means to gratify his sexual desire and abstain from sins. On the other hand, if any person does not get married and also wants to lead a pious life, he has to cross a thorny path and Allah knows when he will fall down.

In a Hadith, marriage has been called 'half the religion'. It has been said by the Holy Prophet (peace and blessings of Allah be upon him); 'When a person got married, he completed half the religion.' (Mishkat)

If we further think over the matter, we can easily understand that a large number of sins are due to perverted sexual behaviour. When a man does not transgress the laws of the Shariah, the chances of corruption are minimized.

Hadrat 'Abdullah bin Jubair (Allah be pleased with him) reported: 'Hadrat' Abbas said to me: "Are you married?" I said: "No". He said: "Get married. Verily, the best of this Ummah, that is, the Holy Prophet (peace and blessings of Allah be upon him) had many wives."
(Bukhari)

Nikah (Marriage), is also the Sunnah of the Prophets and almost all the Prophets got married and led family lives. It has been said in the Holy Qur'an:

> And verily, We sent messengers (to mankind), before thee, and We appointed for themselves and offspring. (13:38)

Ascetic Life

Once the Holy Prophet (peace and blessings of Allah be upon him) said: 'The man who has no wife is destitute.'

The Companions (Allah be pleased with them) enquired: 'Even if they are wealthy?'

He (the Holy Prophet), said: 'Yes, even if they are wealthy.'

Then the Holy Prophet said: 'The woman who has no husband is destitute.'

The people enquired: 'O Allah's Apostle? Even if she is rich?'

He answered: 'Yes, even then she is destitute.'

The above and a number of other Ahadith lay great stress on marriage. The main aim and object of marriage is that it is an effective means for the protection of chastity and morality by the lawful gratification of sexual desire and for the perpetuation of the human race.

Hafiz Ibn Hajar has truly said in his *Fathal-Bari:* 'Marriage is done to break (gratify), the sexual lust, to achieve chastity and perpetuate the race.'
(Fathal-Bari)

Islam discourages asceticism. This is the reason why the Holy Prophet (peace and blessings of Allah be upon him) insisted on the marriage of people who declined to marry.

There is a Hadith that Uthman bin Mazun kept aloof from women and expressed his desire for castration so that he might be relieved of the sexual urge, and worship Allah with full devotion. When the Holy Prophet (peace and blessings of Allah be upon him) came to know of it, he disliked this sentiment and Hadrat Uthman bin Mazun had to change his idea.

There is another Hadith that three people came to Allah's Messenger's house and enquired about his *ibadah* (exertion and devotion in the acts of worship and prayer). They were informed about it and from the information given to them they perhaps arrived at the conclusion that they did not exert much in ibadah. They said: 'We cannot vie with the Holy Prophet (peace and blessings of Allah be upon him) as Allah has pardoned all his sins, whereas we are deeply steeped in sins.

One of them said: 'I shall spend the whole night in worship and prayer.'

The other said: 'I shall keep fast daily.'

The third one said: 'I shall remain aloof from woman and always refrain from marriage.'

When the Holy Prophet (peace and blessings of Allah be up on him) came to know about this incident, he went to them and said: 'Have you said all these things? Listen! By God. I am the most pious and God-fearing among you, but I keep fast and sometimes I am not with fast. I worship and also sleep. I have married and I go to my wives. Anyone who is heedless of my Sunnah, has no concern with me.'

It has been stated in the last few lines of the above Hadith that the Holy Prophet (peace and blessings of Allah be upon him) warned such people as were proud of their act of keeping themselves aloof from women and of their celibacy. The Holy Prophet (peace and blessings of Allah be upon him) repudiated this saying: 'I have married and whosoever is heedless of my Sunnah is not of me." (Bukhari)

Hadrat Abu Dhar (Allah be pleased with him) has reported that one day 'Akaf bin Bashar Tamimi (Allah be pleased with him) came to the Holy Prophet (peace and blessings of Allah be upon him). He said: "Have you a wife?"

Hadrat Akaf answered: "No".

He asked: "A maid-servant?"

Akaf replied: "No."

Thereupon the Holy Prophet (peace and blessings of Allah be upon him) said: "You are rich and can afford it, but are still unmarried. Then surely you are one of the devil's brothers." The Holy Prophet (peace and blessings of Allah be upon him) got him married.

Once Hadrat Abu Huraira (Allah be pleased with him) came to the Holy Prophet (peace and blessings of Allah be upon him) and said: 'I am a grown up man. I run the risk of fornication, but 'I cannot afford marriage.'

He aimed at conveying to the Holy Prophet (peace and blessings of Allah be upon him) the idea that he wanted to be castrated. The Holy Prophet (peace and blessings of Allah be upon him) kept silence. Hadrat Abu Huraira (Allah be pleased with him) again repeated the above question and sought permission; but the Holy Prophet (peace and blessings of Allah be upon him) again gave no reply. Hadrat Abu Huraira reiterated his demand. Thereupon the Holy Prophet (peace and blessings of Allah be upon him) observed: 'What is going to happen has already been decreed. It matters naught whether you marry or do not marry. You have sought permission for a wrong act merely on account of baseless fear.'

Castration is, therefore, unlawful in Islam.

Hadrat Anas bin Malik (Allah be pleased with him) forbade celibacy and exhorted us to marry.

According to some Traditions if a person cannot marry due to economic reasons, he should keep fasts to subdue his sexual urge. Castration is prohibited. Instead, the keeping of fasts serves this purpose.

Islam is against castration and celibacy as both are evil practices. These are nothing short of denying the favour and blessing of Allah which He has bestowed upon man. If these evil practices were allowed, its results would have been alarming for the world today.

Due to the above reasons Islam holds quite a distinct view about women and in Islam ascetic and monastic outlook has no place. Instead of likening a woman to poison, the Holy Prophet (peace and blessings of Allah be upon him) said: 'The whole world is a valuable asset and the best asset is a pious woman.'

A religion which speaks so highly of women considers them to be Allah's greatest favour and reward cannot brook the idea of attaching any filth or impurity to women and keeping aloof from them. That a pious woman is really most valuable, is easy to understand. Does not a woman save a man from many vices and sins? Is she not a source of comfort and pleasure for him and a means of gratification of his sexual desire, after whose proper satisfaction he can apply himself to his work wholeheartedly and with full concentration? The Holy Prophet (peace and blessings of Allah be upon him) said: 'Of the things of the world, the love of woman and scent has been put in my heart and prayer has soothing and cooling effect on my eyes.' (Nasa'i)

A careful study of the above Hadith would reveal that Islam lays great stress on people, especially on its followers, getting married in a lawful manner. It is incumbent upon a person to marry if he wants to control his sexual lust. The significance of marriage in Islam can be judged from the fact that those who shun marriage merely on account of unfounded fear of poverty have been warned in the Holy Qur'an:

> If they be poor, Allah will enrich them of His bounty. Allah is of ample means, Aware.
> (24:32)

Those who entertain unfounded and baseless fears regarding their financial position wonder how they can marry in such a state of penury. How can they provide food, lodging and other amenities of life to their family? Allah, the Almighty removes these fears saying that there exists no such problem as He is the Sustainer, the Provider. It has been said again and again in the Holy Qur'an:

> And will provide for him from (a quarter), whence he hath no expectation. (65:3)

> We provide for you and for them. (6:152)

That is to say, one must not judge the future from the present. When a man attains puberty he should marry, leaving the means of sustenance to Allah. It is possible, the wife may bring wealth and property or that he may get some reasonable job. It is also possible that a married person may develop a keen sense of responsibility after marriage and work hard to increase his earnings.

Maulvi Ashraf Ali Thanvi has mentioned in his interpretation of the Holy Qur'an:

'At the time of marriage the financial position of the person from whom the proposal of marriage is received should not be taken into consideration, if he has the capabilities to earn and feed his family. If he is poor, Allah would enrich him out of His bounty. So poverty should not stand in the way of marriage as marriage does not make a man poor and destitute.'

The above brief commentary removes all the doubts and fears that can possibly arise in the human mind. The Holy Qur'an disentangles man from this cobweb of doubts and fears:

> If ye fear poverty Allah shall preserve you of
> His bounty if He will.
>
> (9:28)

In the above verse, it has been stated that poverty and prosperity are from Allah; but fear of poverty should in no way make a man slack or a shirker of work, because Allah can bestow abundantly of His bounty after poverty. Allah has made marriage incumbent upon man and it is preposterous to shun marriage on account of baseless fears. Allah says that if a person has ability and confidence, Allah will provide the ways and means of sustenance. However, it is the bounden duty of man to strive hard for his livelihood.

While interpreting the above verse Hadrat Ibn 'Abbas (Allah be pleased with him) said: 'Allah, the Exalted, exhorts to many and has made marriage incumbent upon the person who is competent to marry. He also promises abundance to him.'

Hadrat Abu Bakr Siddiq (Allah be pleased with him) said: 'Act upon Allah's Command concerning marriage and obey Him. He will fulfil His covenant.'

Hadrat Ibn Mas'ud (Allah be pleased with him) said: 'Seek abundance and prosperity through marriage as the Holy Prophet (peace and blessings of Allah be upon him) has said: Seek abundance and prosperity through marriage.'
(Ibn Kathir)

Hadrat Abu Huraira (Allah be pleased with him) has reported that the Holy Prophet (peace and blessings of Allah be upon him) said: 'Allah has undertaken to help the three people: A debtor who desires to pay; a person who marries for chastity and a fighter in the cause of Allah.?'
(Mishkat)

Hadrat 'A'isha (Allah be pleased with her) has reported the Holy Prophet (peace, and blessings of Allah be upon him) as saying: 'Marry women. They will serve as a means of bringing wealth for you.' That is, Allah will increase your earnings because of them.

Hadrat Jabir (Allah be pleased with him) has reported that the Holy Prophet (peace and blessings of Allah be upon him) said: 'When a man marries relying upon Allah and seeks His pleasure, Allah assures of His support and blessing.'

Once a person complained of poverty to the Holy Prophet (peace and blessings of Allah be upon him). He advised him to marry. From what has been said above it can be inferred that the Holy Prophet (peace and blessings of Allah be upon him) paid little heed to one's present state of poverty, nor did he hesitate to grant permission of marriage because of this.

The books on Ahadith mention several instances where the Holy Prophet (peace and blessings of Allah be upon him) permitted his Companions to marry despite financial stringency. A Companion who possessed nothing but an iron ring was allowed to marry. Another Companion of his who had nothing, except that he had learnt the Holy Qur'an was granted such permission. Similarly, another person who possessed nothing except a pair of trousers expressed his desire to marry which was granted. The request of another person who possessed only a pair of ladies' shoes was accepted. Not to speak of these things, the permission for marriage was granted to people on providing a handful of barley, dates, etc.

The above Ahadith bear ample testimony to the fact that instances of poverty were not uncommon in the days of the Holy

Prophet (peace and blessings of Allah be upon him) but he still got the marriages of those poor and destitute people arranged. Allah made them prosperous after marriage and provided for their sustenance.

Why does Islam attach such an extraordinary importance to marriage and why did the Holy Prophet (peace and blessings of Allah be upon him) grant permission to the poor and destitute people to marry? All this was done to protect and preserve modesty and chastity and to produce lawful children. Marriage was allowed for the sake of moral elevation and for checking debauchery. If a person cannot at all afford marriage, he should keep chaste.

However, if a man is quite incapable of marrying i.e., he is unable to support a wife or lacks sufficient strength, or a woman is not available, he should wait until he is able to support or get a wife; but during the period he remains single, he must protect his moral conduct. Allah, the Almighty has ordained:

> "And let those who cannot find a match keep chaste till Allah give them independence by His grace." (24:33)

In short, a great stress has been laid by Islam on marriage and on moral character. If one is quite unable to support a wife he must control his sexual desire by keeping fasts lest his base passions overcome him.

> "He who is unable (to support a wife), fasting is incumbent upon him as it controls the sexual lust." (MishkatlKitab Al-Nikah)

It has been mentioned in the Ahadith that several Companions of the Holy Prophet (peace and blessings of Allah be upon him) could not marry due to their financial stringency, despite their need. The Holy Prophet (peace and blessings of Allah be upon him) advised them to keep fasts which protected them from sins. When Allah provided them the means to marry, they got married.

Abstinence from Marriage

This stress on marriage is based on great wisdom. Sexual lust has been ingrained in the human nature. After adolescence, this sexual instinct expresses itself and grows with the passage of time until it takes the form of passion. Awake or asleep or while sitting or standing, this passion does not leave us. There is a tug of war between the heart and the mind. The heart urges for gratification of the sexual lust by hook or by crook, but the intellect warns against such action. In this tug of war, sometimes the heart wins and sometimes the intellect wins. So during the period when a man is single, and is of mature age, he has to undergo this struggle.

But after marriage, one possesses a lawful means of gratifying this sexual desire. This tug of war ends by itself and a man can apply himself to work whole-heartedly and with full concentration, with the result that he is able to discharge his duties efficiently.

There are three main aims and objects of marriage. Firstly, the reproduction and multiplication of the human race. Secondly, the proper discharge of semen which is necessary for the maintenance of health. Thirdly, the derivation of pleasure out of gratification of sexual lust in a natural way. According to the expert medical opinion, sexual intercourse is conducive to health.

Galen, the well known physician, said that fire and air dominate semen and it is hot and wet. If this surplus fluid is not given any outlet, it gives birth to many diseases. Sometimes a man is obsessed with delusions and devilish insinuations; sometimes he runs mad or suffers from epileptic fits. The discharge of semen is conducive to health and protects a man against many diseases. Man is compelled to eject it.

It has been mentioned in Naftsi, an authentic book on Tibb (medical science), that one should have sexual intercourse when the natural urge for this act is at its height. It should not be done half-heartedly, unwillingly or under compulsion or pressure. In the latter case, sexual intercourse is harmful for the health.

Hadrat Shah Wali Ullah (may Allah have mercy on him) has said:

> 'When the quantity of semen is increased, it affects the mind, with the result that it becomes the hobby of a person to cast glances at beautiful and charming women. Their beauty captivates the heart. The thought also goes to the private parts due to which the urge for sexual intercourse grown intense. This generally happens during youth. If a person is unmarried, this sexual urge ultimately induces him to commit unlawful sex. His moral conduct is spoiled and this sexual lust ultimately causes his ruin.'

The Holy Prophet (peace and blessings of Allah be upon him) has said: 'O party of young men! whosoever among you can support a wife, I must marry as it protects the eye (going stray), and chastity.'
(Mishkat)

Hadrat Shaikhul Islam Maulana Madini said to one of his followers:

'I do not agree with your statement that rectification of the innerself is not possible with marriage, as sexual intercourse purifies the heart and removes the spiritual dust.'

The commentator of the book of Qazi A'yaz has observed:

'The sexual lust of every kind darkens the heart save (lawful) sexual gratification which purifies the heart.'

This does not mean that a man should always remain engrossed in this act, transgressing the lawful limits, as extravagance is extremely harmful. The statements of Galen and Nafisi reproduced above affirm that the principle of moderacy in sexual intercourse should never be lost sight of. It should be done only in the case of genuine sexual excitement otherwise, the committing of this act halfheartedly or under compulsion may prove harmful. Nafisi is of the view that excessive indulgence in sexual intercourse decreases the strength and vitality and is harmful for the nerves. Tremor, paralysis, spasm of eyesight occur due to excessive indulgence.

It is a fact that excessive indulgence is extremely harmful for health and we must avoid it. If sexual intercourse is done within reasonable limits, it is conducive to the physical, mental and spiritual health of a person.

So far we have proved that sexual intercourse is imperative for good health, but those who transgress the lawful limits and resort to unnatural and unlawful ways to gratify their sexual lust waste their energy and vitality unnecessarily. There is a stem warning for them. Man is the sacred trustee of the future generation. He who breaks this sacred trust will have to face the dire consequences thereof sooner or later. He may not be aware of its dreadful results but he will have to face them ultimately.

Muhammad bin Zakaria has stated that the natural heat of the bodies of a group of people who were in the habit of gratifying their sexual lust in unnatural ways, had fallen down. They had become dull and slack. They remained dejected, depressed and downcast. They complained of bad digestion.

The health of the people who waste their semen in unnatural ways breaks down. They are rendered impotent and unfit for conjugal life which constitutes a great loss to humanity and nation. Those who indulge in masturbation do immense harm to their body and soul. Woe be upon these wicked people! They have to face dreadful consequences for this vice in this world in various shapes and forms, and also In the Hereafter.

Another obnoxious act is called sodomy. Its evil results also resemble those of masturbation. The nerves of the sexual organs of both the masturbater and sodomite become weak, rendering them unfit for sexual intercourse.

Islam has prescribed severe punishment for committing the indecent act of sodomy. It has been mentioned in a Hadith: 'If you find anyone committing an act of sodomy, kill both the doer and the one upon whom it is done.'

One form of wastage of semen is when a man commits sexual intercourse with his wife through the anus. It has been mentioned in a Hadith; 'Allah, will not have mercy on a person who commits lawatah.'

Another form of breach of sacred trust is the sinful act referred to in the following Hadith; 'If any person copulates with an animal, kill him.'

Social Advantages

In Islam the sexual gratification of desire has been legalised through the institution of marriage. It is permissible in all religions and in the law and constitution of every country. Families and tribes owe their existence to it. If the institution of marriage is abolished, the progress and development of the world would cease and there would be confusion and chaos everywhere.

Everyone is aware that at a certain stage of life man is in need of woman and vice versa. A man seeks pleasure and comfort through his wife, and the woman protects her modesty and chastity through her husband. Thus both of them living together in perfect harmony and cooperation lead a pious and decent life. Both share each other's feelings and sentiments. Both have some weaknesses and unless they are united, they cannot lead a fulfilled life. Marriage is also necessary from the social point of view. It facilitates close relations between the two families and mutual love and understanding between them. If there is no marriage, who will be called father and mother? Where will there be the relation of a brother and a sister? Who will be the husband and wife? There will be no father-in-law or brother-in-law. Whence will come the relation of foster brother? Where will be the family life and relationship? How will the ties of brotherhood become closer?

Non-Muslim Intellectuals on Marriage

So far you have read about the significance of marriage from the religious and medical viewpoint. Now let us see what is the opinion of non-Muslim intellectuals about marriage.

The renowned leader and the first Indian Governor General, Rajagopalachari says about marriage: 'Marriage is essential for a woman. No doubt, medical, engineering, political science are respectable professions but rearing of children and managing household affairs are more respectable jobs. Working in military, factories and civil offices may be important but to make domestic life pleasant and charming is still more important. On the basis of the experience I have gained during sixty years of my age, I am of the definite opinion that perfection of feminine virtues is not possible without marriage and without playing the role of a mother.'

A European lady scholar writes: 'The first and foremost duty of a woman is marriage, rearing of children and household management. It is, therefore, our social duty that we should provide opportunity to every woman to marry and lead a family life if she desires, just as we provide a job to every man who is in search of it.'

A Western thinker, Anthony M. Lividuacy, has written in his book entitled *Protection of Women:*

> 'We must lay a stress on one thing, that the main aim and object of every woman, at a certain stage of her life, should be to marry. The parents should know this fact and bring up their daughters in such a manner as to make them fit for conjugal life. The excellent human virtues of a woman are consummated after marriage and on becoming a mother. All other things are less important in the eyes of a woman. Those who argue that there are more important jobs than marriage, lead her

> astray. They are the worst enemies of humanity.

The above author further writes:

> 'Since a woman is already engrossed in the domestic life and multiplication of the human race, all such people who impress upon her that she has other functions to perform and other problems to solve besides household affairs, put her in trouble unnecessarily. The error of these people should be exposed and openly declared. In short, those who talk of peace and comfort for a woman without marriage and children are liars.'

The above examples have been given by way of illustration only. The necessity of marriage has been felt and admitted at every age and every time. In addition to many other advantages of marriage, the first and foremost advantage is that it guarantees the protection of chastity, virtues of rare value which Allah has bestowed upon man. Now we shall discuss this point.

Four Important Conditions

The Holy Qur'an has mentioned:

> "Lawful unto you are all beyond those mentioned, so that ye seek them with your wealth in honest wedlock, not debauchery." (4:24)

That is, a woman, other than Muharramat, becomes lawful in the fulfilment of four conditions. Firstly, the pronouncement of acceptance from both sides, which has been alluded to in the verse. Secondly, payment of a fixed dower. Thirdly, keeping the woman in a prescribed legal manner so that her moral conduct and chastity remain intact and are not spoiled. Mere gratification of sexual lust is not the object of marriage as happens in the case of adultery. The wife is forever wife and after marriage both husband and wife live together sincerely and remain loyal to each other. There is no concept of Muta (temporary marriage) in Islam. Fourthly, the marriage should not be held secretly but it is preferable that an announcement of marriage should be made publicly. At least one or two men or two women must be appointed as witnesses. Islam strictly prohibits flirtation, courtship or clandestine meeting of men and women.

The person is protected after marriage and becomes immune from moral corruption, which is the real object of marriage. Thus, marriage is not merely for gratification of sexual desire, it serves as an effective safeguard against sin. If this purpose is not achieved, such marriages cannot be called marriage in Islam. It has been mentioned in the Holy Qur'an:

> "So wed them by permission of their folk, and give unto them their portions in kindness, they being honest, not debauched nor of loose conduct." (4:25)

In the above verse, the purpose of marriage has been clearly defined, that they should thereby protect their modesty and chastity and gratify their natural sexual desire by lawful means and avoid adultery, debauchery and disloyalty to their husbands. It has been mentioned in the Holy Qur'an:

> "This day are (all), good things made lawful for you, the food of those who have received the Scripture is lawful for you and your food is lawful for them. And so are the virtuous women of the believers and the virtuous women of those who received the Scripture before you (lawful for you), when ye give them their marriage portions and live with them in honour, not in lust, not taking them as secret concubines." (5:5)

In the above verse, stress has been laid on marrying pious and chaste women. At the time of negotiations of marriage, the chastity of a woman should be given top priority. Similarly, men have been ordained not to resort to sin. Marriage, according to Islam, is a means of protecting morality and its purpose is not merely to gratify the sexual urge, otherwise, there remains no difference between man and animal.

Marriage accords legal sanction to husband and wife to gratify their sexual passion within the limits prescribed by Allah; it is not permissible to take women as concubines and spoil their chastity. If, after marriage, there is any hazard to chastity and fear of deviation from the limits imposed by Allah, the marriage contract can be dissolved. For instance, if the relations between husband and wife become strained and they begin to hate each other or are unable to fulfil the duties they owe to each other, Islam permits dissolution of marriage; but does not permit one to resort to adultery. If the husband and wife cannot pull on together, Islam gives a man the right to divorce a woman who is free to marry another person after divorce. Similarly, a woman can also seek separation (Khul'a) on this account. She has also been given the right to liberate herself from the clutches of her tyrant husband. If she honestly feels that she would not be able to live within the limits prescribed by Allah, she can get divorce from her husband on payment of the dower money or a part thereof.

Due to the paramount importance which Islam attaches to chastity and morality, a person is not permitted in Islam to continue his *Ila'* (vow of separation from wife), and a vow of abstinence from sexual intercourse for more than four months. If he abstains from his wife for more than four months, he loses his right to keep her as his wife. Due to this very reason it has been said in the Holy Qur'an:

> "But turn not altogether away (from one),
> leaving her as in suspense." (4:129)

It is most probable that the suspended woman may transgress the limits imposed by Allah, thus nullifying the very purpose of marriage. The Ahadith also lay great emphasis on protecting of chastity and morality.

Mutual Love

Another important function of marriage is that there should exist mutual love, sincerity and companionship between the two sexes and there should be perfect coordination and harmony between them, which are essential conditions for the progress and prosperity of a family, society and a nation. The husband and wife should play a positive role in the development of culture and civilization. Their conjugal life should be happy and comfortable. The Holy Qur'an has explained this fact in a beautiful manner:

> "And of His Signs is this: He created for you helpmates from yourselves that ye might find rest in them, and He ordained between you love and mercy." (30:21)

While explaining the purpose of marriage, Allah, the Exalted, says that it affords peace and comfort to both husband and wife. Both support each other in difficulty and share each other's sentiments and feelings. Whenever the sexual urge overwhelms them, they gratify their desire in a lawful manner. The Holy Prophet (peace and blessings of Allah be upon him) has said in an eloquent Hadith: 'The woman advances and returns in the shape of a devil, so when a woman fascinates any one of you and captivates your heart, you should go to your wife and have sexual intercourse with her, for it would repel that you feel.'
(Muslim)

Sexual Urge

It is natural for a man having a strong sexual instinct to cast a glance at a woman. Woman has an irresistible charm for man. If the sight of a woman captivates the heart of someone, he has been ordered to have sexual intercourse with his wife and discharge the fluid responsible for this allurement, so that the devil may not dare infuse wicked thoughts into his mind involving him in sin and vice.

The great scholar Nawawi has added the following footnote below the above Hadith: 'The reason for resembling the movements of a woman to those of a devil is that she possesses irresistible charm and attraction for man, due to which she can easily allure him into sin and vice The woman is therefore not allowed to go out except in the case of extreme need. She must avoid moving in the company of men.'

It is thus amply clear that the standard of morality and piety envisaged by Islam cannot be achieved unless the marriage is performed according to the rules prescribed by the Shari'ah.

Part - Two

Equality

Four

Rights and Equality

Prior to studying about the status of women in Islamic society and before dealing with the position of women under Islam, it would be well to examine how the question of women's rights and their claim for complete equality with men came to the forefront in modern times and what the underlying causes were which added strength to women's claim for freedom and equality. Such an analysis is called for in order to ascertain how far women's movement in modern history flourished out of a scientific and rational understanding of their powers, faculties and social functions and how far it represented merely a blind revolt against tradition, custom and artificial social restrictions and was prompted by desires untinged with altruism. It is necessary to make a dispassionate search for rational as well as non-rational factors in the modern women's movement, because otherwise our conclusions are likely to reflect the partisan spirit of one or the other side in the bitter controversy that has raged over women's demands.

An American writer, Mary R. Beard, sums up three divergent viewpoints on the subject of women's place in society in her book, *Woman as Force in History*. She says:

> One is the view that 'the women's problem,' a definition inspecting woman's place in society satisfactory to herself, can only be solved by complete equality with men, and that this equality can only be established under Communism. A second view is that woman must find her greatest happiness and

> contribute most to the state by limiting her ambitions to domesticity and still more narrowly to child-bearing, in order that the population rate may be high enough to keep a given nation secure against crowded societies on its borders, and strong enough within for aggressive action when desired against neighbours or more distant communities; this is the ideology of Fascism. The third view is that woman must have the right to choose her way of life even to the point of self centered interests; this is one among the ideologies of democracy.

Historical Circumstances

Let us now see the actual historical circumstances which gave birth to these three viewpoints on the subject of women's place in society. We shall first deal with the democratic viewpoint which is historically prior to the ideology of fascism and communism.

The eighteenth century was a period of great social and intellectual unrest in Europe. The rising intelligentsia, and the middle classes of Western countries found themselves encumbered with a host of social barriers, economic restrictions and intellectual fetters which were blocking the path of progress in every direction. They were legacies of an age of feudalism which was already past. The feudal landlords, the Catholic Church with its vast power over men's bodies and souls and the Pope, headed the Church organisation, had a vested interest in perpetuating age-old customs and artificial social restrictions which the new spirit was seeking to break through. In these circumstances, it was not unnatural that, for the rising bourgeoisie of European countries, freedom and liberty should acquire a sanctity out of all proportion to their importance in the total scheme of human values. Thus, in the eighteenth and nineteenth-century Europe, liberty and freedom became exclusive sovereign values. The importance of all other ideals was lost sight of and the complementary values of order, discipline and responsibility, without which there could be no real liberty, were ignored and brushed aside as of no moment in the lives of-nations. History bears witness to the fact that when some powerful idea takes root in a civilisation, it permeates every sphere of human life and activity. The same thing happened with the notion of liberty which, extending from the domain of politics, invaded the social sphere and expressed itself in a demand for the readjustment of sex relations. Powerful voices were raised on behalf of the rights of the female sex which had long suffered from innumerable legal and social disabilities. Freedom and equality of, the sexes became accepted principles with the new social reformers.

In France, which was the centre of all revolutionary ideas, the Romantic school of literature and poetry first made an organised drive to popularise the ideal of sex equality. George Sand, who headed this school, was a woman of loose sexual morality. She proved unfaithful to her husband Who was driven to separation. Thereafter she led the life of a libertine forming promiscuous sexual relations with a number of men, among whom was Alfred Musse, a French poet of some renown. In her novels, *Lelia and Jacques*, she severely criticised the institution of marriage and advocated free love. George Sand was followed by another group of poets, novelists and dramatists among whom Alexander Dumas and Alfred Naquet stand out as the most prominent. These writers laid emphasis on the natural birthright of men and women to indulge in free sexual relations without the encumbrances of marriage. Mention must also be made of Mary Wollstencraft who wrote her book, *A Vindication of the Rights of Women*, in 1702. She reflected a more rational outlook which was coloured more, by the altruistic desire to serve the cause of women than open the floodgates of license. In this pioneer work she protested against the unjust and unequal treatment of women and condemned the whole system of law and custom that governed the relations of men and women. Her influence on the-women's movement in France was deep and widespread. These tendencies were reinforced by the Neo-Malthusian movement in England and France which sought to limit the growth of population by popularising the use of contraceptives. The Industrial Revolution in England, by throwing upon the crowded cities a vast army of peasants and rural craftsmen, unable to support their families, further accentuated this process and brought women into the economic field for the first time in history. The radicals and philanthropists of the 'fifties and 'sixties like Robert Owen, Ruskin, Bentham, and John Stuart Mill gave further impetus to the women's movement. In 1861 Mill wrote his famous book *Subjection of Women* in which he argued, with great precision and logic that the subjection of women was the product of age-long custom and did not testify to any inherent inferiority in the female sex. Mill contended that the distinctions between men and women which went to show the inferiority of women in the domains of mental and intellectual productions; were not natural but artificial, that is, a product of subjecting environment. The education and external circumstances in which women were being brought up were, according to him, responsible for their seeming inferiority; all other talk of her innate inferiority, he pointed out, was logical perversion and psychological misunderstanding. Under the stress of these social changes and intellectual movements, family ties loosened and domesticity lost its importance for women who were forced into the economic field by circumstances beyond their control. The ideal of sex equality came nearer, fulfilment than ever, though in ways which boded ill for the happiness, of individuals and the moral health of the community. In the Great War of 1914, a vast majority of the male population in European countries had to join the war services and many of non-military occupations, hitherto regarded as the closed preserve of the male sex, were thrown open to women who became more and more convinced of their ability to compete, with men on equal terms in all fields of life.

In 1941 when America entered the Second World War, millions of American women were taken into the armed forces, placed in uniform, disciplined by officers of their own sex working under naval and military authorities, accorded official ranking and honoured with decorations for bravery under fire; to relieve men for fighting, thousands of uniformed women worked as secretaries, clerks and officials. With skill and courage, women served as doctors and nurses in the battle areas and in war hospitals at home; and many were killed at the fronts while working near or under fire. In all the drives to raise money in aid of the armed services, American women assumed leadership and served in the ranks. They laboured to uphold the morale of the services at home and abroad. They toured the war areas and fronts as entertainers of the men under arms. They entered the war-production plants by millions and made possible the output of munitions and other war supplies on a scale that astounded the whole industrial world.

At the end of the war, American men and women alike in general hoped for a return to civilian life, and this meant a heated debate over public policies to be adopted with regard to 'equality of rights' in the distribution of employments, in the competition for places and rewards in economy and society. The old debate over women's place in society was reopened with added intensity. When in 1944 the War Department of United States issued its booklets for the education of soldiers at round table forums, it included one manual to invite a pointed argument: 'Do you want your wife to work after the war?' In this discussion one side argued that times have changed, that it is good and fitting for women to work that they are competent in any kind of job, hanker after economic independence, and are likely to hang on to a cash nexus for dear life. On the other side were those who argued that woman's place is in the home that her function is child-bearing and rearing and that men will not stand her competition with returned veterans.

Democratic Ideal

So far we have examined the circumstances in which the democratic ideal of equality of sexes arose and gathered strength. Now let us turn to the Communist ideal. The leader of Communism in Russia, V.I. Lenin was ably supported and encouraged throughout his period of struggle by his wife, Krupskaya. When Lenin climbed to power in Russia, Krupskaya who had been a zealous champion of sex equality, helped to drive home, the issue of women's rights as one of the basic issues of the, revolution.

Lenin and his wife both knew very well that the Communist movement could have little prospect of success without the active support of women. And to win their full support, recognition of their right to full participation in the Communist regime was immediately given. In a speech delivered in September 1919 at the Fourth Moscow City Conference, Lenin declared: 'The Soviet Government has applied democracy to a greater extent than any other country, by the fact that in its laws not the slightest hint for any inferiority of women is left. I repeat, not a single state and no democratic legislation has done even half of what the Soviet Government did for women in the very first months of its existence.' In a conversation with Klara Zelkin, a prominent German socialist, Lenin elaborated the doctrine that 'real freedom for women is possible only through Communism.' Women must appreciate this and throw their energy into the Bolshevik Revolution,' he insisted. 'The Communist women's movement must itself be a mass movement, a part of the general mass movement. There can be no real mass movement without women. Unless millions of women are with us we cannot exercise the proletarian dictatorship, cannot construct on Communist lines. We must find out our way to them, we must study and try to find that way.' In Krupskaya's introduction to a Pamphlet by Lenin on Women and Society, the double power of women's revolutionary agitation and the Communist theory of its underlying importance were brought out. Krupskaya wrote, 'Ever since the beginning, of the Soviet rule, equal rights for women have been an object of interest, not only for women but for men as well.' As a result of these ideas, which impressed themselves on youthful minds, Russian women in great numbers agitated and organised at home and abroad for the realisation of their objects. They secured positions in Russia with the secret police and both judged and punished opponents of the Communist Party. After German troops invaded Russia, women who were not members of the Communist Party rushed like members of the party to defend their country. The Russian women, Communists as well as non-Communists, engaged in all phases of armed combat with the foe.

Like the Russian Soviet Revolution, the Fascist Revolution in Italy, Germany and Spain was also confronted with the necessity of winning women's support and their active co-operation in the struggle for Fascist ascendancy. The Fascist attitude to women was explained by Professor Maria Castellani in a volume on Italian Women, *Past and Present*, in which she said, 'Fascism recognises women as a part of the life-force of the country, laying down a division of duties between the two sexes, without putting obstacles in the way of those women who by their intellectual gifts can reach the highest positions.' Adolf Hitler, leader of the German Nazis, formulated the attitude of his movement towards women in a speech at Nuremburg on 15 September 1934, when he said, 'Woman has her battlefield. With each child that she brings to the nations, she fights her fights for the nation.' Such women as Sophic Rogge-Boemer, who called for the military training of women, were suppressed by Hitler and Goebbels in favour of women who devoted their strength and interest to child-bearing. Young women in large numbers responded enthusiastically to indoctrination on this point and entered the numerous maternity homes founded by the Nazis.

We have seen how the Democratic, Communist and Fascist viewpoints about the rights of women and their place in society were in part moulded by certain historical conditions and in part by political expediency designed to secure a larger following by enlisting the support of women. As far as the democratic viewpoint is concerned, it was free from the taint of political expediency but there was present in it from the very beginning a negative urge to sweep away age-long restrictions. Democracy failed, as in other fields, to develop a positive doctrine of women's rights and duties and continued itself to the removal of old abuses.

In contrast with the above-mentioned attitudes towards the problem of sex relations, Islamic teachings in regard to the position of women can be traced to neither of the sources. There was no political necessity for the Prophet of Islam to gain the favour of the fair sex, because the social conditions of Arabia were such that women's influence on the larger affairs of life was bound to be negligible. Nor was the Prophet of Islam confronted by the necessity of enlisting women for fighting a national war of defence or aggression against foreign countries. Therefore unlike Hitler and Mussolini, he had no motive to define women's rights and duties with an eye on the requirements of military defence or aggression. Again, in contrast to democracy, which was the outcome of a negative urge, to sweep away old restrictions that blocked the way to progress, Islam was more concerned with bringing some sort of discipline to a race of wild, freedom-loving Arabs who knew no respect for law and order and obeyed no central authority. The problem, therefore, for Islam was not so much the loosening of artificial bonds, as creating law, order and discipline among a people steeped in license and unacquainted with healthy social or moral restrictions. For all these reasons, Islam treated the question of sex equality and women's rights on its own merits and defined its attitude to sex relations on the basis of human nature rightly interpreted. Islamic teachings on this subject, therefore, spring from the ultimate facts of human nature in its social context. Military necessity, political expediency or merely blind revolt against the past did not in any way affect Islam's solution of the sex problem.

Question of Relationship

The question of the relationship between man and woman and their respective rights and duties is really a part of the larger socio-economic problem of man. Its solution depends on the way in which this larger problem is dealt with by a civilisation. It is wrong, therefore, to study the question of woman's rights and her place in society in isolation from the total context of human relationships in all their aspects. Before we pass any judgment on the particular way in which a civilisation deals with the sex problem, we should consider its total approach to human existence, so as, to, enable us to view its specific solution in their larger and total setting. But for this, we shall have to define the basic attitude of a civilisation towards life in general. In the next chapter, therefore, we shall attempt to define the basic approach of Islam towards human existence, in contrast with that of the Western civilisation, because this approach has decisive bearing on the way in which Islam grappled with the problem of sex equality and the rights of women.

Because of the pressure of many forces every country of the Moslem East, as we have seen, shows some trend of change in the relationship between religion and life. The control of Islam as an iron clad system of rules and traditions is giving way to a more individual interpretation of religion. Since this new spirit of religious liberalism deeply affects the life of women, one constantly feels the desire to know the personal attitude of Moslem women toward their religion, and their share in determining the new religious thought in Islam.

The older generation as a whole in every country tends to be conservative in all religions but this is especially true of Islam. This unquestioning adherence to the literal interpretation of the teaching of their religion is especially characteristic of women in the middle and lower levels of society, regardless of age, and also of the village women of Asia. This great majority of Moslem women, who have remained untouched by Western influence, have been little conscious of any changes in Islam, and have themselves undergone no change in their religious outlook. In fact, they constitute very often a distinct deterrent to change, opposing any deviation from established social customs, which are in their minds identified with religious sanctions. It is very often the orthodox wife or mother who maintains the rigid conservatism of the home, however lax men may become in their observance of religious customs outside the home.

The full meaning of Islam for the devoted Moslem woman is difficult for a mere outsider to understand. This is one veil of Moslem life which the Western observer cannot lift. Accustomed to a different form of religious experience, one from the West may easily draw a false conclusion regarding the relationship of Moslem women to their religion. The small number of women in the mosques in most countries — Turkey is an exception-which offers a striking contrast to the usual predominance of women in churches in the West, might be interpreted as a lack of worship of Moslem women, if one did not know that it is not the public prayers in the mosque but her private prayers at home which have primary significance for the Moslem woman. In her home the orthodox woman will pray, with her face turned towards Mecca, five times daily in the name of the Prophet to the one God, and will cherish the devout hope as a constant follower of Mohammed, that she may make the pilgrimage to the Holy City.

The keynote of the Moslem woman's religion is complete acquiescence to fate; to protest against a lack of privileges is quite foreign to her nature. Islam may have deprived her of privileges but not of responsibilities. Her primary obligation is to accept as the will of Allah, whatever is written on her forehead as her fate. This spirit of fatalism has insured the undisturbed control of Islam over the destiny of Moslem women through the centuries. Today, although the great majority of Moslem women have remained unchanged in their personal attitude toward their religion, a small minority of women has begun to question the relationship between the accepted teaching of Islam and the demands of their modern world. Education inevitably is undermining the characteristic attitude of fatalism toward religion and life. One begins to find in the different parts of the Islamic world Moslem women expressing an independent opinion of the interpretation of Islam, in order to bring religion into accord with modern needs.

Speaking on purdah in a public address, Lady Abdul Qadir, one of the outstanding Moslem leaders of India, said: "Purdah, as observed among certain classes of Indian Mohammedans, is far beyond anything enjoined by Islam and requires modification according to the needs of the day and the rapidly changing times." Another interesting illustration of the modern approach to Islam by a Moslem woman in India is the aggressive challenge to the Ulemas, the authorities of Islam, made by Begum Habibullah, an enlightened Moslem leader in Lucknow in a newspaper article, in which she showed that the Koran does not teach educational inequality and segregation of women.

Indian women are deeply imbued with religion, but their religious devotion today does not cloud the vision of the educated minority, nor even of a larger number, so that they cannot discriminate between religious and social questions. The widespread testimony against child-marriage gathered from Indian women of all classes *by the Age of ass came as a great surprise Consent Commission,* doubtless to many in India and elsewhere who had not realized that there is a Growing spirit of religious freedom among Indian women. The All-India Women's Conference, representing as it does the inter-communal effort of women leaders to release social reform from the bonds of religious tradition, has repeatedly given utterance to the new religious liberalism. In India, more than in any other country of the East, women have been impelled to protest individually and collectively against social handicaps. The active promotion and support of the Child Marriage Act, and the repeated resolutions against polygamy passed by the All-India Women's Conference, are exerting a powerful force toward the freedom of Hindu and Moslem women from these and other social customs, hitherto regarded as determined by religious sanctions.

The Challenge

The fact that women have challenged the inviolability of these sanctions is perhaps no less important than the social reforms themselves. Some Indian leaders are especially concerned to keep their endorsement of social advance in harmony with religious teaching. In the discussion on polygamy at a recent 'All-India Conference, one of the Moslem delegates explained that she favoured the abolition of polygamy, but she wished to call attention to the fact that "it was permitted by their religion only in case of strictest necessity arising, as for example, in the event of there being no issue from the first marriage."

Syria offers an interesting example of an interpretation of the social teachings of the Koran, made by a young Druse girl Nazira Zein-el-Din, in her book, *As-Sufur-Weel-Hijab* (Unveiling and Veiling), which evoked much comment. This book was translated into several languages, widely circulated, and brought the author a trunkful of clippings from all over the world. The Islamic teaching concerning the veil was discussed also in an oratorical contest at the American University of Beirut by Madame Ihsan Shakir El-Kousy, to whom reference has already been made. In her address, which received the second prize, she showed that the Koran does not prescribe the veil. Thus, incidentally she justified her own presence unveiled in a large university.

These two examples, however, are not typical of the .women of either Syria or Egypt as a whole but less so of Syria. There is very little evidence of any analysis of Islam and very little articulate expression on religion by women in Syria: a very small minority of Egyptian women is actively interested in the relation of religion to reform. The attitude of Madame Sharawi Pasha, to whom reference has already been made as the outstanding Moslem woman leader in Egypt, shows general conformity to the prevailing policy in Egypt as regards the promotion of social advance. She has carefully based her demands for social reform on the spirit of the Koran and has not promoted reforms which do not have Islamic sanction. For example, her claims for equality of education for girls have been based on the teaching of the Koran. She has urged a law prohibiting polygamy. Reference has been made to her very effective protest against polygamy in a public lecture at the American University in Cairo last year. But while protesting against polygamy she recognizes the exceptions for polygamy which are granted by the Koran (adultery, childlessness and incompatibility). One has the feeling that this policy of maintaining a careful balance between Islamic teaching and social reform, which is followed by Madame Sharawi and the Feminist Union, is dictated more by political expediency than by religious conservatism.

Among the women of Palestine no deviation from the conventional attitude toward Islam is evident. Moslem women simply reflect the prevailing religious conservatism. However, the interesting feature in the situation, to which reference has already been made in another connection, is that Moslem women pay the price for this conservatism, of which the veil is the symbol, willingly and with a sense of pride; since by retaining the characteristic Islamic customs they feel that they have a certain distinction in contrast to the Zionist community. It is worth recalling the incident showing the counter-influence of Arab national feeling in reference to the veil, when the, group of Arab women unveiled made a protest against Zionism. But as already explained, the veils were later resumed when the habitual spirit of conservatism reasserted itself. The great majority of Moslem women in Palestine, as elsewhere, are not aware of the new conflicting currents of thought.

The attitude of women in Iran and Iraq toward religion, as toward social advance, is one of passive acquiescence. Changes in Turkey have aroused much interest in both countries, and the Turkish method of drastic social and religious reforms has been little questioned in reference to its having an adverse effect on religion. The women of Iraq and Iran have been primarily interested in the achievement of Turkey. Very often in Iraq I heard the statement: "We need a Kamal Ataturk." In Iran the hope was frequently expressed at the time of my visit several years ago, that the Shah would follow Kamal Ataturk's example and issue an order to remove the *chaddur*. In Iran as elsewhere it was erroneously believed that unveiling in Turkey had been made compulsory. This hope has now been realized and, it is interesting to note, that the definite regulations against the chaddur have not apparently caused a widespread religious shock among the women of Iran. Even the conservatives are accepting the new freedom, I have been told, as they accepted the former social restrictions, in an attitude of acquiescence.

In marked contrast to the attitude of women in Iraq and Iran toward Turkey, Moslem women in India have repeatedly asked me with deep solicitude whether Turkey had cast aside Islam. "Have Turkish women lost their religion?" was the question that came alike from the student group and from conservative older women. The new freedom of Turkish women, if secured at the sacrifice of religion, would seem to Moslem women in India to have cost too high a price.

In Turkey women have regarded religious changes together with all other changes, as merely a natural part of the general transformation taking place in Turkish life. There has been remarkably little analysis of the new situation in reference to the effect on religion. During the first crucial years of change the conservatives retained the veil, which older women doubtless associated with religion. But by this time the veil has, I believe, for the great majority lost any religious significance it may have had. However, recent municipal legislation of Adana and some other cities, has doubtless brought a shock to those who still have the feeling of the relationship between the veil and Islam. But they will probably accept the enforced change philosophically, as did a conservative Turkish woman in Adana, whose comment on the new regulation was: "Well, the sin will be charged against those who issued such an order and not against us, because they are forcing us to do this against our wills." This idea that unveiling is an actual sin, is probably held by very few Turkish women today.

The viewpoint of these orthodox Turkish women can scarcely fail to be affected unconsciously by the modern atmosphere, which has become steadily more natural, even in the smaller towns of the Interior. The new type of preaching of the *hodjah* has also had its effect. As a simple Turkish woman in Talas told me several years ago, "They tell us different things about religion today. The hodjahs formerly taught that women must always be veiled and their voice never heard in public. But they say now that these things are not religion." Thus, the most orthodox women have been steadily exposed to the new idea, that social customs are not necessarily, identified with religion.

The educated Turkish woman has adopted such new ideas as a logical part of the modernization of Turkish life. Before the recent period of reform this educated minority was already progressive in religious thinking for, as has already been mentioned in the discussion of Turkish education, the social- religious revolution in Turkey was preceded by a gradual period of preparation. Today due to many forces there is said to be a decline in the formal practices of Islam. "Many people no longer pray five times a day. Everyone is too busy," was the comment of a young Turkish business woman. A young teacher explained why comparatively few young people go to the mosques. "We must make our worship more modern to suit our modern clothes and customs. Praying without shoes and with many genuflections was a good thing in the Prophet's day but does not suit our present kind of life."

Although the private prayers of the formal type are still continued by many Moslem women in the homes and to a lesser extent in the mosque, as has always been the case among women, the turning away from the ritualistic worship by the younger generation is undoubtedly a marked present-day tendency. However, this should not, as has been said before, be interpreted merely as a trend toward irreligion, but perhaps it may indicate the genuine urge for a reform in worship, so that it may be something more than a prescribed ceremonial. "We are beginning to recognize the difference between essentials and nonessentials," a thoughtful Turkish woman said. "The religious forms and social restrictions are not suitable today. These can be changed without destroying our fundamental belief".

Another Turkish leader, talking with a Moslem woman from Jerusalem, who had expressed the belief that Turkey had sacrificed Islam, said, "We have separated religion from externals and made it personal. Religion is not a matter of clothes-the veil and the *fez*. It is not based on form but feeling. The repudiation of Islamic formalism therefore does not mean giving up Islam. The women of Palestine may be more outwardly religious in the orthodox sense of Islam but not necessarily more truly religious in the inner meaning of the term than are the women of Turkey."

In regard to this transfer of emphasis from the external to the more individual idea of religion, a young Turkish woman student in Istanbul University expressed the opinion that there is need now for a more positive interpretation of religion. "Most of the younger Turkish girls will grow up with very little idea of Islam," she said, "since nothing positive has taken the place of the old forms, which have lost their appeal, and since very little attention these days is paid to religion." The need for a more definite constructive idea of religion is probably not as yet generally recognized by the younger generation in Turkey, which associates religion merely with a peaceful existence of quiet contemplation in the shade of mosque walls and not with an intensely active modern life.

However, a number of thoughtful Turkish leaders, both men and women, but perhaps especially women, are beginning to realize the need of a new relationship between religion and life. It is, I believe, not too much to expect that Turkish women, who have gained so much from the social and religious reforms in Turkey, may now make some special contribution to the rethinking of religious values. Their voice, and the voice of Moslem women in other countries, which have been so little heard in shaping religious thought in the past, may help to answer the crucial question in the East today, as to whether the present spirit of religious liberalism in the Moslem world will mean the disintegration of Islam or the beginning of a new era of more vital faith.

Contribution of Islam

It is easier to appreciate what Islam has contributed to the well being of woman and how it liberated them from all those yokes. Islam has regarded the practice of burying a girl alive as a crime i.e., murder. In this respect the Holy Quran says :

> "And when the female infant buried alive is questioned: "for what crime she was killed?" (Quran, 81: 8, 9) (Even her father himself could not give her an answer).

Quran also criticizes parents on how they react when news is brought to them about the birth of a girl. On this the Holy Quran says:

> "When news is brought to one of them, of the birth of a female child, his face darkens and he is filled with inward grief. With shame does he hide himself from his people because of the bad news he has received. Shall he retain her on sufferance and contempt, or

> bury her in the dust? Ah! what evil choice they decide on." (Quran, 16 58, 59)

We shall appreciate the way man, used to deal with different situations and the way he regarded a woman in such an olden society (whether that society be in Arabia), fittest and, strongest. This was more so as man attacked man and man looted man. This was their common law.

Bahiy al-Khuury in his book: *al Marla bainal 'Bayti wal Mujtama-i* (Women between Home and Society) throws light on problem in a very good way:

> "...... Was a man, then, to blame, when he, in those days, arranged his life and other social activities in accordance with the conditions prevailing then, taking into account the invasions that could happen at any moment and the unexpected looting and ... "Was he to blame, 'then, when he went out looting or defending if he, exempted the pregnant, the one who nursed her baby and the like who were weak amongst women?
>
> "To which of the two births would he be happy; about the birth of a baby boy who would ride a horse, take up arms and fight the enemy or of that a baby girl that would not be able to do anything of the sort. Over and above, she would be a burden in the battle and she would have to be protected?
>
> "..... The Arabs did not welcome the birth of a baby girl, and this was so because of the nature of their society. Wars and invasions never ceased and taking revenge never stopped. All these things depended on the male, but a woman was unable to do any of

> these tasks, in addition to it, she was the desired loot for (the) service (of the enemy) in the eyes of the enemy, or she was for his entertainment....

We learn from Hadith (Sayings of the Holy Prophet peace and blessings of Allah be upon him) that a girl should not suffer injustice or inequality. He is quoted as saying what it meant :

> "He who has a daughter and does not bury her alive, or insult her, and does not prefer his son to her, Allah will enter him into Paradise."
>
> (There are many other sayings that encourage the bringing up of girls in, the same way as with equal treatment as the boys.)

According to the teachings of Islam woman is not blamed for Adam's first mistake. In some verses of the Holy Quran Adam is specifically blamed:

> "Then they twain ate thereof, so that their shame became apparent unto them, and they began to hide by keeping on themselves some of the leaves of the Garden. and Adam disobeyed his Lord, so Went astray.(Quran, 20 :121)

(Let us see what Abdullah al-Khayyat in his book, *The Muslim's Guide to Faith* has to say here. He quotes the Apostle (peace and blessings of Allah be upon him) as saying: "every child is born with an upright nature, but his father makes him a Christian or a Magian."

This means that every new born child carries within himself an innocent upright nature...... This is in complete contradiction with the Christian creed of the inborn sin. According to Islam no sin is inherited by a child Even Adam is not considered sinful in Islam. He forgot Allah's orders and had no intention to disobey his Lord's orders as said in the Quran.

Adam and Eve jointly disobeyed. Both repented and both of them were forgiven.

Women's Human Rights

Islam dealt with human rights of women at a time when in some parts of the world conferences were being held to discuss whether she had a soul or not and whether she was human or not, or whether she was to worship God as the man does or otherwise, or whether she will enter Paradise or not.

These conferences took place between the fifth and seventh centuries of the Christian era. It was at this very time that Islam came into being and gave the answer in such an amazing bravery:

> "O Mankind! Be careful of your duty to your Lord Who created you from a single soul and from it created its mate and from them twain hath spread (abroad) a multitude of men and women..." (Quran,4:1)
>
> "He, it, is Who did create you from a single soul and therefrom did create his mate that he might dwell with her in life...." (Quran, 7:199)
>
> "And Allah hath given you wives of your own kind, and hath given you from your wives sons and grandsons, and hath made provision of good things for you. Is it then in vanity that they believe and in the grace of Allah that they disbelieve?" (Quran, 16: 72)
>
> "The Creator of heavens and earth: He has made for you pairs from among your selves." (Quran, 42: 11)
>
> "And of His signs is this: He created, for you helpmates from yourselves, that ye might find, rest in them and He ordained between you love and mercy. Lo, herein indeed are

> portents for folks who reflect."(Quran, 30: 18)
>
> "O Mankind ! Lo! We have created you male and female, and have made you, nations and tribes, that ye may know each other ...."
>
> (Quran-49: 13)

No Discrimination

Islam does not differentiate women from man in terms of religious obligations. It is interesting to find out that a woman has certain advantages (you may call them so if you like) over man in certain cases.

Let us quote some such cases

She is exempted of the daily prayers and of fasting during her menstruation period (monthly course) and for forty days of her confinement after giving birth to a child. She does not have to make up for the missed prayers because of one of the aforementioned reasons. She may not fast during her pregnancy but she is not exempted from prayers and when she is nursing her baby if there is any threat to her health or her baby's she is allowed to miss fasts. She can make up for such missed fasting days whenever she can before the next Ramadan-(the ninth month of Islamic Era and the month in which fasting from food etc., is observed from dawn to sunset for the whole month).

Islam took into account the physical and psychological changes in the natural female function, e.g., a woman might be nursing her babe or looking after him; that it made the attendance of congregational prayers optional for her while it is compulsory for men. A man must attend all the congregational prayers, especially if he happens to live near a mosque or a place where Muslims meet to say prayers. It is not accepted that he says his prayers alone at home, while it is permissible for a woman to do so. Some of the theologians even say it is preferable that she say her prayers at home.

Championing Equality

In the 6th century the greatest event of the history of mankind which shook the very basic ideals and concepts of man and brought about a complete revolution in his thoughts and views and a total change in his character, was the high-spirited and high-hearted proclamation of the Prophethood of Hazrat Muhammad (peace and blessings of Allah be upon him). The result of this revolution was that it not only took a different turn in man's thought, but also gave a new direction to his life. One significant aspect of this new trend of thinking was the 'concept of woman' which underwent a complete change and thereby established the relationship between man and woman on entirely new grounds.

Before the advent of Islam and the arrival of Prophet Muhammad (peace be upon him) and his proclamation of Prophethood, the history of woman was no doubt the history of subjugation and oppression. She was underestimated and condemned as a low and mean creature and was regarded as the root cause of all evils and disasters. Instructions were given to be careful about her and to avoid her like snakes and scorpions. She was bought and sold like animals. She did not enjoy any absolute or independent position in the society and was made subservient to man. She was denied all rights and had to live on the pity and mercy of man. In such a dark period of the history of woman, Islam raised its voice so vehemently that the whole world reverberated with it. Today no one dares say that her previous position was correct and real. It was loudly proclaimed:

> O mankind! Reverence
> Your Guardian Lord,
> Who created you
> From a single soul
> Created, of like nature
> His mate, and from them twain
> Scattered (like seeds) Countless men and
> women:
> Reverence God, through Whom
> Ye demand your mutual (rights).

And (reverence) the wombs
(that bore) for God
Ever watches over you. (4:1)

It was declared that the discrimination which the world has made between one man and the other is false, absurd and baseless. The whole mankind is the offspring of the single human soul. Originally all have the same descent. No one is noble or mean, or low or high by birth. All are equal and enjoy equal position. Any kind of distinction between them on the grounds of family status, race, colour, tribe, region, language, occupation or nationality is null and void.

It was thus a repudiation of the age-old differences and discrimination between man and woman. It brought into light the fact that the very companion of the first man was not of some other kind but belonged to the same species. No different kind of creature was taken for his companionship, rather she was taken from him alone. This first pair gave birth to numerous men and women and among them some or the other kind of relationship existed and thus the whole human generation got spread far and wide. Hence to differentiate and discriminate between man and woman is in fact to differentiate and discriminate between one side of mankind and the other and is the division of the two parts of a single whole. There can be no better elucidation than this for the expression of the equality of man and woman and their equal status.

It is also stated that all human beings are the servants of one God and the children of one and the same father and mother. Therefore on the one side they should worship and obey God and lead their life in fear of Him and on the other, give due respect to the relationships which exist between them. Here, with the honour of man, the honour of woman is also emphasised.

Islam totally repudiated the notion that man is dignified and honoured merely because he is a man and woman is low and mean simply because she is a woman. Both man and woman are equal in the eyes of Islam. Neither the inferiority of anyone nor superiority of anybody is written down for eternity. Whoever is adorned with faith and fair practice emerged successful here and in the hereafter and whoever is devoid of such qualities fails in this as well as in the eternal world:

> Whoever works righteousness,
> Man or woman, and has faith,
> Verily, to him will We give
> A new life, a life
> That is good and pure, and We
> Will bestow on such their reward
> According to the best
> Of their actions. (16:97)

Islam assigns different spheres of activity for man and woman. The field of work of woman is her own house and of men is the world outside. What the Qur'an instructs the honourable wives of the Holy Prophet (peace be upon him) holds true for all such women as believe in Allah and His Messenger.

Generally, two objections are raised against the position of woman in Islam. First, that the great responsibility of household affairs which is imposed upon her, would debar her from participating in the economic and social development. For this reason it is assumed that her position in the society would not be definite, but would be weak and unstable.

Regarding this, it needs to be clarified, that Islam has not barred woman from economic activities, rather it has given permission while imposing on her a few appropriate limitations. Although it is doubtless that her involvement in family affairs affects her economic struggle, Islam offers its own solution to it. Islam has held man legally responsible for the maintenance of his wife and children.

The second objection is that since the great responsibility of the house is vested in woman, she is confined to the four walls of the house. It is conceived that since she is completely engrossed in the home affairs, neither the society would be benefited from her abilities nor would she get any opportunity to contribute her potentialities to society.

This objection is also incorrect and without any substance. Islam has not forbidden woman from other activities which stand beyond the household activities. What Islam virtually intends and emphasises in this regard is that a woman is mainly a queen and fore-runner of her house. Hence, she should not bear the outward burden of the work at the risk of her indoor work. She is allowed to participate in the economic struggle with man while performing her role in the family affairs. Furthermore, she can take interest and contribute her abilities in different fields of life while keeping into consideration her condition, social environment and her own interest. History bears witness to the fact that the Muslim women have manifested their abilities, skill and talent in different fields of life and have left a tremendous impact on the age.

The most important thing is, Islam has assigned woman a prominent position at social level. Hence, she can lead an honoured and dignified life without becoming a victim of any inferiority complex. She can, in fact, offer her fullest cooperation to man in building up a chaste and virtuous society while contributing her potentialities and abilities which she possesses.

Different Spheres

There are two important reasons for which Islam assigns different spheres of activity to man and woman. First, it helps them guard their chastity. When both of them perform their work in the same sphere, it will become difficult for them to lead a life of chastity and modesty. If man and woman mix with each other in educational institutions to pursue education and participate in sports and games, and other recreations in parks and picnic spots and engage themselves openly in markets and in business centres without any checks and balances and meet each other without any restriction and this process of intermingling continues not for a day or two but for years together and in this way all the stages from childhood to youth and from youth to old age will be crossed, it is certain that their physical urges will get excited and flared up and will become uncontrolled and unchecked and ultimately they will become victims of indecent sexual anarchy.

In the present age, wherever free mixing of man and woman has been granted, it has resulted in a disaster. Chastity and honour are ravaged and modesty and decency are crippled. It gives rise to vulgar and ignoble sexual lapses which like an epidemic disease goes to such an extent that it becomes difficult to cure and correct it. And now it is taken as an inescapable social evil. Also all the evil results of it are willingly or unwillingly tolerated.

Chastity and modesty are apparently moral values, and it is on this basis that the direction of the whole society is determined. In a society where no importance is given to these values, man from every direction is taken to debased and evil acts and adultery. It gives rise to a particular kind of culture, civilisation, association, manners and literature, each element of which ignites fire in the sexual emotions of man. Contrary to it, the society which realises the importance and value of chastity and purity is erected entirely on a different standard. Each act of such a society reflects the purity of character, modesty and decency, and piety and purity fills the whole environment.

Islam is very sensitive to the chastity and purity of a man. It forbids free mixing and unrestricted meeting between man and woman. Islam considers it wrong to let man and woman mix with each other in their fields of work and let themselves involve in a severe test from where it is difficult to return. Islam not only forbids the acts of adultery but also prohibits man and woman to go near it.

The Qur'an says:

> Nor come nigh to adultery:
> For it is a shameful (deed)
> And an evil, opening the road,
> (to other evils). (17:32)

The second reason to assign different fields of work for man and woman is that their abilities and potentialities differ with each other. It is a fact that a woman is physically weaker than a man. She cannot bear hardship and strains.

Woman passes through such stages of life which restrict her from performing heavy work constantly. Her menstrual period begins from her youth and continues until she steps into the old age. Moreover, she passes through the most difficult and arduous stages like pregnancy and delivery. All these conditions and stages affect her health, strength and manner and stand as obstacles on the way of constant and laborious work. Now, it is the question of justice that she should not be given any tedious and wearisome works. Islam, therefore, assigns the work which requires more strength and valour to man and the work which is not hard and tedious to woman. Islam solves the problem thus that woman should look after the house while man should perform outside duties.

The very nature, interest and the psychology of woman demands the same sort of work. Woman in herself possesses the qualities of grace, love, patience, devotion and sacrifice more than a man. She fills the whole atmosphere of the family with happiness and order, peace and tranquility and love and affection. But to face the hardships and difficulties of life and to march forward firmly on all ups and downs, strong determination, bravery and intrepidity are the qualities which are required. Man possesses all these qualities far more than woman. The home and the family, however, provide a peaceful environment. The abilities of woman distinctively appear more sharply in the house from which full advantage can be derived. Man can face the complications and problems of life. For this reason man should be given such responsibilities as require more courage and valour.

It is no fairness to woman that she should be taken out from her natural field of work and be pushed into an unnatural field of work. It is not advantageous for her, rather a great loss.

The pains of menstrual period, pregnancy and delivery are unavoidable. Man can hardly assist her in all these difficulties and complications. It is, therefore, not a fair play if she is also given the responsibilities of man.

The woman is the queen of the house. She gets all the love and affection from her father, brother and husband and all the members of her family and all her rights are protected in the house. If woman does not bear the responsibility of the house, she cannot claim her rights. Thereafter she will have to work in such a field to pass her life which will not be in fact her own field and where she will have to face such a partner at every step who will be stronger than her. Then, it can be hardly expected that she will surpass man.

The place of honour and dignity of a woman is her own house, not the market. But in the present age, the importance of house and family is not fully recognised. It is the reason that the important role of woman in the house is interpreted as an injustice to her or that it gives her a low and mean position in the society or to deny her rights which she possesses or to condemn her constantly to the lowest position though a family is the basic unit of every society. The importance and significance of the house stands far ahead than of an office or a bazaar. The service which a woman renders in building the inner environment of her house is more important than the service which she can render outside. Here some aspects of her work are mentioned.

Services of Woman

1. Today, man is engrossed in innumerable political, social, cultural and other problems. Other factors like health, diseases, poverty, difficulties also coincide with these problems. Sometimes for earning and living, man struggles too severely, bears all kinds of pains and faces innumerable difficulties. For maintaining and uplifting his family, he overcomes insurmountable hardships. In such a state of affairs, he deserves mental peace and content. It is the home which can provide him with all this peace and rest. If he does not get peace even at his own home, it becomes too hard for him to live: Islam teaches that a woman should make her home a 'peaceful dwelling' so that man should forget all his tensions and complications after reaching his home and prepare himself for a fresh struggle after breathing an air of gratification.

2. It has become an established fact that there is no better nourishment for a child than the milk of his mother. If a mother does not stay at home and engages herself in outside activities, she cannot set herself for breast-feeding. In this way the proper nourishment of the child for a considerable period even after the age of breast-feeding depends on mother. For the proper bringing up of the child, it is not just enough to give him proper nourishment but the child abundantly needs the love and affection, sympathy and an earnest devotion of his mother. If he is devoid of love and emotions from his nearest environment, his whole personality gets affected and even if his personality blossoms it will develop in a very wrong direction. It is the heart of mother which is the source of inspiration for the child. Nobody else can take the place of woman for playing a decisive role. If the mother remains outside the home, the child would yearn for the love of his mother and he will not get it.

3. For the basic education and training of the child, mother is most suitable. For the purpose of education of the child, it is necessary that his teachers should be very loving and devoted to him, and should be acquainted with the nature and psychology of the child, and tolerate all his mischiefs and check him with love and patience. The most important thing is that the child should also love the teacher and consider even the bitterest scolding of the teacher to be good and beneficial for his well-being and tolerate even the harshness of the teacher. These sorts of feelings do not prevail between any two persons other than between mother and child. Let us look at another aspect. From educational point of view, it is extremely important that there should prevail an intimate and cordial relationship between the teacher and the child. The stronger this relationship, the better and beneficial it would be for the child. Perhaps, because of this reason, classes of higher standards are not much liked in schools because there the relationship between the teacher and the child is weaker in most of the cases. Comparatively, the classes of the lower standards are liked much because here this relationship is found to be stronger. In this manner the mother can provide basic

education for her children which they cannot possibly acquire even at school.

Most of the children do not obtain proper education because they do not get better tutors at home or their parents are not able to afford tutors for them. Furthermore, most of the parents do not get proper tutors for their daughters. If the mother is capable enough to educate her children and even feel that it is her responsibility to give proper education to her children, the expenditure which is incurred on education will also get curtailed and help solve many other problems.

Here, one important point from the Muslim outlook on education is that today little attention is being paid to religious education. Very few children obtain religious education. Consequently, the child is sent to school when he has reached the age of school going. He does not get any opportunity even the preliminary religious instructions. Therefore, even the children of some good and God-fearing people remain ignorant of the basic religious tenets. The reason behind all this is that the father does not get time to give them religious instructions and the mother either herself lacks such education or does not take interest in education. If the mother is thoughtful enough and also capable of giving education to her children, they will not be ignorant of their religion, even after obtaining education in schools.

Even for training the children, the role of the mother is most important and significant. It is the mother who stands as an ideal for a child. The child observes the morals and etiquette of his mother day and night and moulds his behaviour noting the behaviour of his mother. The child maintains the same sort of relationship between himself and others on the mode of the relationship which his mother maintains between herself and others. Mother is his virtual model in this aspect and plays a decisive role in moulding the character of her child.

The fact is that the construction of a society depends upon the construction of a house. This is the reason that Islam has completely relied upon woman to construct her house. Islam does not wish to thrust on her other burdens along with this responsibility. The woman is freed even from the financial responsibilities. In the light of Islam, the construction of their house is no less important than Jihad. Hazrat Anas related that once a group of women asked Prophet Muhammad (peace be upon him) that men perform some acts and attain the reward of Jihad, what we should do to get such reward which men get through Jihad in the way of God? Prophet Muhammad (peace be upon him) replied that woman who sits at home receives the reward of Jihad in the way of God. What a great reward.

Five

Liberty and Equality

Liberty and equality are concepts which have been very much misused by the modern world. There is no doubt that human progress depends to a large extent on freedom and equality, and a society which creates artificial inequalities and places unnatural obstacles in the way of human freedom slowly degenerates and dies out. But it is equally true that real freedom does not lie in unrestricted license and presupposes as its inevitable corollary certain wholesome natural restrictions. Similarly, equality cannot mean a total obliteration of diversity arising from the natural and inborn differences between man and woman. Real equality can be based only on an inequality of function where each individual and each sex is entrusted with the tasks to which its natural endowments and inherent qualities qualify it most. The Western civilisation has placed undue and exaggerated emphasis on self-assertion and self-expression for the historical reason that its fundamental concepts arose out of a struggle against artificial repressions. The result is that the assertive and expressive tendencies of human beings have brought about internal conflicts which threaten to its foundation the very structure of civilisation. A balance between self-expression and self-repression, freedom and order, uniformity and diversity should be achieved to put human society on a stable basis. If this is true in the large spheres of human relations, it is equally true in the sex relations of men and women. An expert on sex psychology like Havelock Ellis says: 'We have always to remember that the whole art of living lies in a fine balance of expression and repression. For repression - understood in a wide sense and not merely in the special sense sometimes given to it by psychoanalysts - is as central a fact of life as expression. We are constantly at the same time repressing some impulses and expressing other impulses. There is no necessary penalty in the repression, for it is essential to expression.

Islam has placed certain restrictions on men as well as on women in order to regulate their sex and family life both of which it regards as the foundations of a stable and progressive civilisation. The restrictions on men and women differ in accordance with their varying functions in society. To the extent that these functions differ in the case of the two sexes, their rights and responsibilities also differ and the restrictions they are required to observe also differ. The advocates *of a bald and dead equality* who do not believe in the functional differentiation of the sexes will cite them as a proof of unequal treatment. Actually, these restrictions arise out of the different social responsibilities of either sex. If it is true that motherhood is one of the essential responsibilities of women, that sexual aberration in women leads to more complications and more serious consequences than the misconduct of men; if, again, it is true that men and women differ in the types (not degrees) of their natural gifts and that the physical powers of women are attuned to particular types of work only, then it is easy to see that, within the general framework of fundamental sex equality, their rights, duties and the channels of their self-expression and self-repression should also differ.

Functional Difference

Saner intellectuals even among the Westerners have always recognised the functional differentiation between the two sexes. They also admit that women are better fitted for particular types of work than men, and ill-suited for other tasks. For example, the American authoress of *Male and Female*, Margaret Mead, discussing this point in connection with her researches into the life of savage tribes, writes: 'Thus if the theorist about men and women's natural work-rhythms had based his theories on *Jatmul*, he would easily have come up with a picture of man as the lineal descendant of a nomadic hunter, capable of strong output of effort, but demanding long periods of recuperation, and a picture of women as better fitted by nature for the routine tasks of everyday life, unresisting and unrebelling against a world in which their work was never done and their hands were hardly ever at rest.' Proceeding further, the same authoress says: 'If research finally demonstrates any genuine difference in the capacity to tolerate monotony, or to benefit by working in irregular spurts of energy, we still have to consider whether the most felicitous results are obtained by constructing a society in which women's work, while more monotonous and demanding, is also keyed up to the cycle of menstruation and pregnancy, and men's work, less monotonous and demanding, is the work that can be depended upon in any emergency, since men are subject to no such periodic rise and fall in capacity as women. Possibly we may find instead that if all work is keyed low enough so that women do not suffer too inappropriate demands during their periodic fluctuations in capacity, but men are not prevented from constructing crises if they find them congenial, the gain in adaptation of rhythm between the sexes may be greater than any loss that comes from not pitching the work-rhythms of each sex as perfectly as possible to their distinctive periodicities.'

Now this periodic rise and fall in the capacity of work among women is an undeniable physical fact that alters their function in society and excludes them from certain kinds of work. A civilisation which keeps this fact in view in the allocation of rights and duties will naturally suggest different social restrictions for women with a view to preventing them from transgressing their natural sphere of duties.

A more important physical factor which has a decisive bearing on the functions of women and marks out a different path of life for them is the physical periodicity of women arising from menstruation. Menstruation is by no means an ordinary phenomenon of local manifestation. It is but the most obvious symptom of the general monthly waves which periodically flow through a woman's body, affecting to a greater or lesser extent all her organs. The observations of a great many medical authorities have shown that during the process of menstruation most significant physical and mental changes are observed in women. The whole nervous system of women is affected during this period and it is the nervous system upon which depends the normal functioning of the general physiological well-being of women. Vemilow in his *Biological Tragedy of Woman* says that women's mental equilibrium is upset during the period of menstruation. He records his observation that a woman street-car conductor pulls out the wrong tickets and is muddled in counting the change. A menstruating moto-woman drives the street-car slowly and with hesitancy, becoming confused at crossings. The lady typist's fingers strike the wrong keys. The woman dentist cannot find the proper instrument. An actress is not in the right mood and makes wrong gestures. Writing in *Man and Woman*, Havelock Ellis observes that there is at this period greater impressionability, greater suggestions and more or less diminished self-control. It is at this time that sudden caprices, fits of ill-temper, moods of depression, impulses of jealousy, outbursts of self-confession are chiefly liable to occur. At times menstruation produces abnormal and diseased conditions. There may be so high a degree of physical pain and disability that the woman is really an invalid for several days every month. On the basis of these facts Havelock Ellis had to utter a note of warning that 'it is no longer possible to regard the physiological periodicity of women and the recurring menstrual function as the purely private concern of the woman whom it affects'. Such a view necessarily leads to the conclusion that the public activities work and employment of women must be conditioned and limited by their physiological peculiarities. It cannot be that men and women are treated as equals in the field of industrial employment or in the matter of political activity. If an attempt is made to create an artificial equality which in fact does not exist, it is likely to break down with serious consequences.

Motherhood is another important factor in the life of women which conditions, limits and particularises their sphere of activity. In the modern world, a large number of well-to-do women, under the influence of a wrong conception of equality, have increasingly turned away from this noble life-vocation. Various theories and suggestions have been propounded to prove that motherhood is not essential to the life and happiness of women and that alternative institutions can be evolved which will free the mothers from the burden of rearing and training their children, thus allowing them greater liberty of movement and enabling them to share with men the larger activities of social and political life. While no sane person will maintain that women should be kept confined to domestic life or should in no case participate in the wider spheres of collective activity, many will agree that the duties of motherhood form the primary concern of a woman's life, and a society which allows its female members to plunge into the wider spheres of life at the cost of their primary avocation is bound to suffer from maladjustment. It is only women who are already past the age of motherhood and can easily spare time and energy for other duties that should be really welcome in the political and industrial fields. But by far the largest number of women cannot escape, *if they ace to fulfil their function in society—the burden of their primary biological and social responsibility.* Of course, the more fortunate among them, by reason of their economic condition or limited family, can do, if they are so minded, part-time work in other fields but not in a way which might disturb their main functions. The saner elements among Western writers and thinkers have not overlooked this aspect of the matter and we shall give a few brief quotations from them.

Writing about the depth of maternal instinct in women, Havelock Ellis says: 'Most people, certainly most women, feel at moments, or at some period in their lives, a desire for children,' and in women the longing for a child may become so urgent and imperative that we may regard it as scarcely less imperative than the sexual impulse. Van de Veide writes: 'To be a woman means to have the desire to become a mother both physically and mentally.' He admits that 'there are women, and presumably always have been women, although their number may be relatively very small, who feel such a strong antagonism to motherhood that they refuse to marry for that reason,' but he adds: 'The absence of the maternal instinct in the modern woman is really nothing but a pose. The maternal instinct exists in spite of this, although there may be only one child

.... Where it really is repressed, because some women think it fashionable, or because of decadence or love of pleasure, it will also be, seen that such repression has its revenge sooner or later. A more than temporary repression of the mother instinct is, practically speaking, impossible.'

A prominent American authoress Margaret Mead writes in, *Male and Female*: 'Women may be said to be mothers unless they are taught to deny their child-bearing qualities. Society must distort their sense of themselves, pervert their inherent growth patterns, perpetrate a series of .. outrages upon them, before they will cease to want to provide, at least for a few years, for the child they have already nourished for nine months within the safe circle of their own bodies! The same writer quotes the experience of a psychiatrist working in the United States who said: 'I have never seen a woman who was socially and physically able to have children and who refused to have children, who did not suffer psychologically from that refusal.'

Writing about the nursery and other institutions for the education of children in order to relieve mothers of their educational responsibilities, Havelock Ellis says in his book, *On Life and Sex:* 'The idea has been put forward (first of all by Plato in the famous fifth book of his Republic) that the infant should be removed from its natural parents and placed in the hands of nurses skilfully trained in all the science and art of modern hygiene in general and puericulture in particular. Certainly, it is possible to find innumerable parents who are completely and lamentably ignorant of this science and this art. This may be specially so in those lands of communistic tendency, like Soviet Russia, where the Platonic ideal is most commended. But to be content to leave the mothers in ignorance and to train up in the knowledge of the duties of maternity a body of women who are rot intended to be mothers, except for other women's children, seems a perverted attempt to escape the difficulty. It is not calculated to benefit, and still less to render happy, the real mothers, the artificial mothers or the children. An institution on so unreal a foundation cannot possibly compete with one on a sound biological basis which is just as susceptible to any necessary cultivation and development as the other.... The legitimate method of approaching the problem-as is constantly becoming more widely recognised-lies in training the real mothers and, so far as possible, before they have begun to be mothers.... The establishment of Schools for Mothers, in some countries facilitated by law, constitutes a noble step along this path.'

Wider Sphere of Social Activity

In regard to the advisability and fitness of woman for work in the wider sphere of social activity, Havelock Ellis expresses an opinion which agrees with our own view which we have given above, namely, that women who have had the experience of motherhood and whose maternal duties are over have more justification as well as ability to take part in such activity than those whom motherhood calls for dedication to domestic duties. Writing in his book, *On Life and Sex*, Ellis says: 'There is nothing that is so much needed as the "maternal in politics," or in all sorts of non-political channels of social service and none can be better fitted for such service than those who have had an actual experience of motherhood and acquired the knowledge that such experience should give. There are numberless other ways besides social service in which mothers who have passed the age of forty, provided they posses the necessary aptitudes, can more profitably apply themselves than in hampering or pampering their adult children. It is by wisely cultivating their activities in a larger sphere that women whose chief duties in the narrower domestic sphere are over may better ensure their own happiness and the welfare of others than either by fretting and obstructing or by worrying over their own children who are no longer children. It is quite true that children may go astray even when they have ceased to be children. But the time to implant seeds of virtue, the time to convey a knowledge of life, was when they were small. If it was well done, it only remains to exercise faith and trust. If it was done ill, nothing done later will compensate, for it is merely foolish for a mother who could not educate her children when they were small to imagine that she is able to educate them when they are big.

Writing about the desirability of close mother-child relations during the period of infancy which is completely non-existent in collective social institutions where women, other than mothers, take care of children, Dr. Westermarck writes: 'According to Havelock Ellis, the mortality of artificially fed infants during the first year of life is seldom less than double, and sometimes as much as three times that of the breast-fed, or even more. He also points out that the advantages for an infant being suckled by its mother are greater than can be accounted for by the mere fact of being suckled rather than hand-fed, bemuse the infant's best food is that elaborated in his mother's body. This has been shown by Vitray, who found from the statistics of Astel-Dien at Lyons that infants suckled by their mothers have a mortality of only twelve per cent, while in the case of infants suckled by strangers the mortality rises to thirty-three per cent.'

It may be said that the progress of science may so lighten the manual burden of women that even after discharging their full responsibilities at home, mothers may be enabled to spend a larger and larger portion of their time outside their homes in social, political and industrial activity. While nobody would grudge such a situation, provided: it means equal facilities for all mothers and not merely for a few born with silver spoons in their mouths, it is after all not so certain that the increasing use of mechanical devices would bring about the desired change. The following quotation from Margaret Mead is worth-reading in this connection: 'There was a time also when in the first fine flush of laundries and bakeries, milk deliveries and canned foods, it did look as if American life was being enormously simplified. A vacuum cleaner was a great addition to a home that kept the standard of a carpet-sweeper and a broom, laundries were a godsend to a household whose routine of sheet-changing was geared to the old-fashioned wash-tub, and bakeries to homes in which the making of bread had dominated one whole day. But just as our new medical palliatives are creating new vulnerabilities and new disease states, so the new equipment has not led to more leisure, more time to play with the baby, more time to curl up and read by an open fire or to help the P.T.A., but has merely combined with other trends in making the life of the American home-maker not easier, but more exacting. Most urban living women do not realise that, as the Bryn Mawr report shows, house-keeping activities consumed 60-65 hours a week in a typical farm family, 78.35 in urban household in, cities of over 100,000. This was in pre-war days, and in a world that has been moving steadily towards a forty-hour week on the job.'

Now, if these facts are true, they show that even the mechanical improvements of an industrial civilisation cannot release mothers for whole time work outside their homes, and a pattern of social life which seeks to make men, and women equal in this respect is bound to produce unpleasant consequences. There remains one final argument to justify the full participation of women, in fields other than the sphere of domestic life. It is said that special gifted women should be given full opportunity to utilise their gifts for social and political service and to that extent they should be absolved of the responsibilities of motherhood and domestic life. This is true. But it should not be overlooked that special gifts can be multiplied and passed on to future generations on a wider scale, if the specially gifted woman undertakes the responsibilities of motherhood. So the argument in favour of exempting such women from the burden of motherhood falls down, because the social service which such women can render may be more effectively rendered if they can become proper mothers. A woman who has borne two gifted children and brought them up under her gifted training really does greater service to society than if she exercise her sifts in other ways. Of course, if she can combine motherhood with social or political service, nothing should be allowed to stand in her way, because then her utility will increase tenfold. But motherhood is the essential vocation of a woman's life which should not be sacrificed for any other consideration.

It is in view of all the facts and considerations we have stated above that Islam has laid down certain social restrictions both on men and women. Some of them are common to either sex, while some are different and arise from a particular conception of womanly duties. On the whole, the Islamic pattern of life is one in which woman has her main functions confined to home life. This does not mean that she is completely debarred from going out or taking part in wider activities, as the old-fashioned Muslims maintain. But there is no doubt that Islam disapproves of a social pattern in which women neglect their primary and essential functions or plunge into wider spheres of activity at the cost of their primary duties. Women who have the time and the ability to do useful service in the social or political field are not prevented by Islam to enter these fields, provided it does not prejudice or impede their functions at home. Let us now examine in more detail what these restrict ions are which Islam places on the liberty of men and women in, the interest of sexual purity and the stability of family life.

Common Restrictions

Among the common restrictions on men and women, the first relates to the duty of behaving with modesty in public. About this the Qur'an says: 'Say' to the believing men that they cast down their looks and guard their private parts; that is purer for them. Surely Allah is aware of what they do. And say to the believing women that they cast down their looks and guard their private parts and do not display their ornaments except ... to their husbands, or their fathers, or the fathers of their husbands, or their sons, or sons of their husbands, or their brothers or the sons of their brothers, or their sisters' sons, or their women or those whom their right hands possess, or male servants not having need (of women) or the children who have not what is hidden of women, and let them not strike their feet, so that what they hide of their ornaments may be known' (xxiv. 30-31).

In these verses, apart from the common duty of casting down ones looks in public, where men and women may both be present, the Holy Qur'an has laid down two special restrictions on women, namely, that they shall not make a display of their elegance and ornamentation or behave in such a way as to draw the attention of men towards their ornaments and beauty. The Prophet said that the first look which is generally involuntary is pardonable, but not the second look, which is cast for further sexual satisfaction.

This is meant both for men and women. Similarly, a tradition quoted by Abu Dawud says: 'O 'Ali! do not have a second look after the first one, because the latter is not punishable, but the former is.'

Another restriction which is common to both sexes is the compulsory duty of keeping certain parts of the body covered. These parts which should be kept covered in any case and not exposed to any person, except to the wife or the husband, or when medical or other pressing necessities require exposure, are called *Satr*. For men, the portion of the body beginning from the knees and extending to the navel has been fixed as *Sam*. A tradition of Daraqdtni reported by Abu Ayyub Ansari says: 'What is above the knees and what is below the navel should be kept covered.' Another tradition reported by 'Ali states: 'Do not expose your thighs to anyone and do not look at the thighs of a living or dead person.' For women the entire body, excepting hands, feet and face, is included in the Satr. A tradition of Abu Dawud says: 'When a woman reaches the age of puberty, no parts of her body should be kept exposed except the face and the hands extending to the joints of the wrist.' Just as men have been forbidden to wear pure silk to prevent luxurious living, women have been forbidden to use thin clothing which, instead of covering and hiding the features of their body, makes them all the more prominent. Asma bint Abu Bakr, the sister of the Prophet's wife, Ayeshah, once came to the Prophet wearing a thin dress which did not properly cover her body. The prophet at once turned away his look and said: 'Asma! when a woman has reached the age of puberty, it is not proper that any part of her body should be seen except her face, hand and feet.' Another tradition states: 'God has cursed those women who remain naked era after putting on their dress.' Similarly, the corpus of traditions collected by Muslim contains one which states: 'Women who remain naked even after putting on dress and draw others into temptation or walk and move in an alluring manner shall not enter paradise, nor get even its scent.'

There are some special restrictions on men circumscribing their freedom of action with a view to guarding their chastity and sexual purity. The entry of men in the houses of other persons is forbidden except with the permission of the inmates. The Qur'an says: 'O men who believe! do not enter the houses of other people until you have asked their permission and when you do enter, salute them' (xxiv. 27). Further, with a view to guarding against the possibility of men finding the female members of their own house without proper covering, it is laid down that no male member should enter his house at night, in the early morning and during midday time of siesta and rest without previous notice. The Qur'an says: 'And when the children among you have attained to puberty, let them seek, permission as those before them sought permission' (xxiv.59). Strangers of the male sex are required to be circumspect, if they have to ask for something from the female inmates of a house. The Qur'an says on this point: 'And when you ask of them any article, ask of them from behind a curtain; this is purer for your hearts and for their hearts' (xxxiii. 53). Another restriction is that no man or woman is permitted to remain alone with a member of the opposite sex except his or her partner, but women who have passed the age of child-bearing or those with whom, owing to intimate blood-relationship, marriage cannot be contracted are excepted: for example, brothers, sisters, parents, nephews, nieces, etc. A tradition reported by 'Aqabah b. 'Amir states. Do not go near women when they are alone. One of the Ansar asked: What about, the husband's elder and younger brothers? The Prophet said: 'Intimacy with them is to be avoided as death.' Another tradition says: 'Do not go near any woman in the absence of her husband because Satan is circulating as blood in your veins.' 'Amr b. 'As reports a saying from the Prophet: 'The Prophet of God forbade us to go near women except with the permission of the husband' (Tirmidhi). Tirmidhi gives a further tradition saying: 'No man should from this day go near a woman unless there are one or two persons with, him.' Touching of women is also forbidden, except in cases of grave emergency endangering life or health. A tradition says: 'if a person touches a woman with whom he has no legitimate relations, his hands will be burnt on the Day of Judgment.' Whenever a woman or a party of women came to the Prophet for taking the pledge of Islam, he refused to stretch his hands. Once Umaymah bint Ruqayqah came with a few women to take the pledge and asked the Prophet to give his hand. The Prophet refused saying: 'I do not shake hands with women; verbal declaration, is enough for them.'

All these restrictions on men are intended to guard sexual purity. If chastity is of any real and lasting social value, there is no doubt that such restrictions are justified, as they prevent men and women of various disposition from failing into temptation. For those who have already been corrupted and become used to sexual indecency, these and other restrictions are of no avail.

We now come to special restrictions on women. Two of them we have already mentioned, namely, that women should not display their beauty and finery to anyone else except their husbands and a few intimate relations with whom they cannot enter into marriage: for example, brothers, fathers, nephews, etc., and that shall not strike their feet in such a way as to draw the attention of men. Other restrictions are specified by the Qur'an in the following verses:

> O wives of the Prophet! you are not like any other women if you fear God, be not soft in speech lest in whose heart is a disease yearns, and speak good word. And stay in your houses and do not display your finery like the ostentation of the days of Ignorance.(xxviii. 22)

> O Prophet! say to your wives and your daughters and the women of the believers that they let down on their bosoms their overgarments.
> (xxx. 59)

> Say to the believing men that they cast down their looks and guard their private parts; that is purer for them. Surely, Allah is aware of what they do. And say to the believing women that they cast down their looks and guard

> their private parts and do not display their ornaments except what appears thereof, and let them wear their head-covering over their bosoms and not display their ornaments except to their - husbands, or their... (xxiv. 30.31)

In the first verse women are forbidden to indulge in alluringly soft speech which may raise amorous hopes in the person spoken to. This is a necessary and natural safeguard, as speech is one of the primary sources of sexual excitation. In the opinion of Van de Velde, speech has an overpowering, effect on sexual passions. Writing in the second chapter of his *Ideal Marriage*, he observes: 'The tone-colour of a voice, and the intonation of a single word and it may be a word with no special meaning or associations in itself-may excite incredible intensity of desire. The unique and precious significance that a woman's voice can give to "you" or "thou" can suffice to overwhelm a man's powers of endurance and control, or to bring about the climax of erotic expression in the organism.' Women have, therefore, been ordered by Islam not to speak in a soft or sexually sweet tone.

The second verse prescribes a certain mode of dress for women which is designed to guard themselves and the member of the opposite sex from falling into sexual temptation. This injunction has been further clarified in the following verse which says that women should keep all, portions of their body fully covered except such as must necessarily become exposed. Explaining this injunction Maulana Muhammad Ali writes a note (1751) on pages 701-02 of his translation of the Holy Qur'an (1935 edn.): 'To guard the relations between males and females and to check a too free intermingling of men and women, the Qur'an now lays down another injunction in addition to that which requires both sexes to go abroad with their looks cast down. One part of the injunction is common to both sexes: both must keep their looks cast down and both must guard their private parts. Both men and women must observe some further directions. The injunction which relates to women in particular is to keep their ornaments concealed. There is a difference of opinion as to what *zinat* or ornament means. According to some it includes the beauty of the body, while according to others it is exclusively applied to external adornments (Razi). The use of the same word in the concluding portion of the verse, let them not strike their feet so that what they hide of their ornaments may be known, clearly supports the latter view. But even according to those who include the beauty of the body in the significance of zinat, it is permissible for a woman, to have her hands and face uncovered (Razi), as being allowed under the exception, what appears thereof, as without uncovering these it would be impossible for women to take part in any business; the rest of the body and the ornaments upon it, whether in the form of tight clothes or of gold and silver ornaments, are to be kept concealed by a long head-covering or, say, an overcoat., According to Kashshaf. . . except what appears thereof means. . except that which it is customary and natural to uncover. The customs of different societies, would therefore allow a variation, and one rule cannot be laid down for all. According to Qaffal the meaning of the word is... except that which a person discloses usually, and in the case of women this means the face and the two hands (Razi). Thus, a woman when going out should have herself covered over by an external wrapper or an overcoat, it being permissible to leave the hands and the face uncovered. The exposure of such parts as the neck, the bosom or the arms is forbidden, as also the display of decorations.

The modern 'civilised' society has taken precisely to those forms of dress which expose and do not conceal a woman's beauty. The Qur'an which regards chastity as one of the basic moral and social values has directed its injunctions against these ultra modern forms of dress which are meant more to reveal than to conceal. The justification for these restrictions lies in the hidden springs of sex psychology. Let us quote Van de Velde again on this point. He says in *Ideal Marriage*:

> The male costume of modern times is not as a rule specially sexually accentuated.
>
> The exact contrary is the case with female dress, which of late has followed primitive

> and tropical patterns, and aims not at concealing but at enhancing physical charms. From the earliest times, and even when it had to serve as covering from intense cold, it has tended to accentuate and follow the lines of secondary sexual characteristics. Examples are numerous: for instance, the low-cut bodice -'decollete' of the seventeenth and eighteenth centuries: take corset, which in its original form literally lifted and pressed forward the bosom, in a dangerously painful fashion; and the wasp-waist, which was constructed in order to emphasize the curves of the bust and the hips. Or, again, the 'Tournure' or 'bustle' of the eighties, which was at first only meant to discreetly indicate the roundness of the feminine posterior-in itself an important sexual attraction, but which became so exaggerated and unwieldy that it ended by giving the ladies of the most fashionable society a deplorable resemblance to Hottentots.
>
> Fashions such as those of the Directoire and contemporary periods, which, instead of uncovering the largest possible amount of epidermis, drape the covered portion in light and clinging fabrics, which suggest rather than conceal outlines and give additional suppleness to movements, have a particularly alluring effect — much more so than that of nudity. Women have always recognized and utilized this form of charm in their veils shawls and shawl-dances, etc.

In view of these facts, it is impossible not to agree that the Quranic restrictions on female dress are not only rational but necessary.

One of the Quranic verses quoted above states that women should stay at home and not wander about displaying their beauty and finery. This verse does not mean that they should never go out and remain in perpetual confinement, since otherwise the Quranic injunctions about dress and movement of women would become meaningless. The injunction emphasises the fact that their home should form the centre of their interest and activity and there should be no unnecessary intermingling of the sexes in daily life. This interpretation is supported by a famous tradition of the Prophet in connection with 'Umar's objection against the appearance of the Prophet's wives outside their homes. Once Sauda, a wife of the Prophet, came out on some private business. Umar recognised her and complained to the Prophet that she was not observing the Quranic restrictions, whereupon the Prophet replied: 'They are permitted to go out for satisfying their real wants.'

Apart from restrictions on dress and speech, as indicated above, women are also forbidden to use scents or perfumes when going out. A tradition from Tirmidhi's collection states: 'The Prophet of God said that a woman who uses scent or perfume when passing through streets is a profligate woman.' A tradition of Muwatta by Imam Malik says: 'When a woman goes to mosque for offering prayers, she should not use perfume or scent.' Here again Islam has shown great insight into sex psychology. Perfumes and odours play a great role in exciting sexual emotion. The subject has been discussed in detail by Van de Velde in his *Ideal Marriage* in which he explains how women have always known the sexual effects of odours and perfumes and utilised them for different purposes. Van de Velde goes so far as to remark: 'I am of opinion that experts who use perfumes as aphrodisiacs for their own emotions - perhaps without being fully conscious of this aim-are generally women.'

Rules of Decency

Within the home also men and women are required to observe certain rules of decency. Although the sex relations of husband and wife are not subject to any kind of restrictions, the Prophet has given directions that even in their utmost privacy, husband and wife should conduct themselves with decorum and refrain from acts of mere animality. Thus, according to a tradition of Ibn Majah, the Prophet is reported to have said: 'Whenever one of you goes to his wife, he should not uncover himself completely like asses.' A wife of the Prophet, according to Tirmidhi, reports that she never saw the Prophet completely naked. The same ideal of decency and chastity finds expression in the restrictions placed on men and women in their family life. These are explained in the following Quranic verses:

> O you who believe! let those whom your right hands possess and those of you who have not attained to puberty ask permission of you three times: before the morning prayer, and when you put off your clothes at midday in the summer, and after the prayer of the nightfall; these are three times of privacy for you; neither is it a sin for you nor for them besides these times, because some of you must go around waiting upon others; thus does Allah make clear to you the communications, and Allah is Knowing, Wise.
>
> And when the children among you have attained to puberty, let them seek permission as those before them sought permission; thus does Allah make clear to you His communications, and Allah is Knowing, Wise.
>
> And as for women advanced in years who do not hope for marriage, it is no sin for them if they put off their clothes without displaying their ornaments; and if they restrain themselves, it is better for them
>
> (xxiv. 58-60).

Here the Qur'an has laid down three rules for the observance of the male and female members of the house. Women who have attained puberty are usually found half-dressed or lightly dressed at night, during midday in the summer or in the early morning. The male members of the family, with the exceptions already stated, as well as male servants should not enter their rooms or come inside the house without previous notice. Barring these stated periods, they are free to move about as they like. It automatically ,follows from this that the Qur'an desires that women should keep themselves fully dressed during business hours, so that no opportunity of temptation occurs for males or females. But women who have passed the age of childbirth are exempt from this restriction. Children when they reach the age of puberty are also required to observe these directions.

It is clear from all that has been said above with regard to the Islamic restrictions on the dress, movement and social intercourse of males and females that Islam insists on the segregation of sexes to the utmost extent compatible with individual and collective self-preservation. Its pattern of society is one in which men and women do not intermingle too freely. For each sex a certain sphere of life has been allotted within which it should concentrate its energies, leaving other fields for the opposite sex. If intermixture becomes necessary at any time, even then it is necessary to avoid too much freedom and laxity and observe the minimum requirements of decorum and sexual purity.

Now, the question is whether this Islamic pattern of sex life is compatible with industrial efficiency and military preparedness, two factors on which in the modern world depends the collective self-preservation of a community. We shall discuss each of these factors separately.

In regard to industrial efficiency, it should be borne in mind that all efficiency, interest and dynamic energy in men and women depend, to a very great extent on a healthy and happy private and family life. We have already discussed the question whether it is possible to dispense with the institution of the family and shown that, on the testimony of Western thinkers and sex psychologists themselves, it is very difficult to envisage a time when the family will disappear as an organised unit of collective life. If the family is a permanent feature of human civilised life and cannot be satisfactorily replaced by alternative institutions, it is self-evident that its stability and betterment should have the first claim on a nation's attention. If the family becomes disorganised and is not able to throw out healthy and happy individuals, not only will industrial efficiency disappear, all other spheres of human activity will suffer a setback on account of ill-equipped, unhealthy, irresponsible and unhappy individuals who come to these fields. A pattern of collective life which weakens and disorganises the family, in the interest of increased material and industrial productivity, is certain to suffer on the whole and, keeping all other factors in mind, more than others from social and economic maladjustments, because it undermines the very foundation on which the individual's health and efficiency depend. Unhappy, ill-adjusted and uprooted individuals lacking the drive, initiative and moral idealism, which only a healthy and happy family life can create, will hardly be productive in the full sense of the word, materially or spiritually, in any field of life they enter. Before we form any opinion as to the desirability of bringing women in the industrial field as whole time workers, let us consult the experience of industrialised countries. It would seem that the entry of the female sex in the industrial field has had positively harmful results on the 'family organisation of Western countries. Dr. Sallivan observes in his book *Akoholism*:

The employment of women in the ordinary industrial occupations not only involves a disorganization of their domestic duties, if they are married,, but it also interferes with the acquisition of housewifely knowledge during girlhood. The result is that appalling ignorance of everything connected with cookery, with cleanliness, with the management of the children, which makes the average wife and mother in the lower working classes in this country one of the most helpless and thriftless of beings, and which, therefore, impels the workman whose comfort depends on her, not only to spend his free time in the public house, but also tends to make him take to alcohol as a necessary condiment with his tasteless and indigestible diet.

Both directly and indirectly, therefore, the employments that withdraw women from domestic pursuits are likely to increase alcoholism, and, it may be added, to increase its greatest potency for evil ... namely, its influence on the health of the stock.

Again, Arnold Toynbee, the renowned British historian, says in an article published in March 1949 issue of World Review:

Failed Efforts

Certainly our recent efforts to solve our 'problems in strictly materialist terms have failed and made caricatures of all our brave plans. 'We have made enormous strides,' we say, 'in the development of labour-saving machinery,' and so we have. But one of the odd results of this progress is that women today are overworked as never before. Wives in America can no longer get household help or afford to devote themselves exclusively to the home. As a result the woman of today does two jobs: one as wife and mother in the home, one as employee in the office or factory.

During the war in England, this double working of women was almost universal. And such a trend is not a hopeful one. In history the ages of disintegration were unusually the ages in which women had left the home. In fifth-century Greece, the high point of classical history, women stayed in the home. But after Alexander's time when the city states were breaking up, there was a feminist movement like our own.

Commenting on the female craze to copy and imitate men and prove themselves equal to their power and capacity, Oswald Schwarz remarks in his *Psychology of Sex*:

> If women try to compete with men they try the impossible, impossible because it is against their intrinsic nature and against the trend of history. The best they can achieve is equality in action in such superficial strata as, for instance, the economic sphere.

Sensible Western thinkers have never approved of the existing sex and social patterns in Western countries. Their ideas and opinions are much more akin to the pattern of life advocated by Islam. For an example, we quote Anthony M. Ludovici who writes in his famous book, *Women, A Vindication*:

> It seems eminently desirable to emphasize more than we have emphasized in the past the ideal of matrimony for every woman up to a certain age, and bring home to parents that marriage is what they must train them for. . . . Anything else that she may do must always be second best to this; and those who, by misrepresentation and appeals to vanity, persuade her while she is quite young that there are callings better than, or at least as good as, motherhood for, her, are enemies not only of women but also of the species.

The same book also contains the following passage:

> Immersed as woman obviously is up to her, shoulders in the business of life and its multiplication, let it be said openly and unequivocally that all those who teach her that any other business is her business, although who, in the face of the dilemma of modern problems, confuse her with tales about a true womanhood away from life and its multiplication; all those, in short, who beguile her with promises of happiness, contentedness or even comfort, without her primary adaptation to man and the child, are liars both unscrupulous and criminal.

It is clear from the above quotations that the promiscuous herding together of men and women in factories, besides disorganising family life, has been productive of other evils such as alcoholism, sexual laxity, etc., which, in their combination, have more than nullified the benefits arising from increased industrial productivity. All this should not be taken, however, to mean that Islam desires women, to be wholly confined to domestic life. There is no such restriction in Islam on the activities of women. They are free, to do any work that benefits themselves or their society either materially or spiritually, provided, first, they do not neglect their primary duties as wives and mothers, and, secondly, observe the rules of decency explained above. In general, this means that part-time activities, other than domestic ones, are most suitable for women, if they can spare time and if such activities do not lead to too much intermingling with men., Co-operative family concerns in which a number of women belonging to different families or to one large family take part, are ideally suited for mothers and wives. If it becomes necessary to engage male workers in such undertakings for supervision, teaching or training, men of advanced age can be selected for the purpose. Part-time work in factories can also be performed by women if there is a separate section exclusively meant for them. Women whose maternal or domestic functions are over and who can do whole time work in other fields are not debarred from outside, activities. Such is, the pattern of Islamic social life and it is one which, without breaking up or disorganising family and home life, gives full scope to the abilities and energies of the female sex.

Women as Soldiers

Let us deal now with the question of military preparedness and Islam's attitude in respect of the participation of women in military service. Individual and national self-preservation in time of crisis and emergency alters the normal course of life and individuals as well as communities are forced to deviate from their principles of life when the threat to their existence becomes too serious. In consequence, they have to do things which they would never like to do in the normal course of their existence. It is the sign of a virile individuality and virile civilisation that even if it has to deviate under the pressure of extreme emergency from the standards of conduct that it holds dear, it does so most unwillingly and only in the measures required by the necessities of the situation-neither more nor less; and when the threat to its existence has passed, it hastens to revert to its original pattern of conduct. Islam, being a practical religion and claiming to be the natural way of life, recognises that situations may arise where things otherwise unlawful may have to be legalised as a temporary measure, but it takes care to ensure that its followers do not develop a liking and relish for illegality under flimsy pretexts. Therefore, while it allows temporary relaxation of normally accepted standards, it enjoins on Muslims not to regard them as more than passing concessions and to make use of them except to the extent made absolutely necessary by the requirements of the situation. Examples of this attitude are found in the Islamic commands with regard to wine and exposure of the private parts of a Muslim male or female. Wine has been absolutely prohibited by Islam, but if a person on the point of death can be saved by being made to drink wine, its use is legally justified. Similarly, Islam has given strict injunctions to its followers not to expose their private parts under any circumstances. As explained above, the Prophet even enjoined on married couples not to become completely naked during sexual intercourse. But if a man or woman is threatened with extreme danger of ill-health or one's life is in peril and the threat to life or health cannot be averted except by exposing one's private parts before a doctor for medical treatment, such an act becomes fully legitimate. Islam has adopted that same attitude with regard to the intermingling of the sexes in times of extreme national emergency or during an actual war. During such times, it relaxes all the restrictions as and when required and to the extent made necessary by the situation. When the emergency has passed, the normal restrictions are again made operative. But even during a war or emergency, Islam requires the Muslim males and females to follow as far as possible the rules of decency and avoid unnecessary intermingling. According to the Islamic attitude of life, the Muslim individuals, male and female, and the Muslim brotherhood exist not for mere self-preservation and self-enjoyment. The primary object of human existence in general and of the Muslim community in particular is to live and act for the preservation and growth of moral values and to uphold the spiritual ideals of social fairplay, justice, decency, cleanliness in thought and action.

> You are the best of the nations raised up for (the benefit of) men. You enjoin what is right and forbid the wrong and believe in Allah
>
> (iii. 109).

> Those who, should We establish them in the land, will keep up prayer and pay the, poor-rate and enjoin good and forbid evil. (xxii. 41)

> And thus We have made you a nation of the middle path that you may be bearers of witness to mankind and (that) the Apostle may be a bearer of witness to you. (ii. 142)

Sexual purity and chastity are among the fundamental social values upheld by Islam. In themselves they may appear to be of secondary importance, but they affect one's social conduct, one's ideas of justice, honesty and fairplay and in fact one's whole gamut of action in a thousand and one ways. They are, therefore, regarded by Islam as occupying a position of primary importance in its total scheme of values. How is it possible then for a community which claims to be the guardian of morality and spirituality to sacrifice them for the sake of safeguarding and ensuring a bare carnal existence. Suppose the Muslims ensure their self-preservation at the cost of these or other moral values, would it be a soul-satisfying existence? As Jesus Christ, one of the greatest Prophets of God, remarked: 'What does it avail if a man gains the whole world but loses his own soul?'

In view of these facts, Islam has enjoined, while permitting temporary relaxations, that great care should be taken during an emergency to see that these relaxations are neither misused nor used in a way which is unnecessary for individual and national self-preservation. As far as possible, intermingling of the sexes should be avoided even in times of war and resorted to only to the minimum extent compatible with the needs of collective self-preservation.

Keeping in view these safeguards and precautions, let us explain the freedoms granted to women during a national emergency.

During the early period of Islam when the Muslims were engaged in a life-and-death struggle with the forces of disbelief, women used freely to take part, in helping the warriors of Islam. Short of actual fighting which was unnecessary for Muslim women, because the women on the other side too did not join battle, they did everything such as nursing, carrying food and water and looking after other needs of the army. Bukhari quotes a tradition stating that when the Prophet received wounds during the battle of Uhud, his daughter, Fatimah, dressed up his wounds and carried water to him. It is clear that, under these conditions, she could not have observed any normal restrictions on the dress and movement of the female sex. Similarly in the chapter on Jehad and Siyar, Bukhari states on the authority of Anas b. Malik, that during the battle of Uhud when the nonbelievers inflicted a crushing defeat on Muslims, 'Ayeshah, the wife of the Prophet, and Umm Salim, an other Muslim lady, raised up their gowns to the knees and carried water to the wounded. This shows that the normal restrictions on the dress of the females can be abandoned during a war to the extent made necessary by the exigencies of the situation. Again, a tradition found in the Muslim's collection states: Umm 'Atiyyah says: 'I took part in seven battles with the Prophet of God, and I used to cook food for the warriors, supply them with medicines and dress up their wounds. Anas also reports that the Prophet usually took with him in war Umm Salim and other women of the Ansar and these women administered medicines to the wounded and kept them supplied with drinking water. That the Prophet saw nothing objectionable and even approved of women fighting for Islam is evident from another tradition also which says that the Prophet used to visit the wife of 'Ibadah b. Samit who was related to him. One day the Prophet slept in her house and on waking up began to laugh. The wife of 'Ibadah asked him as to why he laughed. The Prophet said that he saw in a dream a number of men and women travelling in a ship and heading for a battle with the non-believers. The wife of 'Ibadah requested him to pray that she be one of those warriors. Accordingly, the Prophet prayed for her. During the reign of Mu'awiyah, the wife of 'Ibadah actually voyaged to the battlefield, but when she landed on the coast she fell down from her horse and died.

All these reports establish the fact that women are permitted to take part in war with men. There is nothing to prevent women from participating in actual fighting if this becomes necessary. During the Prophet's time the Muslim women did not do actual fighting because it was not necessary, if the other side also did not employ women to fight its battles. But the Muslims may be faced nowadays with enemies who recruit women in regular fighting service. Should this happen, Muslim women can also do actual fighting as Islam does not prohibit it.

Last Question

Only one question remains to be discussed. Modern war requires intensive training both for actual military service and for auxiliary services. How can Muslim women be trained in the art of war and nursing, etc., if intermingling of the sexes is to be avoided? The obvious solution is to train initially a batch of women advanced in age for military and auxiliary services with the help of male experts. When a sufficient number of women have acquired skill in the different fields of military or medical services, they can train a large number of women without the help of men.

Six

Equality of Gender

As a term, equality is hard to define. There is a sense in which all human beings are equal, but in actual life, we find that no two human beings are really equal in all respects. There are differences of tastes, temperaments, faculties, powers and outlook, all of which cannot be traced to differences of environment or upbringing. It is apparent that the rights and duties of men and their social position flow from these inborn differences. In spite of the fundamental and essential unity of all human beings, it is impossible in practice to level down all differences and inequalities, because some of them are the outcome of native differences. Inequality leads to injustice and oppression only where artificial impediments, whether in the shape of laws and customs or traditions, are super-added to natural inequalities so as to prevent men and women from developing their native capacities to the full. It is the task of religion, state and law to remove all hindrances to human development and create an environment where only natural inborn differences and inequalities may fix a man's station in life.

The ideal of sex equality should also be studied from, the same angle. If by sex equality is meant that artificial customs, traditions and laws which prevent the female sex from playing its full part in collective life and developing its inherent capacities to the maximum extent should be removed out of the way, there is hardly any individual of sound understanding who would disagree. But if sex equality means that the type of mental and bodily faculties, psychological make-up and temperamental equipment possessed by the two sexes is identically the same and that men and women exist and have their, being not as complements to each other but as competitors and rivals in a common sphere of action, then it is an ideal about which most people would disagree. As we shall discuss later, even modern writers and specialists on sex are not agreed on this point.

As far as the Holy Qur'an is concerned, it promulgated the doctrine of human equality, including sex equality, in a comprehensive verse which negates all inequalities due to sex, race, colour, nationality, caste or tribe. Says the Qur'an:

> O people! be careful of (your duty to) your Lord, Who created you from a single being and created its mate of the same (kind) and spread from these two many men and women. (iv. .1)

This is a declaration in plain terms that, in essential human dignity and fundamental rights, all human beings of whatever sex or race or nationality stand on a footing of equality, because they all ultimately spring from a single source.

When Islam appeared in Arabia, women held a very low position in society. They were treated not only as social inferiors but like slaves and chattel. When a man having many wives died, the latter were inherited by his sons like movable property. It was a mark of dishonour for any man to have a daughter, and many preferred to bury alive their female children rather than face social opprobrium. It was Islam and the teachings of the Holy Prophet which dispelled the prevailing idea that women were inferior to men or that female children deserved any treatment different from that meted out to male issues. The Qur'an asserted the dignity of women by declaring:

> They are an apparel for you and, you are an apparel for them (ii. 188).

Here, again, the Qur'an lent support to the basic equality of women and men by declaring that each sex complements the other, and neither is inferior in status and dignity. The word 'apparel' may be interpreted to mean either 'protection' or 'dignity and beauty'. The verse would mean, therefore, that men and women protect each other from sin and dishonour or it may mean that woman lends dignity and adds beauty to the existence of man, as, man does to that of woman. Similarly, the Qur'an heaped scorn on the Arabs' traditional attitude towards the female sex in the following verses:-

> And when a daughter is announced to one of them his face becomes dark and is full of wrath. He bides himself from the people, because of that which is announced to him. Shall he keep it with disgrace or bury it (alive)- in dust? Now surely evil is what they judge. (xvi. 58-59).

With a view to contradicting the notion that women have no rights, the Qur'an came out with the plain and unambiguous declaration:

> They have rights similar to those against them,
> in a just manner. (ii. 228)

In consonance with this spirit of equality the Prophet of Islam constantly reminded his followers that female children should be treated exactly in the same manner as male issues. Prior to Islam, daughters were looked upon with disfavour and as a kind or economic and social burden. The result was that male members of the family enjoyed a respect which was denied to those of the fair sex. There were marked differences, in the treatment and upbringing of sons and daughters. All this was discouraged by the Holy Prophet (peace be on him) who upheld the rights of female children and insisted on their being treated on a footing of equality. For example, according to a report of Ibn 'Abbas, the Prophet's cousin, he is said to have declared: 'If a daughter is born to a man and he brings her up affectionately, shows her no disrespect and treats her in the same manner as he treats his sons, the Lord will reward him with paradise' (Kanz al'Ummal, p. 277). According to another report from Anas b. Malik, the Prophet said: 'Girls are models of affection and sympathy and a blessing to the family. If a person has one daughter, God will screen him from the fire of the hell owing to his daughter; if he has two daughters, God will admit him to paradise, if he has three, God will exempt him from the obligations of charity and Jehad' (ibid). Abu Hurairah, a revered companion of the Prophet, says: 'The Prophet of God said that if a person has three daughters whom he provides for and, brings up, God will surely reward him with paradise.' According to 'Abdullah ibn Mas'ud, the Prophet is reported to have said: 'If a daughter is born to a person and he brings her up, gives her a good education and trains her in the arts of life, I shall myself stand between him and hell-fire' (ibid.). Not content with moral exhortations intended to assert the equal rights of free women, the Prophet went so far as to declare. 'A person who has a female slave in his charge and takes steps to give her a sound education and trains her in arts and, culture, and then frees her and marries her, he will be doubly rewarded' (Bukhari, Sabih, Kitab al-Nikah).

Moral and Spiritual Development

The Holy Qur'an has at more than one place made it plain that in regard to moral and spiritual development, men and women stand on a level of perfect equality. There are no limits to the moral progress of a woman as that of a man. For example, the Holy Qur'an says:

> Men shall have the benefit of what they achieve and acquire and -women shall have the benefit of that which they similarly achieve and acquire (iv. 32).

And again:

> And whoever does good deeds, whether male or female, and he or she is a believer, these shall enter the garden and they shall not be dealt with a jolt unjustly. (iv. 124)

In regard to religious duties, the Qur'an recognises no distinction between men and women. Their obligations towards God and man are similar in many respects,. and, therefore, their position and status in the eyes of God are also not dissimilar. Says the Qur'an:

> And as for the believing men and the believing women they are guardians of each other; they enjoin good and forbid evil-and keep up prayer and pay the, poor-rate, and obey Allah and, His Apostle; (as for) these, Allah will show mercy to them, surely Allah is Mighty, Wise.
>
> Allah has promised to the believing men and the believing women gardens beneath which rivers flow, to abide in them and goodly dwelling in gardens of perpetual abode; and the best of all is Allah's goodly pleasure; that is the grand achievement. (ix. 71-71)

It follows that if men and women have equal, duties in regard to prayers, the payment of Poor-tax and, most of all, in the enjoining of good and the forbidding of evil in all their social, economic and political forms, it is necessary that they should have equal educational opportunities. How can a woman enjoin the good in politics or forbid men from bad politics, how can she raise her voice against ruinous economic policies or advocate, beneficial economic reforms, if she is not mentally and spiritually well equipped for the supreme religious duty? It should also be remembered that Islam makes no distinction between secular duties and religious duties. According to the teachings of Islam all duties, whether they concern politics, economics or social well-being in general, are religious duties, in no way different from prayers, fasts and the organisation of social charity. It is, therefore, a plain deduction from the above verses that men and women should be regarded as equal in the fields of politics and education, etc., and, consistent with the discharge of their special responsibilities in their particular spheres, they should receive equal rights in all these fields of action.

The, Prophet not only enunciated this general doctrine of sex equality involving,equal educational opportunities but also practised it. Innumerable are the traditions of the Prophet which show that women like men, used to come freely in the presence of the Prophet for putting questions and addressing inquiries on all sort of social, religious and economic matters. The Prophet used to answer their queries and enlighten them on all live issues. Arabia, in particular and the world in general, was so backward in those days that there were no organised educational institutions even for boys, not to speak of girls. So the Islamic attitude towards female education can be studied only from the casual remarks of the Prophet and his permission to women to approach him freely for inquiries on matters of religious, economic and social importance. There is no doubt that the Prophet encouraged women in the spirit of understanding and inquiry. His wife, 'Ayeshah, was herself a very learned woman, and during the reign of the first four Caliphs her advice, even on political matters, was eagerly sought by the rulers of Islam. On Islamic jurisprudence she was and is still regarded as a great authority. In his collection of traditions, Muslim reports that Ayeshah praised the women of Ansar for their spirit of inquiry and learning, saying, 'How praise-worthy are the women of Ansar that their modesty does not prevent them from attempts at learning and the acquisition of knowledge'; (Muslims, Sahih, Kitab al-Taharat). This statement was occasioned by the fact that the women of Ansar were more eager than others to learn from the Prophet and they used to address frequent inquiries to him. Instead of discouraging them, the wife of the Holy Prophet characterises as highly praise-worthy their eagerness for learning and inquiry.

The Holy Qur'an further stresses the equality of women, in regard to the possibilities of spiritual progress by quoting from history the examples of women who reached spiritual eminence by their own efforts:

> And Allah sets forth an example to those who believe the wife of Pharaoh when she said: My Lord, build for me a house with Thee in the Garden and deliver me from Pharaoh and

> his doings, and deliver me from the unjust people.
>
> And Mary, the daughter of 'Imran, who guarded her chastity, so we breathed unto her of Our inspiration, and she accepted the truth of the words of her Lord and His Books, and she was of the obedient one.
>
> (lxvi. 11-12).

The Holy Qur'an further declares that women have been the recipient of special gifts from God so that nothing stands in the way of their reaching the highest pinnacle of spiritual progress:

> And We revealed to the mother of Moses. (xxviii. 7)
>
> And (remember) when the angels said: O Mary, surely Allah hath chosen thee and purified thee and selected thee (for His special blessing) of all the women of the world.(iii. 41)

Despite the great stress it has laid on the essential and fundamental equality of men and women and their equal rights in all matters, of vital concern, the Holy Qur'an does not believe in that conception of sex equality which ignores the natural differences, special aptitudes and specific powers and faculties of men and women with the resulting of men for some kinds of work and the equal fitness, of women for other types of activity. On the whole, the Holy Qur'an regards men and women as complementary to each other, one sex making up what the other lacked. This is evident from the following verses of Holy Qur'an which underline the purposive nature of sex differences:

> He it is Who created you from a single being, and of the same (kind) did He make his mate, that he might incline to her. (vii. 189)

> And one of His signs is that He created mates for you from your selves, so that you may find quiet of mind then and He put between you love and compassion. (xxx. 21)
>
> Men are the maintainers of women because of that excellence which Allah has given to some of them over others and because they spend out of their property. (iv. 34)
>
> And they (women) have rights similar to those against them in a just manner and the men are a degree above them. (ii. 228)

Significant Points

The main points to be noted here are, first, that the female sex must be a source of comfort and peace of mind to its male counterpart; secondly, that men and women excel each other or are superior to each other in some respects and that in the general affairs of life men are partially, but not absolutely, superior to women. These general statements involve certain indirect conclusions which are of the greatest importance to social happiness. The Qur'an, it seems, first sets forth a general doctrine of sex equality and then qualifies and defines it with the assertion that this is not a bald and undifferentiated equality but one involving special rights and duties both for men and women, within the framework of their special responsibilities: both sexes are absolutely equal to each other.

Now, what are the conclusions to be drawn from the qualifications mentioned by the Holy Qur'an? It is emphasised by the Holy Book that the female sex is a source of comfort and quietness of mind to the male sex. This can happen only if men and women are united in a more or less permanent based of interests which finds expression in a life planned and based on some idea of the future which requires them to co-operate and not to compete, and integrates them as complements in an ordered whole. These considerations involve a pattern of life of which Marriage, Family and Children are the most important factors because there can be no other abiding interest to hold together two individuals of different sexes. A mere community of intellectual interests or identity of special aptitudes is an insufficient bond even for that microscopic minority to whom, these things matter most. For the large majority of men and women these can hardly provide any link unless they are supported and strengthened by the desire for family life and children. It is obvious, therefore, that Islam does not envisage any social pattern from which family and children have been excluded, and since these two factors involve special functions for women and special responsibilities for men, equality of rights in Islam means an equality which is adjusted to and qualified by the special duties and responsibilities of each sex.

Concept of Gender Equality

Again the Qur'an recognises the superiority of both sexes over each other in some respects. To the extent that men are superior to women and women to men in certain matters, the doctrine of equality must be, qualified with due regard to natural, facts. About the special position of men, the Qur'an makes two statements. First that men are the supporters or sustainers of women in a sense. But it must be noted that this implies no natural superiority on the part of men, nor any inherent inferiority of women, because it is a purely, economic arrangement dictated by natural necessities. The Qur'an, however, accords a slight superiority to men, in general by saying that men are a degree superior to women. This superiority of men relates both to the domestic and political fields. In domestic life, final authority must rest with one sex or the other. There cannot be two co-equal authorities here as elsewhere. Similarly, in the political field also final decisions should rest with men in general, because men are by nature gifted with a wider vision and also because their comparative freedom from certain natural limitations, which absorb a considerable amount of female time and energy, enables them to devote more attention to political affairs.

Having stated the Islamic conception of sex equality, we shall examine whether the qualifications made by Islam to the general doctrine of sex equality find any support from modern writers on the subject of sex. The question ultimately resolves itself into one of differences between men and women in regard to their faculties, powers, aptitudes and temperaments. If there are such differences and dividing lines, then the doctrine of perfect sex equality can be true only with the qualifications set forth by the Holy Qur'an and to the extent of these qualifications there ought to follow a scheme of life in which men and women, apart from general and equal rights and duties, must be assigned special rights and exclusive responsibilities. Many modern writers on sex, would generally agree with the above proposition. For example, Dr. Alexis Carrel, a French Nobel Prize winner, says in his famous book, *Man, the Unknown:*

The differences existing between man and woman are of a mere fundamental nature. They are caused by the very structure of the tissues and by the impregnation of the entire organism with specific chemical substances secreted by the ovary. Ignorance of these fundamental facts has led the promoters of feminism to believe that both sexes should have the same responsibilities. In reality, woman differs profoundly from man. Every one of the cells, of her body bears the mark of her sex. The same is true of her organs and, above all, of her nervous system. Women should develop their aptitudes in males. Their part in the progress of civilization is higher than that of men. They should not abandon their special functions.

There are a large number of equality enthusiasts among us now who are either unwilling to recognise such radical differences between the two sexes or accepting them grudgingly, insist on their removal and obliteration by conscious efforts. What these people fail to note is that the peace of mind and comfort on which the Qur'an has laid stress in the relation between the two sexes is the outcome of these very differences. If they could possibly be removed, sex life and marriage would lose much of their charm. On this point we would quote the American writer, Margaret Mead, who says in her book, *Male and Female:*

> Our tendency at present is to minimize all these differences in learning, in rhythm, in

> type and timing of rewards, and at most to try to obliterate particular differences that are seen as handicap on one sex. If boys are harder to train, train, them harder; if girls grow faster than boys, separate them, so the boys would not be damaged; if women have a little less strength than man invent machines so that they can still do the same work. But every adjustment that minimizes a difference, a vulnerability, in one sex, a differential strength in the other, diminishes their possibility of complementing each other, and corresponds symbolically to sealing off the constructive receptivity of the female and the vigorous outgoing constructive activity of the male, muting them both in the end to the duller version of human life, in which each is denied the fulness of humanity that each might have had. Guard each sex in its vulnerable moments; we must protect and cherish them through the crises that sometimes are harder for one sex than for the other. But as we guard, we may also keep the differences. Simply compensating for differences is in the end a form of denial.

This sound advice of a writer who herself happens to be a woman and belongs to an advanced country of the West must serve as an eye-opener to those extremists who, in their blind enthusiasm for sex equality, are advocating all sorts of ridiculous reforms and denying the beneficial effects of sex differences as well as the complementary position of man and, woman in respect of each other.

This same American writer, commenting on the increasing entry of women in professional field (of course, under a wrong conception of sex equality) further remarks: 'It is of very doubtful value to enlist the gifts of women if bringing women into fields that have been defined as male frightens the men, unsexes the women, muffles and distorts the contribution the women could make, either because their presence excludes men from the occupation or because it changes the quality of the men who enter.'

It would seem, then, that the doctrine of sex equality cannot be pushed to a point where it means that men and women are equally, fit for all fields of employment or that the indiscriminate entry of women in the professional fields would have no undesirable social effects.

In regard to the Quranic statement that men and women excel each other in some respects and are, therefore, unequal to that extent, we shall quote another American woman writer, Mary B. Bread, who gives a very interesting account of the discussions held on this point by American psychologists, in her book, *Woman as Force in History*. She writes:

At its ninth spring meet the Eastern branch of the American Psychological Association held-sessions on the attitude of men and women towards men.

The meeting lasted for two days and nearly one thousand persons were reported attending its session. The main discussion revolved round the results of a questionnaire submitted to an equal number of men and women. By means of this survey designed to explore opinions of men and women about women, the conclusions was reached by its promoters, that both sexes were in a remarkable agreement in favour of equal social rights for both sexes and a wide disagreement in evaluating the emotional stability and originality of women.

In the discussion which followed, a statement of the survey's findings, men and women participated and according to newspaper accounts, 'seven out of every ten men, and an equal proportion of women, believed that men were less influenced by emotion than women in their judgements.' To the statement that 'women are more interested in the trivial things of life than men,' 91.7 per cent of the men and 92.1 per cent of the women gave their assent.

The discovery or assumption that women differ from men governed discussions of the subject by members of the Psychological Association which assembled at Palo Alto a, few years ago, and much importance was attached to glandular differentiations.

'What is the psychological difference between a boy and a girl?' was the question on which they attempted to focus their remarks. The question had been put before the members of the Association for meditation in advance of this meeting. Indeed, a report, framed by two men and one woman of Stanford University, was ready for the guidance of the discussion. Its burden was that the 'original constitutional' equipment of girls and boys differs. And in women, it asserted, the whole glandular system is 'more precarious' than in men. But mental balance is 'superior in the male'. Whys and where-fores of the divergence in mental balance were 'probably' traceable to the basic physical differences, some speakers averred. As the discussion was reported in the Press, its upshot was the consensus that 'women in general have made no relative progress against mental irregularities since they began throwing off conventional restraints at high speed.'

Men are Better Fitted

Now, if the above conclusions are true, it means that men, being less amenable to emotional influences and possessing a more stable mental balance, are better fitted for political activity which requires calm reasoning and lesser susceptibility to emotional influences. Similarly, these conclusions also establish the fact that, being mentally more stable, men are bound to remain superior in intellectual pursuits which require persistent and continuous work. These facts make it clear that the ideal of sex equality cannot be accepted without important qualifications and reservations based on the ultimate facts of the psychology and nature of the two sexes.

Let us now see what Havelock Ellis, one of the greatest modern authorities on the, psychology of sex, has to say about the special nature and characteristics of woman. In *Man and Woman*, Havelock Ellis has considered impartially a great amount of available data as to the intellectual and other capacities of the two sexes. He says that abstract though a woman is, on the whole, marked by a certain docility, and receptiveness. Even in trivial matters, he says, the average woman accepts statements and opinions more easily than a man; and in more serious matters, 'she is prepared to die for a statement or an opinion, provided it is uttered with such authority and action that her emotional nature is sufficiently thrilled'. Further, Ellis points out that woman craves more for sympathy than man and that she has not the same sturdy independence like him. This is a statement which leads support to the Quranic view that men are the maintainers of women, because even if it were possible for all women to become economically independent of men, their emotional nature and craving for sympathy would involve most of them in partial dependence on men. In man, on the other hand, there is no such gravitating force to incline him towards the fair sex, unless it, be sexual attraction or the bond of children. Ellis illustrates his statement on this special characteristic of women'by giving a list of famous women of genius who have put forth their best efforts only in sympathetic and intimate association with another person of the nude sex. Thus Madame Curie, the most distinguished woman of science in modern times, was the wife of a distinguished scientific man who shared in her investigations. Mrs Browning wrote her finest poems after she knew Robert Browning. The whole of George Eliot's fiction and other imaginative work was written in the company of a man (J.H. Lewis) who shared her scientific as well as literary tastes.

Taken as a whole, Havelock Ellis considers that the qualities of intelligence in men and women are not of identical character or value; but there is no question of superiority or inferiority. Their respective intellectual qualities fairly balance each other. Thus men, he says, are better able to apply what they have leamt; they are much more inclined, to support what they have learnt; by reflection or further investigation. They have a precise knowledge in their own department, are without doubt more apt to supplement the prescribed course of reading by independent scientific research, take more interest in scientific pursuits and have greater power of observation. Women, on, the other hand, dislike the essentially intellectual process of analysis, because, says Ellis, they instinctively feel that 'analysis may possibly destroy the emotional complexes by which they are largely moved and which appeal to them' This is, why women do not favour rigid rules, principles and abstract propositions. They are more impulsive and believe in its rightness. There are not all defects of the feminine mind, says Ellis; they are innate sexual differences pointing to the ineptitude of women for science, however numerous and, brilliant the exceptions.

Those characteristics, in his opinion, are 'probably correlated with instinctive and emotional qualities which may fairly be regarded as organic'. Ellis then proves that emotion is not, as popularly supposed, a purely mental phenommon. It has its reactions upon man's vascular and muscular system, however self-controlled a man may be. 'No amount of self-control on coarser expressions of emotion alters the case, for even to unscientific inspection the passion of the self-controlled man reveals itself by some quiver of muscle, some quickening, of the heartbeat.' Here he lays down an important truth that emotion depends on physical organisation. Woman's heart, is easily excited under the influence of stimuli by which man's heart in a state of health is unaffected. And he gives a proof of the greater, excitability of woman's heart by pointing out that there is a distinctly greater increase in the number of pulsations on awakening from sleep in women. Even the complex phenomenon of hysteria is due to weakness of resistance of the vaso-motor system. And the special tendency of women to be affected by the disease of the eye called 'glaucoma' is, he says, accepted by all authorities to be due to the disturbances which emanate in generative organs.

He then points out that woman is more liable than man to convulsive manifestations. It is based on an.abnormal readiness or, in other words, an undue affectability. Frequent appearance of blushing in women is due to the greater affectability of their vaso-motor system. Convulsive tendency of women is testified by the facility with which they yield to tears and laughters. Tears are not produced by pain even when amounting to agony, but occur when 'sympathetic nervous system is most developed and most impressionable'.

Irritability, which Ellis calls 'irascibility,' is another form of affectability which 'has been quite legitimately attributed to women.' How far is this affectability in women, their, greater emotionality, organic and, therefore, ineradicable, and how far is it the product of external circumstances and, therefore, capable of modification? Ellis says that affectability in women may be decreased to some extent, but that 'there is, however, a limit to this sexual equalisation of affectability, remains extremely probable.' And he further emphasises that the comparatively large extent of the sexual sphere in women and of the visceral regions generally, the physiological tendency to anaemia, the existence of inevitable periodicity of function in women, conspire to famish a broader basis for the play of emotion, which no change in environment or habit could remove. And he quotes Hymen that-'all the most characteristic features of women's nature are correlated with emotionality, and half of women's psychic nature would remain unexplained if we struck out this factor.' Affectability in women, therefore, is an innate quality which, according to Havelock Ellis, may be reduced to finer and delicate shades but can scarcely be brought to the male standard.

It is not only Havelock Ellis who holds this opinion on the differences between men and women. There are other psychologists who think almost in the same terms. Thus, Bloch says that 'psychologically also man and woman are different beings;' and Forel expresses a similar opinion. Kisch who has made an elaborate and deep study of woman's sexual life remarks: 'The intellectual changes undergone by the girl at puberty are no less extensive and characteristic than the physical. In brief, the girl is transformed into a young woman endowed with all the attributes, mental and bodily, characteristic of femininity.' Dr. Winge, a Norwegian physician, quoted by Weith-Kundsen, says: 'The difference of sex is fundamental.

Both bodily and mentally the difference between the typical woman and the typical man is all-pervading-the difference is by no means confined to sexual organs.' And Weith.-Kundsen himself remarks: 'Man and woman are not equal; they have never been equal and they never will be. On the contrary, the difference of sex is so deep-going that two men of different civilized races are much more nearly similar in their nature than are men and women belonging to the same race.' Dr. Lambrose Gina writes in her book, *The Soul of Woman*, that not only man and woman are different in height, in structure of the bones and in the muscular system, but they are also different in the quality and quantity of air and food that they absorb, that they are subject to different sicknesses, their desires are different and finally they differ in their mental and moral tendencies. She further remarks, 'Progress, evolution and life are possible only through differentiation.'

After quoting these authorities, the author of *Whither Woman* -V.M. Rege writes: 'There is, therefore, no escaping of the fact that there are certain inherent psychological differences which sharply distinguish man and woman. Here there is no question of their relative superiority or inferiority. They only point to the fundamental differences of the sex in their function and mission. In their zeal to show equal educable capacity and intelligence, the English and American women are utterly misguided in demanding the same education for girls as for boys. It is now proved beyond doubt that woman has as much intelligence as man in, pursuing the highest possible education. And this is exactly what has misguided the modern woman. She has misunderstood her own nature, needs and functions. She has allowed herself to be exploited by male-like ideals. She has come to conceive in womanliness something inferior and lacking, so that she has held before her as model all that the male is doing. She has become ashamed of her womanliness and wishes it better if she had been born a male. These ideas have created a false standard before her, and consequently she has identified her personality with that of man. She has ignored that she has an independent personality, quite different and entirely equal to man and which, if she developed, would develop into perfect womanliness.'

In the sphere of sexual morality, it has been observed by modern protagonists of sex equality that it is unjust to apply two different standards in respect of men and women; that if sexual laxity in men is not regarded as a very serious offence, there is no reason why it should be so regarded in women. This is true up to a certain limit and Islamic teachings have never made any discrimination in this respect between males and females. Thus adultery, according to Warn, in both men and women, is legally an equal offence punishable with equal penalties. But even in this sphere unalterable facts of nature tilt the balance in favour of men. Discussing this question, Dr. Westermarck says in *The Future of Marriage in Western Civilization:*

> But even if public opinion would, in the future, grant complete sexual freedom to the unmarried of either sex, the indulgence of it by girls would still be attendant with serious disadvantages already pointed out. There would undoubtedly be exploitation in women by men; girls who remained virgins would still be preferred as wives, and the others would run the risk of being used for temporary purposes. Feminists advocating equal freedom for men and women seem to overlook the benefits that the men would derive from it; they would find it easier to gratify their desires in a more agreeable manner than through intercourse with prostitutes, and at the same time to acquire sexual experience is considered useful for their future marriage. When speaking of the 'injustice' of different moral demands on men and women, those advocates also fail to notice that this difference is ultimately due to a difference in the sexual instincts of the two sexes.

The ideas expressed above are more or less in line with the Islamic conception of sex equality; As we have shown in the beginning of this chapter, Islam upholds the essential human dignity and fundamental equality of the two sexes, but, along with the common rights and duties of men and women in which both are equal, it concedes some separate rights and prescribes some separate duties for men and women, in accordance with its view that each sex has its specific functions in society and is charged with an independent mission for the preservation and advancement of the human race. Within the limits of their special mission and functions in society, both men and women will have different rights and responsibilities and neither sex should feel jealous of the other if this involves lesser rights for one sex against the other in a strictly limited sphere and on easily understandable terms capable of adjudication in law-courts. This is the meaning of the Quranic verse:

> And do not covet that by which Allah has made some of you excel others; men should have the benefit of what they earn and women shall have the benefit of what they earn.
>
> (v. 32)

Specific Individuality

According to Islam, there is a specific sex individuality in man and woman which they must preserve and cherish, because it is this individuality which gives them honour and dignity and enables them to fulfil in an effective manner their specific role in society. Where this specific sex individuality, instead of being regarded as a source of honour and dignity, is sought to be pulled and effaced, as if it involved an inferiority in men or women, it produces a dead and colourless equality which is, in effect, a denial of real equality, as it makes for less differentiation and, therefore, for less progress. There are clear instructions of the Holy Prophet on this point which stress the need for preserving sex individuality. Thus Abu Dawud records it on the authority of Abu Hurairab, a companion of the Prophet, that the Prophet uttered a curse on men who imitate women in their dress and manners and similarly on women who abhorred their femininity by trying to dress and act like men. Similarly, at another place, Abu Dawud has recorded that the Prophet severely condemned those women who tried to appear and behave in the form and likeness of men.

Consistent with the exercise of their specific individuality and of the special functions flowing therefrom and involving special rights and responsibilities, both sexes have equal rights and are looked upon by Islam as distinct legal personalities. A wife, even after having come in partnership with her husband, is a separate legal person in Islamic law capable of suing and being sued in her own individual capacity and entitled to sue her own husband for any infringement of her just rights. This is a position which was not accorded to the female sex in Europe and America until the nineteenth century and this too after a great deal of agitation against the existing legal disabilities of women. Blackstone, who was the greatest exponent of the English Common Law and has profound influence on legal theory and practice both in England and America, maintained that the legal position of a married woman was one of unity with husband. In *The Legal Rights, Liabilities and Duties of Women*, Professor Mansfield summarised the Blackstonian thesis as follows:

> The first great principle of Scripture, the unity of husband and wife, is repeated by the law. They are, in law, one person ....Upon it, as observed by Blackstone, depend nearly all legal rights, duties and disabilities acquired by marriage.

Commenting on Blackstone's dictum, Mary B. Beard says in her book, *Woman as Force in History:*

> When Blackstone spoke of the husband's rights over the real and personal property of his wife and of her disabilities in law, he was technically correct, within fixed limits. On its face, the statement meant that, in case of

> litigation, the husband asserts certain rights over the real and personal property of his wife, and if the wife contests them or the said rights are drawn in question at Common Law, the Common Law Courts will enforce the husband's Common Law rights, unless the husband and wife have made agreements to the contrary before and after the marriage, or a relative of the wife has safeguarded the wife's rights by the creation of a trust or otherwise, which agreements or trusts made in due form are valid in equity and will be enforced by courts of equity. In other words, in the absence of valid agreements and actions to the contrary, the husband may, if he so desires, or his creditors and other litigants may assert a husband's rights over the wife's property and within the limits set by the specific rules of Common Law, the Common Law Courts will enforce them in case of litigation.

This was the position of a married woman in Europe and America until about 150 years ago. She could lose her rights on her own property, if the husband wished to deprive her of them because the law did not recognise her as separate legal personality. Islam, on the other hand, from its very inception, gave the married woman a separate Legal status with full property rights. Little wonder that a wrong conception of sex equality and extremist stand in respect of female freedom resulted from the sense of utter frustration generated by such great social and legal disabilities. But how could the Muslim women be justified in going to the same extreme length and preaching a conception of sex equality which lacks all scientific and natural basis, as evidenced by latest researches on sex psychology.

Raising Dignity

Islam stands for honour. The sum total of Islamic teachings is to raise human dignity and respect. It relieves mankind from disgrace and provides higher and honourable place in human society. It imparts the lesson of human dignity. Islam directs humanity to prostrate before Allah alone for the achievement of—superiority over other creations. Mankind is the masterpiece creation of Allah. The following verses of the Holy Quran testify this fact :

> Verily We have honoured the children of Adam. We carry them on the land and the sea, and have made provision of good things for them, and We have preferred them above many of those whom We created with a marked preferment. (17 : 70)

> Surely We created man of the best stature. (95 : 4)

> "When thy Lord said unto the angels : Lo : I am about to create a mortal out of mire. And when I have fashioned him and breathed into him of My spirit, then fall down before him prostrate. The angels fell down prostrate, everyone save Iblis; He was scornful and became one of the disbelievers."(38 : 72-75)

In Islam the welfare of mankind depends upon right thinking and right practice. It is sheer ignorance to degrade woman simply because she happens to be a woman, and man is considered a heavenly creature simply because he happens to be a man. Islam has explained it in very clear words that human dignity rests upon piety and virtue. Hence, who is more honourable, man or woman? This question is well answered by the Holy Quran :

> "Whosoever doeth right whether male or female, and is a believer, him verily We shall quicken with good life and We shall pay them

> recompense in proportion to the best of what they used to do." (16 : 97)
>
> "Lo! Men who surrender unto Allah, and women who surrender, and men who believe and women who believe, men who obey and women who obey, and men who speak the truth and women who speak the truth, and men who persevere (in righteousness) and women who persevere, and men who are humble, and women who are humble, and men who give alms, and women who give alms, and men who fast, and women who fast, and men who guard their modesty, and women who guard (their modesty), and men who remember Allah much and women who remember Allah hath prepared for them forgiveness and a vast reward." (33 : 35)
>
> "And their Lord hath heard them (and He saith): Lo! I suffer not the work of any worker, male or female, to be lost. Ye proceed one from another. So those who migrated and were driven forth from their homes and suffered damage for My cause and fought and were slain, verily I shall remit their evil deeds from them and verily I shall bring them into gardens underneath which rivers—flow a reward from Allah, and with Allah is the fairest of rewards." (3 : 195)

The Holy Quran distinctly explains the characteristics of the Momineen (The faithful followers of Islam) who submitted their lives, property and desires to the Will of Allah:

> "(Triumphant) are those who turn repentant (To Allah) ' those who serve (Him), those who praise (Him), those who fast, those who

> bow down, those who fall prostrate (in worship), those who enjoin the right and who forbid the wrong, and those who keep the limits (Ordained) of Allah, and give glad-tidings to believers! " (9 : 12)

At another place, the pious wives of the Holy Prophet (S.A.W.) have been 'commanded to develop such qualities in them without which they would not be able to remain in his Nikah. And the Holy Prophet (S.A.W.) would easily find such wives who would possess such virtuous qualities.

> "It may happen that his Lord, if he divorces you, will give him in your stead wives better than you, submissive (to Allah) believing, pious, penitent, inclined to fasting, widows and maids." (66 :5)

Now, it becomes crystal clear that according to the Holy Quran, piety and virtue are the only criteria for the achievement of successful life in the Hereafter. None, whether man or woman can accomplish his or her goal without fulfilling this condition.

The Holy Quran points out that man and woman both have helped and cooperated with each other in the development of human life. Both have equally shared the burden of life. Their union has brought the civilization into existence. No nation or movement of the world can neglect either of them. If man and woman are responsible for the establishment of the authority of Truth and its enforcement, they are equally responsible for the spread of vices in the world, The Holy Quran says:

> "The hypocrites, both man and woman, are one and the same. They enjoin the evil, and forbid the right; and they withhold their hands from spending in the cause of Allah. They have forgotten Allah and so He hath forgotten them. Indeed, the hypocrites, are the transgressors." (9 : 76)

> "And the believers, men and women are protecting friends one of another; they enjoin the right and forbid the wrong, and they establish the prayer and they pay the poor-due, and they obey Allah and His Messenger, as for these, Allah will have mercy on them. Lo! Allah is Mighty Wise." (9 : 71)

Since it is admitted that the revolutions in the civilization of the world are brought about by both, man and woman, no logical argument can degrade one and upgrade the other. Besides, it will be foolish to eliminate either of them from the civilization and march forward. No person can play any role in life after having paralysed one half of the body.

Degraded and Outcast

Before the advent of Islam, the world had degraded the woman and had almost outcast her. She was thrown in such deep abyss that there seemed no hope of her redemption. Islam boldly remonstrated against this injustice and emphasised that life needed both man and woman. Woman is not created to be derided and cast aside. Like man, woman also has her purpose and right to exist. And the Nature is achieving its aim with the help of man and woman both. As the Holy Quran says:

> Unto Allah belongeth the Sovereignty of the heavens and the earth. He createth what He wills. He bestoweth female (offsprings) upon whom He will, and bestoweth male (offspring) upon whom He will; or He mingleth them, males and females, and He maketh barren whom He will. Lo ! He is Knower, Powerful. (42 : 49-50)

Islam lifted woman from the abyss of disgrace and granted her rights and facilities. Abdullah-bin-'Umar (R.A.A.) relates:

> During the life time of our Prophet, Muhammad (S.A.W.) we did not talk to 'our woman freely because we feared revelation against us. When the Holy Prophet (S.A.W.) passed away, we became frank with them. (Bukhari, and Ibn Majah)

Whereas, all other religions deprived woman of right even to live.' Islam granted her rights almost on a par with man. It also warned that all those who strive to snatch her rights away, will surely be, accountable to Allah on the Day of Judgment.

> And when the girl-child that was buried alive, is asked For what sin she was slain?(19 : 8-9)

The Holy Prophet (S.A.W.) has issued numerous instructions in favour of woman, the favour which she could not receive even from the so-called modern upholders of the woman's rights. The Holy Prophet (S.A.W.) has said :

> Allah has forbidden you, disobedience unto your mothers, refusal to sanctioned rights, accumulation of wealth from all sides and burial of living daughters. (Bukhari)

The Prophet of Islam (S.A.W.) has also said:

> "A man who has a daughter and he neither despises her nor buries her alive nor prefers son to daughter, Allah will admit him in Heaven." (Abu Daud)

Abu Sayeed (R.A.A.) relates that the Holy Prophet (S.A.W.) said:

> "Whoever brought up three daughters and treated them well, the Heaven is for him." (Abu Daud - Tirmizi)

The world condemned woman, but Islam honoured her. The Holy Prophet (S.A.W.) raised her status and assigned her respectable place in the human society. He (S.A.W.) said :

> "In worldly things, I like woman and perfume,
> but coolness of my eyes lies in salat (Prayers)".

Once the Holy wives were travelling on camels, the Holy Prophet (S.A.W.) said to the camel driver.

> "Carry these glasses very carefully."

About Fatimah (R.A.A.) the Messenger of Allah (S.A.W.) has said :

> "My daughter is my flesh, any trouble to her
> will cause pain to me."
>
> (Bukhari, and Muslim)

Once Hazrat Aisha (R.A.A.) was asked whom did the Holy Prophet (S.A.W.) love most? She replied, Fatimah (R.A.A.).

On another occasion, somebody asked the Holy Prophet (S.A.W.), 'Who is your most beloved person?' The Holy Prophet (S.A.W.) replied,' Aisha (R.A.A.).'

Thus we see that the Holy Prophet (S.A.W.) loved his wife Aisha (R.A.A.) and his daughter Fatima (R.A.A.) most. And the sayings of the Holy Prophet (S.A.W.) explicitly explain the aim of Islam with regard to the treatment of fair sex.

Revolution in Thinking

The teachings of Islam revolutionized the thinking of those men who buried their daughters alive and felt no shame in doing so. They began to love and nourish their daughters, those who refused to shelter their own daughters, became the guardians of other's daughters. Those who were devoid of love and affection for women, now loved and cared for them.

On the occasion of the Battle of Uhud, Jabir's father told Jabir (R.A.A.), "My Son! I may be martyred in the forthcoming battle, so I advise you to look after my daughters." Consequently, Jabir (R.A.A.) who was still young, married a widow owing to the responsibility of his sisters. The Holy Prophet (S.A.W.) asked him, "Why did you not marry a young woman?" He replied, "O Prophet of Allah (S.A.W.) My father was martyred in the Battle of Uhud and he has left behind his nine daughters who are my sisters. Therefore, I chose such woman for my marriage, who could look after them well." The Messenger of Allah (S.A.W.) replied, ,You did a good deed." (Bukhari)

It is related that after the martyrdom of Hazrat Hamza (R.A.A.), three persons claimed to have the right to look after his daughter. The first was Hazrat Ali (R.A.A.) who claimed his right to look after her because she was his cousin (sister). The second person was Hazrat Jafer (R.A.A.) who said that his claim was better than that of Hazrat Ali (R.A.A.) because she was not only his cousin (sister) but her maternal aunt was his wife. Hence, she could be brought up in better way. The third man was Hazrat Zaid (R.A.A.) who filed his petition on the ground that she was his brother's daughter and that none else can have better claim than her own uncle.

(Bukhari, and Muslim)

ᵗhe examples which the history of other nations
: is the only religion that raised the status of
.ent in the world.

According to Islam, society is responsible for the protection of human rights and maintenance of law and order. Its duty is to chop off the hands of the oppressors and unjust. The Quran says:

> "And there is life for you in retaliation, O men of understanding, that ye may ward off (evil)."
> (2 : 179)

The law of Shariah awards death penalty to murderer whether he has murdered a man or a woman, because the life of woman is as sacred as that of man. The laws given to the people of Yaman by the Holy Prophet (S.A.W.) included the death penalty to the murderer of woman also.

> "Undoubtedly (men) murderer of a woman shall be sentenced to death."

> It is stated that a Jew crushed the head of a girl and killed her. The Holy Prophet (S.A.W.) ordered him to be put to death in the same manner (Bukhari and Muslim)

> Once, all those men who murdered a woman, were put to death by the order of Hazrat 'Umar Farooq (R.A.A.)
>
> (Al-Ahkam-ul-Quran, Jassas)

If a woman pardons a murderer of her relative, the other relatives have no authority to nullify her consent for forgiveness. Not only this, she can offer protection to an enemy during the emergency of war and this act of her cannot be considered unlawful. The Holy Prophet (S.A.W.) has said

> "Undoubtely, a woman can shelter an enemy for the benefit of Muslims." (Tirmizi)

On the occasion of the conquest of Holy Mecca, Umm Hani said to the Holy Prophet (S.A.W.), "O Messenger of Allah (S.A.W.), I have provided protection to Ibn Hera, but Ali (R.A.A.) says that he will kill him under any circumstance."

> The Holy Prophet (S.A.W.) replied, "Umm Hani Whomsoever you have protected, he is under my protection too." (Bukhari)

Similarly, Islam permits woman, within the limits of Shariah, to participate in the financial affairs and derive benefits.

No man can interfere in this matter. Even her husband has no right to make use of her personal wealth. Likewise, woman has no right to enforce her will for the use of the wealth of her husband. There is a distinct injunction of the Holy Quran :

> "And covet not the thing in which Allah hath made some of you excel other. Upto men a fortune from that which they have earned and unto women a fortune from that which they have earned. (Envy not one another). But ask Allah of His bounty. Lo ! Allah is Ever Knower of all things." (4: 32)

According to the Holy Quran the Law of Inheritance is:

> "Unto the men (of a family) belongeth a share, of that which parents and near kindred leave, and unto the women a share of that which parents and near kindred leave, whether it be little or much a legal share." (4 : 7)

The ancient religions were not prepared to give equal status to man and woman. Therefore, they formulated separate laws for them. But Islam does not make this distinction. In Islam, man and woman both are equal before law. The Holy Quran says:

> "Lo ! We offered the trust unto the heavens and the earth and the hills, but they shrunk from bearing it and were afraid of it. And man assumed it. Lo ! He hath proved a tyrant and a fool. So Allah punisheth hypocritical men and hypocritical women, and idolator men

> and idolator women. But Allah pardoneth believing men and believing women, and Allah is Forgiving, Merciful." (33 : 72- 73)

> "And it becometh not a believing man or a believing woman when Allah and His Messenger have decided an affair (for them), that they should (after that) claiming say in their affair, and whoso is rebellious to Allah and His Messenger, he verily goeth astray in error manifest." (33 : 36)

Equal Rights

Islam has granted equal rights to both, man and woman. It provides equal opportunity to both of them for the progress and prosperity of life. It guarantees the protection of their lives, property and honour.

The spouses are equally inter-dependent. Therefore, there is no question of honour for man and dishonour for woman. In Islam both are equally honourable. There is no distinction on the basis of sex. In fact they are created for each other to live in harmony and co-existence. As the Holy Quran says :

> "They are raiment for you and ye are raiment for them." (2 : 187)

The relation between man and woman is not of hatred but of love. Man is incomplete without woman and woman is incomplete without man. They are the source of peace and harmony to each other.

According to the Holy Quran

> "And of His signs is this : He created for you help-mates from yourselves that ye might find rest in them, and he ordained between you love and mercy. Lo ! herein indeed are portents for folk who reflect." (30 : 21)

Part - Three

Rights

Seven

Fundamental Rights

The question is; What are the rights and obligations of a woman? It is a very complicated and delicate question of the modern age. The discussions and debates on this topic, both in the past and the current, if collected together would most likely fairly equip a small library. But all these discussions have failed to satisfactorily answer the question. Rather, it would not be wrong to say that they have further complicated it. In answering this question Islam too has taken a certain stand. It has not come as a reaction to the present day activity, but has existed from the earliest times. It was there yesterday, exists today and shall remain extant till the end of days. This stand of Islam was totally against that which had existed and recognized for centuries and was in vogue throughout the world. The Islamic stand has love, sympathy and help and cooperation for woman, her age and the nature of her relationship with man, recognition of her personality in her own right (separate from man), protection of her life, property, honour and dignity, her economic and political rights and also responsibilities in keeping with her strength and capabilities. It can be safely asserted that it provides fully for the development and perfection of her personality. And the complications by the present day stand on her position and status in the social life are also removed.

Irrational Attitude

In relation to Islam the behaviour of some people is irrational and partial. Owing to their peculiar religious and political thought and views, they cannot bring themselves to recognize excellence of Islam. They totally ignore the positive role of Islam in connection with woman. Prejudice and narrow mindedness are the two most dangerous diseases. Those afflicted with them fail to notice facts and realities of great importance. And even after observation try to conceal them. But realities cannot be concealed. Facts must stand out in spite of our efforts to overlook them, and must get them recognized sooner or later. So long as the radiant truths and crystal clear teachings of the Quran and Hadith and the juristic and legal discussions of Islam which have been in practice for decisions on all sorts of problems for centuries, exist, the favours of Islam to woman cannot be denied.

Some people are of the opinion that Islam did correct and reform the miserable position of woman in the Jahili (Ignorant) society and conferred on her certain rights which had been denied to her earlier, but still it failed to do full justice to her. It denied to her the rights it conferred on man. Thus, failing to establish equality between the sexes.

Many an Objection

The rights conferred by Islam on woman are subjected to many objections from the point of view of the superiority of man in Islam. He is the guardian and supervisor in the household, he can marry more than one wife, has the right to divorce the wife, the woman receiving only half the share of man in the inheritance, she has been unjustly treated in the laws pertaining to evidence, Qisas (retaliatory punishment equal for equal), Diyat (blood money for loss of life and lesser injuries) -all these and so many other objections have been levelled against the Islamic Law. Those raising these objections desire that those laws should be repealed, the superiority (higher position) of man be done away with and the woman be granted all those rights exercised by man in the household. Both should have equal authority in all domestic affairs. The woman should be brought on a par with man in her share of inheritance, she should have the power to divorce and she should be able to get rid of her partner as and when she is pleased. In case of divorcing her, man should bear expenses of her upkeep life long. In the presence of one wife, man should be barred from marrying another. At times they do not hesitate in claiming for the woman the right to have more than one husband, the way man can have more than one wife. The woman should get all those political and social rights which a man enjoys. All these objections result from ignorance of the Islamic teachings. It is a pity so many of the highly educated and so-called intellectuals share this ignorance. The very wide and comprehensive concept of life given by Islam and the way it has helped build the edifice of the personal and collective life automatically removes the objections raised against it.

These objections are not of recent origin, they have been thrown in the face of the Muslims since long and the practice continues with greater fury now. During this period efforts have been made to remove them. And it is really deplorable and a contravention of intellectual honesty that these objections are being repeated as if they were being presented before the world for the first time and the Muslim thinkers have been dumb-founded. This leads us to think that at the back of this practice there is very little desire to understand Islam and the greater part of their interest is centred on making it the target of (destructive) criticism. What would have been the reasonable course for them was to have given serious thought to the Muslim rejoinders to their objections and any short-comings in them pointed out. This would have opened avenues for mutual understanding, removal of misunderstandings and Islam would have been understood in its proper perspective.

All these objections are raised by those whose minds are stuffed with the immoderate view of equality of sexes, presented by the West which has them in its tight grip. This is no more a view but has been under experiment for long and its results are before the world in the form of sexual vagrancy and ruination of the family and corporate life. But overlooking these results of those experiments they are advocated in a manner to show that not only is it a harmless view but emancipation of woman from all ills is associated with it. If Islam cannot keep pace with it, it is the demand of our intellect to say good bye to it, although the experiment in the recent history of mankind has brought to light the value, utility and purity of the Islamic view. Whenever that Western view of the equality of sexes is reformed and its immoderation removed, it must approach very close to the Islamic view. Rather it would be more correct to say that Islam alone can reform it and remove its shortcomings.

The Islamic stand has been so violently attacked by its opponents that so many Muslims too paying lip service to Islam, have been influenced and are daunted by their objection and find many infirmities in the Islamic teachings.

This class of brow-beaten persons comprises various grades. It is not so easy to classify them. Some of them, they may or may not admit it, are those who want to get rid of these "decadent" and "impracticable" laws. To them the destiny of woman is pointed today by the West and not by Islam. She can never advance on the path of progress so long as she is confined to the "enclosure" of Islam. For such progress she will have to run about free among those 'meadows' prepared for this purpose by the West. A Muslim, so long as he subscribes to Islam, cannot subscribe to their wishes and endeavours. For him the laws prescribed by the Shari'ah are the limit which he is not permitted to overstep. If ever he is guilty of breach in this respect, he regards himself a criminal and answerable to Allah and it will be his endeavour to retrace his steps for re-entry to this limit. It is the demand of his belief in the Divine Faith. At the moment all the laws of the Islamic Shari'ah are not the subject of our discussion. We are at the moment concerned only with those relating to familial life. The Quran has called these laws as the limits prescribed by Allah at various places in and has sternly forbidden the believers to violate them.

At one place, while mentioning divorce it has been observed :

> These are the limits ordained by Allah; so do not transgress them, if any do transgress the limits ordained by Allah, such persons wrong (themselves as well as others). [8] —Al-Quran II : 229

Laws of divorce are also mentioned in 'Sura-Talaq' (65) and immediately after that it is observed :

> How many nations that insolently opposed the command of their Lord and His Messengers did we not call them to account, - to severe account -And we chastised them with a horrible chastisement. Then did they taste the evil result of their conduct, and the end of their conduct was Perdition. Allah has prepared for them a severe Punishment (in the Here after). Therefore, fear ye Allah Oye men of understanding- who have believed ! -For Allah hath indeed sent down to you a Message, -
> [9] —Al Quran LXV: 8-10

After this menace can any Muslim think of opposing the right of women, familial laws or any law of the Shari'ah for that matter?

There are others whose minds are not so overwhelmed by the Western concepts and views that they may reject the Quranic injunctions as old and time barred. But they are labouring under the erroneous notion that gone are the days when the Islamic Shari'ah was revealed and conditions today are totally changed. Insistence on centuries old principles and traditions is unnecessary. This is the age of advancement and competition. The stand taken by Islam, relating to woman, is not the one that can let her compete in the modern age, and her lagging behind in this race means retardation of the entire nation. So what is needed is to amend the Islamic Laws to fall in line with the modern trends. To them it is "*ijtehad*". And under the changed conditions 'ijtehad' is a must. Those who refrain from such 'ijtehad' have to put up with the taunts of ill-information and conservatism from these iconoclasts.

Advocacy for Amendments

And then there are those who go even further and say, wearing a mask of simplicity and innocence that Islam is a modern religion. It has conferred on the woman all the rights of the modern age, but the conservatives have interpreted the Quran and the Hadith in a way reminiscent of the days of slavery. So a modern and progressive interpretation of the Quran is badly needed. Who is there that will not applaud them for this understanding, insight and enlighenment? These simple-minded intellectuals of the modern age !

Those who desire amendment in the Islamic Law in the name of "ijtehad" most probably presume the Islamic Law to be like man-made laws which can be amended and repealed as and when the law maker so desires. The Islamic law on the other hand has been revealed by Allah and permits not of an iota's change by any one. It was not given even to the Prophet to whom it was revealed.

> But when our clear signs are rehearsed unto them, those who rest not their hope of their meeting with us, say: "Bring us a Quran other than this or change this." Say: "It is not for me of my own accord to change it: I follow not but what is revealed unto me : If I were to disobey my Lord, I should myself fear the chastisement of a Great Day (to come)." [10]
>
> —Al Quran X: 15

The other thing is that man-made laws are the product of time and the existing conditions. They are not free from the limits of time and space. They are very flexible and change with the times. Flexibility in the man-made laws is not their merit but a defect that makes them impracticable under changed conditions. But any one who has studied Islam even cursorily with an open mind cannot deny the fact that the Quran has presented itself as an eternally abiding faith which cannot change till the end of time. As for Ijtehad it is something altogether different. It does not aim at changing the evident Quranic injunctions but framing other new ones in the light of these (Quranic) injunctions. The work cannot be undertaken with unlimited freedom but will have to bind itself with certain strict limits.

Why a Worry?

Here a question persistently strikes us : why are these 'reformers' so much worried about the rights of women and social reform among the Muslims? There are many evils in the Muslim community, that of creed, action, morality, dealings etc., but why do they evince so much interest in and anxiety about Muslim women's aggrieved state? Why do other more serious problems not engage their attention with so much anxiety and compassion?

From a casual study of the minds of these "philanthropists" we learn that to them the end and object of man's life is and should be that appointed by the West. For this purpose they have adopted also the same course. A salient feature of it is that religion and faith are meaningless terms. They do not concern our life and have little bearing on it. If any one is interested in religion, he may follow it in his private life. The collective life should, however, be free from that "paraphernalia." So long as man is entangled in the bounds of religion he shall be rotting in the dark ages of the past. The avenues of progress shall remain closed on him. He has no right to live in the modern age.

They want to take the entire Muslim Ummah on this path. Towards this end perhaps they regard the social reform more useful. And with a hue and cry over this issue of Muslim women's right they probably expect to achieve greater success. For, to them, so long as the Muslim woman is held bound by the norms of old concepts, and is teaching and preaching to the younger generation loyalty to Allah and His Apostle, the strong bonds of religion cannot become loose enough to detach the Muslim Ummah from their faith and its practice, not withstanding their lack and zeal and strict adherence. Their turning away from it is possible only with the woman changing her orientation vis-a-vis the faith, and holding aloft the banner against it in the struggle for her rights. Since they have so far not achieved any success in their endeavours and for that matter should not expect to succeed, they give vent to their pent up feelings of anger and grief against the standard bearers of Faith, calling them names like conservatives and old fashioned revivalists and fundamentalists. Every uttered and written word of theirs is an authority and the modern times have made arrangements for their wide publicity. Thus these "cultured outbursts" and "polite downpour" without hesitation or restraint!

Some of them are people with a religious bent of mind and in real earnest desire to keep away from the unhappy experiences of the Western civilization but its onslaught from every direction is so powerful that they themselves are not entirely free from its pestilential influence. Gradually and totally unawares, their ways of living are changing and the Western, civilization surreptitiously creeping into it, its grip is getting more and more tight on them every day. But even at this critical stage they are happy with the idea that in spite of their participation in the race of the blind pursuit of Western civilization their own culture is free from its evils and shall remain immune in future also. But this is false self-assurance and sort of a pious wish which shall at best be short-lived. If they have not so far been forced to swallow the acrid fruit of the West, it is due to the counter-balancing effects of the Islamic Faith that its evils have not surfaced yet. When these salubrious effects disappear the Western civilization, with all its evils, shall descend into their courtyards. Those not roused to activity to guard their houses, on observing the first signs of a deluge, cannot escape inundation. Nobody can save them.

Already Granted

It is usually observed that a weak person has to strive hard and struggle against the opponents for obtaining his or her rights. Without fighting for them it is very difficult to get even the natural rights. They are not even recognized. The modern society recognized some of the basic rights after tiring debates and discussions, disputes and altercations and violent protests (the Suffragist Movement). This recognition and grant of woman's rights is accepted as a boon of the modern age whereas this is a blessing of Islam conferred on her (without her asking for it). To begin with Islam gave her those rights which had been denied to her and she had been silently suffering long as a result of this deprivation. They were not conferred on her in response to her demand for them. Her protest had continued and her cause was being advocated and promoted and representations were being made on her behalf. Rather, they were given to her since they were her natural rights, and she ought to have been enjoying them, without any body granting or any one else receiving them as charity. They have been and are free for all like light, air and rainfall. Islam was under no compulsion to confer them on her, but it granted them to her since she was the oppressed and aggrieved party and helping and supporting the aggrieved and the suffering, it regarded as binding on it.

We mention below some of the rights that Islam has granted to woman. Islam does not rest contented with the sanction of rights in so many high-sounding legal terms (usual with the stingy and petty natured man), but through persuasion and admonition, it also creates a congenial milieu for their fulfilment.

Right to Live

The women was in no better condition in Arabia than in the rest of the world. Certain tribes of Arabia buried their daughters alive. The Quran admonished them in very strong terms for this villainy and hardheartedness, granted her the right to live and declared that whoever lays hands on this right of hers (to live), will have to account for this felony of his. The Quran says :

> When the female (infant) buried alive is
> questioned for what crime she was killed; [1]
> —Al Quran LXXXI : 8-9

On the one hand, the perpetrators of the heinous crime of taking the life of the innocent girls were threatened with hell-fire and on the other, those abstaining from it and treating them on an equal footing with the sons given the glad tidings of entry to heaven. Abdullah Ibn Abbas reports the Prophet (S.A.W.) to have said :

Allah shall reward the Muslim with entry to heaven who neither buried his daughter alive, nor meted out ignoble treatment to her, nor treated the son preferentially compared to her.

Along with these moral backings Islam also instructed them to respect the right of woman to live, just like that of men, and for any breach of this ordinance armed her with Qisas (retaliatory punishment — like for like) for which the Islamic state was made responsible. Qisas means that if somebody is oppressed or suffers an excess, he or she has the right to seek redressal, so much so that if some innocent person is murdered, his or her relatives have the right to retaliate and take the life of the murderer. This law covers both man and woman. The Quran says:

> We ordained therein for them. - "Life for life, eye for eye, nose for nose, ear for ear, tooth, for tooth and wounds equal for equal." But if any one remits the retaliations by way of charity, it is an act of atonement for himself. And if any fail to judge by what Allah hath revealed, they are wrongdoers. [2] —Al-Quran V : 45

Islam revived this Law of Torah (old Testament) and it became part of the Islamic Shari'ah. This law not only protected woman against tyranny but put a stop to all sorts of tyrannies and excesses against every weak individual and class and provided justice to them.

Right of being Brought Up

According to the Islamic law, every child is born with the natural right of being provided with the necessities. Upbringing of children and their proper care is a lengthy and tedious job and it is noticed that the extra loving care lavished on the boys is stinted or sparing in the case of girls. Islam branded this attitude as undesirable, inducing the parents particularly to her proper upkeep and loving care, declaring it as an act worthy of great reward. 'Ayeshah (R.A.A.) reports the Prophet (S.A.W.) to have said :

Whoever is put to test with girls as offspring, and he treats them kindly, they will become a source of protecting him from hell-fire.

This tradition mentions 'Ehsan' in connection with the girls, which is a comprehensive word meaning, their upbringing, their education and training, kind treatment and loving care, all together.

Anas (R.A.A.) reports the Prophet (S.A.W.) to have said:

> The person who brings up two daughters until they attain maturity, on the Day of Reckoning, myself and he will be like this. And saying these words he brought his fingers together.

Now look at the legal aspect of the issue. According to the Islamic Shari'ah the support and upkeep of the offspring devolves on the father. Offspring includes both boys and girls (without any distinction). Therefore, he cannot deny any of them, this birth right of their's (proper upbringing). So we find in the Quran under the subject of breast-feeding the following injunction :

> And he (father of the child) shall bear the cost of their (mothers giving suck) food and clothing. [3] —Al Quran II: 233

The jurists have furnished details of the ordainment. The erudites of the Hanafite school have opined that the responsibility of support, care, education and training in case of the boys is up to the age of majority. And there it ends. However, the responsibility of upkeep of the female offspring shall remain liable even after her attaining majority, until such time as she gets married and has a home of her own. Others are of the opinion that this responsibility is to be divided between the father and the mother after the daughter's attaining majority. Two thirds is to be borne by the father and one third by the mother. Similarly, the responsibility of any major girl, if she is without means of support shall be the responsibility of the closest eternally prohibited relation. However, if any of them has property of her own, the expenses of her upkeep shall be met from that source. Nobody else shall be held responsible for bearing her burden.

Right to Education

The progress of man is associated with education. If he is not equipped with knowledge, he lags behind in the struggle of life. He is neither elevated in thought nor can he make any material progress. But a sufficiently long period of history passed by leaving her uneducated, for education was not deemed necessary for her. This field used to be the exclusive domain of man. And among men too only some particular classes were benefited by it. The woman lived in thé darkness of ignorance, far from the high pedestal of knowledge and learning.

It was Islam that made the doors of education open on men and women alike. All the impediments of the way were removed and all sorts of facilities provided to promote its cause. It drew, attention towards female education in particular, creating inducements for it, declaring it an act worthy of reward in the Hereafter. Abu Sa'eed Khudri (R.A.A.) reports the Prophet (S.A.W.) to have said :

The person who brought up three daughters, embellished them with education and training, married them off and remained benevolently inclined to them even after their marriage, (Allah Willing) paradise is ensured for him.

Islam addresses both man and woman. It had made each one of them duty-bound morally to devotional acts and observance of the Laws of Shari'ah. It is not possible to live up to these demands without knowledge. For the woman the relationship with man is of great importance, since the relations are very complicated and also of a delicate nature. They comprise woman's rights as well as her obligations. So long as she is ignorant of them, she can neither discharge her duties nor can she protect her own rights from usurpation.

The jurists are of the opinion that for both man and woman basic knowledge of the faith is essential. If the woman is ignorant, it is the husband's duty to inform and educate her or make some alternative arrangement for her education. If the husband fails in this duty she would herself seek and attain that much needed knowledge, for, it is her legal right. For this purpose she can go out of her house too if necessary, but of course within the moral limits prescribed by Islam. The husband has no authority to stop her from such pursuit of knowledge.

This attitude resulted in the early phase of plan in the education of men along with the female education. Among the companions of the Prophet (S.A.W.) we come upon a fairly large number of the female companions well-versed in the knowledge of the Quran and the Hadith. Deduction of religious principles and practices and pronouncing religious verdicts in the light of the Quran and Hadith is not such an easy job. But there were also women who were capable of it. Among them 'Ayeshah, Umm Salmah, Umm 'Atiyah, Safiyah, Umm Habibah, Asma' bint Abu Bakr, Umm Sharik, Fatimah bint Qais, Khaula bint Tawait (R.A.A.) and others are most prominent.

Right to Marry

Just as the woman was denied the right to speak and express her opinion on any important issue or problem of life, she could not give utterance to her own will or desire in the matter of being given away in marriage. Her parents or elders of the family made such decisions and married her off to whomsoever they liked. And she could not refuse or even protest. Her objection or opinion in this particular matter was considered extremely undesirable and most improper (violation of feminine decorum). The society interpreted it in ways reflecting on her moral character. Any remark on her part relating to her marital arrangement and rejecting the selection of the elders was considered a sign of her dissoluteness.

It is usually said that giving her a free hand in the matter of matrimonial arrangements is against her own interests. She is likely to take faulty decisions due to her immaturity and lack of experience. Her parents or guardians more experienced and having better knowledge of men and matters, are less likely to err in their decisions. Moreover, they are her well-wishers and cannot deceive her.

Undoubtedly there is truth in it that her guardians can make a better selection of the partner in life for her, but it cannot be denied either that the guardians are guilty of excesses in this regard, and so often they make these matches a means of serving their own selfish ends. At least, it is difficult to deny the fact that the parents or guardians do not keep before them norms to which their daughter attaches great importance. Therefore, it would not be in the fitness of things to leave the selection of partners for girls entirely to their guardians.

It is a fact that the entering of a girl in a contract of marriage with some man is an important event. Both of them start a new phase of life and the match had better be in order with the mutual consent of the principal parties concerned (instead of leaving it entirely to the seconds). It would not be proper and reasonable to impose upon the girl the decision about her future life against her wishes.

Islam has certainly attached importance to the guardian of the girl being given in marriage, but it has also stressed the point that her permission is essential in a marriage tie. If the ward happens to be a widow or a divorced woman her explicit consent (spelt out in so many words) is necessary. In case of a virgin, however, her silence is to be deemed her consent and concurrence. Abu Hurairah (R.A.A.) reports the Prophet (S.A.W.) to have said :

> The widow or a divorcee shall not be given in marriage without asking for her opinion (about the match) and a virgin without her consent.

The companions submitted that a virgin shall not give utterance to her opinion. How are we to obtain her permission? The messenger of Allah (S.A.W.) said, "Her silence is her consent."

If a guardian of a woman gives her away in marriage and she disapproves of it, it would stand null and void. So we find that when Khansa' Bint-e-Khizam was given in marriage against her wishes (she complained) and the Prophet (S.A.W.) nullified the contract.

Many more such cases have come for mention in the Hadith literature. A minor girl can be given in marriage by her guardian. But the jurists are of the opinion that on attaining the age of majority she may retain or reject it at will.

Right to Dower

Islam has ordained man that the woman, he marries, must be paid her dower, without which *nikah* is not valid. The concept of dower (*mahar*) existed during the period of Jahiliyah also before the advent of Islam. But the Arabs had practically deprived her of it in various ways :

1. The guardian of woman regarded her dower as his own property and took possession of whatever she was given as dower. The Arabs regarded the daughter as a disgrace to themselves, and the news of the birth of a daughter overwhelmed them with grief and shame. But from this angle it was a source of happiness also to them that her dower would increase their wealth. That is why they called the daughter Al-Nafijah.—The means of increase, and in her birth they were congratulated : 'Happy birth to you of one who will increase your wealth'. Since they accepted only camels as dower, this meant that on marriage she will get camels for them as her dower and they will thus increase their wealth of camels.

2. It was also a common practice that on the death of a person, his son from a different mother would cast a sheet of cloth over the widow (not his real but a step mother) and declare himself the owner of that widow also along with the father's inheritance. This declaration confined his claim over that woman. Neither any other person could claim her nor she could herself do any thing against the step-son's will and claim. If he was serious about marrying her, he did so against the dower earlier paid to her by his deceased father. And in case he consented to give her in marriage to any other person,

her dower would be his, depriving her totally of her legitimate right.

3. At times taking advantage of the week position she was given less than the usual dower in vogue. 'Ayeshah (R.A.A.) says that an orphaned girl under the care of a person, if she was beautiful and had property of her own and the guardian wanted to marry her, he would do so in preference to other suitors, and against much less dower than others were ready to pay her. The Quran put a check on this practice, instructing them to either pay their full dower according to usage or marry some one else (and not their poor helpless ward).

4. During the period of Jahiliyah (Ignorance) there was yet another stratagem for getting rid of a woman's dower which has been called 'Shighar' in Hadith. This was a clever trick played on poor helpless women in as much as a person gave his daughter in marriage to another person on condition that he in turn would give his daughter in marriage to him. And in this cross-marriage neither of them paid either woman any dower (one cancelling the other).

Islam put an end to this unjust practice. Abdullah bin 'Umar R.A.A. says:

> The Prophet has prohibited 'Shighar'.
> In another report it has been said:
> There is no 'Shighar' in Islam.

In the report quoted by Bukhari the exchange of daughters without dower has come for mention. In another report quoted by Muslim, exchange of sisters too has been narrated. Both these are as examples, otherwise as remarked by Imam Navavi the Ulama are unanimous on it that exchange of nieces, paternal aunts and cousins like uncle's daughters also come under the same prohibition.

There is consensus of the Ulama that this practice of Jahiliyah has been declared unlawful by Islam. But they differ on the issue that the marriage contracts made on this basis shall be lawful or declared illegal and shall not hold.

A report of Abu Daood says that Abbas son of Abdullah Ibn Abbas (R.A.A.) gave his daughter in marriage to Abdur Rahman bin Hakam and he did in turn marry his daughter to Abbas, making this cross-marriage the dower (they cancelled each other). When Mu'awiyah (R.A.A.) learnt about it, he wrote to his governor of Madina, Marwan, that they should be legally separated as it is Shighar and prohibited by the Prophet (S.A.W.).

Imam Malik, Imam Shafi'i and Imam Ahmad R.A. and some others declare such a marriage illegal. Imam Abu Haneefah and Sufyan Thauri (R.A.) are of the opinion that the *nikah* is valid but both women shall be entitled to dower according to usage. To them the fault lies here in usurpation of dower which can be removed by its payment to both of them, according to the usual practice among the women of their class and status.

Thus, Islam declared dower to be the exclusive property of the woman and removed all the false and unjust claims on it one by one. It openly declared :

> And give them, the women, (on marriage) their dower as an obligation. [4]
>
> —Al Quran IV: 4

Allamah Abu Bakr Jassas says in its exposition :

> Dower is her property. She alone has a right to it. Her guardian has no claim to it.

The Islamic Shari'ah has prescribed no limits on the amount of dower. It can be increased or brought down according to the financial status of the person entering the marriage contract. However, it certainly is its inclination that it should be an amount that the man can easily pay. The jurists differ on the issue of fixation of the minimum amount of dower. Those belonging to the Hanafite school of jurisprudence put it at ten dirhams and not less than that.

Right of Maintenance

Before her marriage the responsibility of the up-keep of the girl devolves on the father. After marriage her maintenance becomes the concern, and a binding one too, of the husband. According to the Shari'ah, the maintenance of the wife is compulsorily the responsibility of the husband, without consideration of his financial status. The Hanafite school says that if the husband and wife are both wealthy, the maintenance of the wife shall be according to her status in life. In case of the wife being at a lower level financially, her maintenance shall be the mean between the rich and the poor. But if the reverse is the case, he shall spend on her according to his means and any deficiency shall become a liability as credit due from him to be paid to her at his convenience.

If the woman is rich, a servant shall be provided to her. If the wife does not want to live together with the husband's relations, she can demand a separate house (or an apartment in the same house but affording her privacy). It is her legal right and the husband has to meet it.

In this connection it would not be improper to mention here that according to the Hanafite Fiqh service to her husband and doing household chores is not the duty of the wife. If she undertakes it, it is courtesy from her and the urge of her moral virtue. She cannot be compelled to it.

Right to Work

Islam has granted the woman freedom of economic pursuits in the form of business, profession and work (any of the public services). She is permitted to undertake trade, agriculture, financing, industry, service, teaching jobs, journalism and writing and compilation of books — in fact all permitted. trades. For this purpose she can come out of her house too if necessary. However, it imposes certain restrictions on her in this connection. There are two objectives behind these checks on her. In the first place, her activity outside should create no confusion and interference in the order of the household and the normal life of the family circle and its stability and harmony should not be disturbed. And secondly the woman should be able to do an existence of modesty and chastity. Her economic effort and work in this direction should not put her under conditions which can hazard her strict adherence to moral limits.

Right to Property

There were many nations of the world that had denied right of ownership to their women. She had no share in the family property. Rather, even her own earnings were not left to her. Whatever she got through her own efforts was regarded the property of the father, husband, sons or other members of the family. Islam recognized the right of woman to ownership of the property and any meddling with it was declared wrongful and unlawful. According to it just as a man has a right to honestly earned wealth so has a woman right to own and use her lawful earnings.

> To men is allotted what they earn and to women what they earn. [5]
>
> —Al Quran IV - 32

Whatever a woman gets from her parents, husband or the offspring under the law of the Islamic Shari'ah or whatever she obtains through her own economic effort, she is the rightful owner of it all, and is entitled to spend it as she likes. She can spend on her own person, her husband and children, parents and other members of the family of her own free will. She can also invest it in charitable acts. She has also the right to the sale and purchase of property, forming trusts, gift it to others and can bequeath it at her own discretion. Nobody can interfere in these matters.

Right to Honour

Honour and dignity are a valuable asset of man. Playing with it and high-handedness cannot be allowed. Attacks on the honour and dignity of a woman have been a common practice and due to her weakness she has not been very successful either in protecting them. There are two forms of attack on her : Qazaf (slandering) and fornication. Qazaf means to question the honour and dignity of some woman and tarnishing her fair name by accusing her of dissoluteness and fornication. According to Islam it is a great crime and a moral sin. The Prophet (S.A.W.) has mentioned one of the seven mortal sins in these words:

> It is Qazaf or slandering chaste innocent believing but indiscreet woman.

As a legal measure against it Islam imposed the severe punishment of eighty cuts of the lash for calumniating a woman with illicit sex and such a person shall be debarred from appearing as a witness. Allah says :

> And those who launch a charge against chaste women and produce not four witnesses (to support their allegations), -flog them with eighty stripes - and reject their evidence ever after : for such men are wicked transgressors, except those who repent thereafter and mend (their conduct) ; for Allah is Oft-Forgiving. Most Merciful. [6]
>
> —Al-Quran, XXIV: 4-5

Now taking the issue of fornication and molestation of women, under the Islamic law, any person found guilty of raping a woman forcibly, in case he is unmarried shall receive hundred cuts of the lash and shall be stoned to death if he is married. However, if the woman as his partner cooperates with him she shall be liable to the same punishment.

Right to Reckoning

Undoubtedly Islam has exempted the woman from collective and political responsibilities. (The issue shall be taken up at length later on). But this exemption does not mean that she shall remain totally unconcerned with these affairs and evince no interest in the collective welfare. The Quran has ordained both man and woman to enjoin good and forbid evil :

> The believing men and women are one of another: they enjoin what is just and forbid what is evil. [7] —Al-Quran IX: 71

Enjoining good and forbidding evil has very wide and far-reaching demands. Call to Faith and preaching is also a part of those demands alongwith the reformation of the ummah and criticism and calling people to account, the rulers being also included in it. It is the responsibility of a woman to meet all these demands within her own limits of action. History bears testimony to the fact that women of the early phase of Islam realized this responsibility and fulfilled it.

Right of Inheritance

In the pre-Islamic day's, Arabian society rights and privileges were totally denied to woman, being exclusively a man's domain. Their argument in this behalf was that she was weak incapable of enhancing family's resources and a hindrance rather than an asset in the defence against the enemies, her own and that of the family. She could not bring in spoils of war home to improve the economic condition of the household and the tribe. And so she could not be the recipient of a share in the family's substance. Similarly boys of tender age were denied any portion of the bequeathal of the family on those very grounds. Only able-bodied young men (war-worthy) who could face the enemies in the field received their share of inheritance.

The Arabian society was not alone in keeping the woman deprived of her share in inheritance. The other social orders of the world on the basis of these and other pretexts kept her out of it, only the male offspring and the first born getting away with it in its entirety. (Even in this so-called age of enlightenment with elaborate charters of woman's rights, children's rights and human rights and what not, the nations regarding themselves the most sensible and just, believe in and act on the self-invented principle of primoprogeniture. It can be witnessed in broad daylight in all the vestiges of monarchies of the world. And all feudal societies do the same unashamed in this democratic age).

Islam raised its voice against this gross injustice to the weaker sex, proclaiming aloud that woman had as much right to her share in the inheritance. The Quran declared:

> From what is left by parents and those nearest related there is a share for men and a share for women, whether the property be small or large,- a determinate share. [61]—Al Quran IV: 7

And along with this instruction on principle it also appointed the share of men and women. Some details are to be found in Hadith and Fiqh (Islamic jurisprudence). The objection raised here is that equality has not been maintained between the sexes and man has been endowed with greater right to it than the woman. But this is a baseless objection levelled against the Islamic Law because of the ignorance of its underlying wisdom and intrinsic value. So long as one does not have the details of this law of inheritance and their wisdom before him, it is difficult to understand it in its proper perspective and misunderstandings are most likely. Here we shall try to present some details of the Islamic Law of inheritance and later an attempt will be made to bring out some of its underlying wisdom.

Islam has restricted the inheritance strictly to the family, and has specified the rights of the members the family with gradation depending on closeness to the deceased. The first and the foremost among the shareholders is the progeny of the person leaving behind property. Allah says in the Quran :

> Allah (thus) directs you as regards your children's (inheritance) : to the male a portion equal to that of two females :[62]—Al Quran IV: 11

This brings out the following points for our consideration: Progeny includes both boys and girls. The inheritance is not the exclusive share of the boys. The girls also have their right to it. One boy's share shall be equal to those of two girls. Suppose the deceased has a boy and a girl. The property left by him shall be divided into three equal portions, one third going to the daughter, and two thirds to the boy. With two girls and one boy, the property shall be divided into four equal parts two parts (2/4) or half going to the two girls and the remaining half to the boy. Allah says :

> If only daughters two or more, their share is two thirds of the inheritance. [63] —Al Quran IV : 11

This is about a situation where there is no male progeny and there are more than two girls. The girls here shall get two thirds. Here more than two daughters have come for mention, but if they are two their portion remains the same, two thirds.

If there is no male progeny and only one daughter she shall be entitled to half the inheritance. Allah say :

> If only one, her share is a half. [64] —Al Quran IV : 11

This leads us also to the point that if there is only one boy he must get the entire property of the dead since his share is twice that of the girl. When an only girl gets half of it, the only boy, common sense demands, should get twice that or full property. However, in case of more than one boy, it will get divided among them since there is no basis for distinction between one brother and another.

Rights of Parents

After the progeny the parents have priority in the matter of rights to the property of the deceased. The Quran has stated their rights thus :

> For parents a sixth share of the inheritance to each if the deceased left children; if no children

> and the parents are the (only) heirs, the mother shall get a third. If the deceased left brothers (or sisters) the mother has a sixth. [65] — Al Quran II

The following principles can be derived from the verse: In the event of the deceased having progeny, even if it is an only boy or a girl, the parents shall get one sixth. Grandsons and grand daughters and even their descendants come under progeny. And in the absence of the progeny of the deceased, the mother shall get one third and the father two thirds. The deceased has no progeny but two or more brothers (of whatever relationship), the mother's share shall become one sixth, the rest going to the father. Brothers and sisters shall have no share whatsoever. And after stating the rights of the parents, it has been said :

> (The distribution in all cases is) after the payment of legacies and debts. You know not whether your parents or your children are nearest to you in benefit. These are settled portions ordained by Allah: And Allah is All-Knowing, All Wise. [66]—Al Quran IV : 11

That means legacies shall be attended to on a priority basis and debts shall be paid (before distribution). When these two liabilities are fully settled, then only what remains of the inheritance shall be distributed.

Rights of Husband and Wife

The rights of the husband and the wife have been declared in the Quran in these words :

> In what your wives leave your share is a half, if they have no child, but if they leave a child, ye get a fourth, after payment of legacies and debts. In what ye leave, their share is a fourth, if ye leave no child; but if ye leave a child,

> they get an eighth; after payment of legacies
> and debts. [67] —Al Quran IV : 12

The verse brings out the following: The husband shall get half of the inheritance of his wife in case she has no children (from this husband or any other before that). Grandson is also progeny. There is consensus on it. The husband shall get one fourth of the wife's property if she has children (from the same or some other husband). The wife shall get one fourth from the property of the deceased husband if he leaves no children. The wife shall get one eighth if the husband leaves children after him (no matter whether borne to him by this wife or any other wife).

Right of the Step-brother and Sister

The children, parents, husband and wife shall be inheritors in every case. Others follow suit. Among them brother and sister have precedence. Brothers and sisters are of three kinds : *'aini, 'allati* and *akhyafi*. Among these three 'aini (real) brothers and sisters have precedence over the rest. If they are absent 'allati brothers and sisters (same father but different mothers) shall be the inheritors. The shares of akhyafi brothers and sisters (same mother, different fathers) are specified, on which there is consensus of the ummah and they have been stated in the following verse :

> If the man or woman whose inheritance is in question, has left neither ascendants nor descendants, but has left a brother or a sister (Akhyafi), each one of the two gets a sixth; but if more than two, they share in a third, after payment of legacies and debts; so that no loss is caused (to any one). Thus, is it ordained by Allah; and Allah is All Knowing and Most Forbearing. [68]—Al Quran IV: 12

This means that Akhyafi brother or sister, each, will be entitled to one sixth. If they are more than two, then they all will be entitled to one-third equally. There will be no difference in the share of brother and sister.

Rights of Real and Step-brothers and Sisters

The rights of real and step brothers and sisters have been stated in these words :

> Say: Allah directs (thus) about those who leave no descendants or ascendants as heirs. If it is a man that dies, leaving a sister but no child, she shall have half the inheritance : If (such a deceased was) a woman who left no child, her brother takes her inheritance : If there are two sisters they shall have two thirds of the inheritance (between them). If there are brothers and sisters, (they share) the male having twice the share of the females; Thus doth Allah make clear to you (His Law), least ye err, and Allah hath knowledge of all things. [69]
>
> Al- Quran IV: 176

This shows that if the deceased has a son (grandson and male progeny in the descending order) or father, grandfather, and others in the ascending order, the brothers and sisters shall have no share in the inheritance. If they (progeny or parents) are not there, the inheritance shall be divided among them like this: If only one sister she will get a half. If only one brother, he will be entitled to the entire property. If two or more sisters and no brother, they will get two thirds. If brothers and sisters both are there, the share of a brother shall be equal to that of two sisters.

If the deceased has daughters only their predetermined shares (half if only one, and for more than one two thirds' for them and the rest shall go to the brothers and sister according to the predetermined principle of one man's share equal to that of two women). If there are only sisters with the daughters, after apportioning their shares the rest shall be given to the sisters.

These are the broad principles of inheritance which the Quran has enunciated. Their details are to be found in compilations of Hadith and Fiqh. We are not going to discuss them here.

Basis of Inheritance

Now, we shall try to briefly explain the bases on which the Islamic Law of inheritance rests, which will bring out some aspects of their underlying wisdom. Inheritance is divided among the members of the family. Blood relationship and that through nikah have been made the basis of consideration in the apportioning. The family is a definite unit, kept intact by heritage and blood ties. The natural feelings of love, sympathy and cooperation exist among them. They are practically partners in all matters involving benefit and detriment of the family, help in promoting their interests and come to their aid in solving knotty problems. That is why the family attachments of a person are very firm and strong. He or she keeps its well-being upper most in all the benefits accruing to him or her individually. His economic effort too is to a large extent for the family. Therefore, normally he regards the family as partner in his substance and its rightful shareholder. Usually, husband and wife are not blood relations of each other. However, they are so close that they become part of the unit of family. Hence, they inherit from one another and this is certainly natural and justified.

The members of the family directly related to the deceased must and do get their share in his/her property, never deprived of it under any circumstances, be they men or woman. The following come under this category: The children of the deceased, both boys and girls. The parents of the deceased. Either of the husband or wife who survives.

Among them, As'habul-Fara'iz shall receive their due shares. The remaining portion shall go to 'Usbah.

The reason behind precedence of these members over others is evident enough. A person regards them too close to himself and factually too it is they who are closest to him. All his life, directly and intermediarily it is they, he has to and does deal with. In spending on them, his hard earned wealth, he feels a pleasure and sort of mental peace and tranquillity. It is his earnest desire that even after his passing away they should inherit his property and none other than they should take possession of it. It is a natural sentiment and cannot be declared wrong or misplaced. And all that the Quran has done is to give it legal sanction.

Even among these most closely related family members Islam has given precedence to the right of offspring over those of the parents. Their needs and financial demands on them have been kept in view in this regard. The children are the rightful successors of their parents. After their passing away they shoulder many of their responsibilities and promote many of the projects left unfinished by them. And over and above these there are many responsibilities of their own with which they have to grapple and have to find means to meet them, planning their future in the light of the existing conditions. Apparently enough their needs of wealth are far greater than those of the parents of the deceased. And the parents (grandparents of the children) themselves are inclined to help the children (their grandchildren) in every possible manner in preference to others. However, if there is no offspring the parents gain importance and their rights have priority.

If the man and woman stand on an equal footing in the matter of relationship to the deceased, one man's share shall be equal to that of two women, like son and daughter, brother and sister. It does not at all reflect in any way on the inferiority of woman and superiority of man. Had there been any such concept woman's share would have been permanently kept at a minimum or none at all and she would have stood totally deprived of any share in the inheritance, whereas in fact none of these things is true. The reason behind it is that Islam has associated inheritance with financial responsibilities. According to Islam man has to shoulder all the financial responsibilities, whereas woman has been totally exempted from them. To illustrate let us take an example of a young man and a young girl. The boy (young man) spends on the support of his wife and children. May be he has to support his parents, both or the surviving one. There is a likelihood of his extending help to his poor brothers and sisters and some other relatives in need of help. Thus, whatever he earns is drained through these channels. As compared with him the girl (woman), if she is well off she may be spending on herself at the most, since she has not been burdened with anybody else's responsibility. And after marriage the expenditure on self too ends, the husband taking over her maintenance. The fact is that if the responsibilities of both are kept in view, neither the boy gets more (than necessary), nor the girl is given less than her need. A just balance has been maintained between them.

Similarly, the share of the wife is half that of the husband. Here too the woman is free from liabilities. Moreover, she gets *mahar* from the husband and all the ornaments and other gifts she receives on marriage and other occasions add to her property. In the event of the husband's death the wife gets her share of inheritance and vice versa. If after the wife's death the husband wants to remarry, he will have to pay, the second wife her mahar and take over the responsibility of her maintenance. But if the widowed wife intends to remarry she will get her mahar from the second husband and he will have to maintain her also. Thus, wouldn't it be just and proper that the woman should get in the inheritance half that of the husband ? And wouldn't it be gross injustice to the husband that his share be kept equal to that of the woman ? That is exactly what Ibn Katheer has said in the following words :

Allah, the exalted, has fixed the share of man equal to that of two women because he has to bear the burden of maintenance of the woman, the difficulties of trade and earning his livelihood and other hardships of this type, it is in the fitness of things that he should get twice that of woman.

Allamah Rasheed Raza Misri says:

> The underlying wisdom in allowing man a share equal to that of two women is that he has to spend on his own support as well as on the maintenance of his wife and so two shares

> for him. The woman spends her substance on herself and after her marriage her maintenance too has to be borne by her husband. For consideration of the burden of maintenance under certain conditions the share of woman becomes greater than that of man.

In this way lightening the burden of woman in the matter of financial responsibilities, in some cases of inheritance woman's share has become reduced to half of that of man. Under the circumstances neither man complains that he has been overburdened with responsibilities, nor can woman question why her share has been reduced to half. As against this, if they had been placed on an equal footing in their shares in inheritance, man would have been justified in making a demand that a woman should also be involved in financial responsibilities. This division of rights and obligations is exactly in keeping with the natures of both of them. A better division is unimaginable.

Hafiz Ibn Qayyim, along with the financial responsibilities of man, points to yet another aspect that since man during his life-time is benefited much more by man, in the event of his death man's share should be more than woman's share in his inheritance. He says:

Man receiving greater share in the inheritance is manifest enough. He stands in greater need of substance than woman since he is the supervisor in the family (he has to shoulder the responsibilities of woman's maintenance). Moreover, man is benefited much more from man in his life-time. Allah, often specifying the rights in inheritance and keeping them at different levels, pointing to this fact has said : you don't know which of the two, your parents or, your offspring is more beneficial to you. When during the life-time of the deceased he had been benefited by man more than by the woman, and he also stands in greater need of money, he deserves precedence in his share from inheritance.

Where the financial responsibilities of man get lightened, Islam does not discriminate between the sexes. In case the deceased has children the shares of both mother and father are the same. One very evident reason is that the right of the progeny has precedence. The second reason is that a person whose progeny has come to have progeny of its own, his financial responsibilities get minimised. He, at this stage comes to take the position of the patron of his grandsons and grand daughters. However, if the deceased has no children who have priority in his property, the father in that case having children (brothers and sisters of the deceased) will have greater right to inheritance than the mother of the deceased since his responsibilities too can be greater.

Islam has based the division of inheritance on the principle that among the blood relations the closer to the deceased the greater his precedence over others. Those far removed shall be entitled to it only in case close relations are absent or after their having received their shares, there is still some property left. Under the principle the woman closer to the deceased may be entitled to' greater share than male relatives not so closely related. Suppose the deceased has a daughter and a brother, the property shall be equally divided between them. If only one daughter and two brothers, the daughter shall have half and the remaining half will go to the two brothers. If two or more than two daughters two thirds shall go to them and one or more brothers shall get only one third.

These detailed discussions refute outright the objection that justice has not been meted out to the woman in the distribution of inheritance. Neither there has been any partiality or biased treatment in dealing with man, nor has the woman been let down in the form of iniquitous treatment. Islam on the one hand has attached importance to woman's close relationship with the deceased and on the other it has kept in view the financial responsibilities of man. On these bases the woman is the recipient of greater share in the inheritance in certain situations and not so great in others. And in certain other situations they stand on the same plane. This is unparalleled equilibrium between closeness of relationship and financial responsibilities. And this exemplary balance is that outstanding characteristic of the

Islamic Shari'ah which bestows on it a unique characteristic not enjoyed by any other religion or ideology.

Other Rights

There are several verses in the Holy Qur'an that say in a clear cut way that kindness to one's parents is next only to Allah. But there should be no Shirk (polytheism) under whatsoever a banner. In this respect Qur'an tells us amazingly :

> "We have enjoined on man kindness to parents; but if they (either of them) strive to force thee to join with Me anything of which thou hast no knowledge, obey them not ...."
> (Qur'an 29: 8)
>
> "Thy Lord hath decreed that ye worship none but Him and that ye be kind to parents. Whether one or both of them attain old age in thy life, say not a word of contempt, nor repel them, but address them in terms of honour. And out of kindness lower to them thy wing of humility; and say: "My Lord ! Bestow on them thy Mercy even as they cherished me in childhood."(Qur'an 17: 23)

If there is conflict between our duty to Allah and our duty to our parents and those in authority, we are to obey Allah and disobey them in a kind, considerate and courteous way. We should never be arrogant, We learn this from the coming verses of the Qur'an:

> "And We have enjoined on man (to be good) to his parents. In travail upon travail did his mother bear him and in years twain was his weaning. Show gratitude to Me and to thy parents. To Me is thy final goal.
>
> "But if they strive to make the associate in worship with Me things of which thou hast

> no knowledge, obey them not; yet bear them company in this life (and consideration....)."
> (Qur'an 31: 14-15)

The mother is the one who suffers more than the father especially at the early stages of the child. The child remains in her womb for nine solid months. At this period she undergoes several physical and psychological changes. Some of the mothers become sick and anaemic, while other pregnant women suffer in different ways.

After that she gives birth. Here she can get some sort of material aid from others such as nannies, baby sisters and a hundred and one other evils of our twentieth century Jahilia. The only person to look after a baby is the mother. Feeders are the worst things to use. They are the carriers of all the diseases that attack our children especially in a backward society. Worst of all is that the bottle feeding media lacks the Heavenly maternal feeling that a child feels when he suckles from his mother's breast. That is why some of our scholars say that if a child does not complete a 24 months suckling period the father is to compensate him (giving him a share from property).

Because of all the troubles that a mother faces, the Holy Qur'an teaches us to be very kind to them. Let us read the following verse:

> "We have enjoined on man kindness to his parents, in pain did his mother bear him, and in pain did she give him birth. The carrying of the child to his weaning is (a period of) thirty months. At length, when he reaches the age of full strength and attains forty years, he says: "O my Lord ! Grant me that I may be grateful for Thy favour which -Thou hast bestowed upon me, and upon both my parents ...." (Qur'an 46 -.15)

The Messenger of Allah (may Allah give him peace) is quoted as saying what it meant:

> "Paradise is under the feet of mothers."

> "It is the generous in character who is good to women., and it is the wicked who insults them."

It is reported that a man came to the Apostle of Allah (peace be upon him) and asked him the following :

> "O Messenger of Allah, who is the most worthy of my company?"

The Prophet said, "Your Mother."

The man asked, "Who is the next?" with the same answer, "Your Mother." It was repeated with the same reply, only in the fourth time did the Prophet change his answer and said, "Your Father."

We learn from such Ahadith (Sayings of the Prophet-may Allah give him peace) how Islam honours and respects the mother.

> "........ But consort with them in kindness, for if ye hate them it may happen that ye hate a thing wherein Allah hath placed much good."
>
> (Qur'an 4: 19)

May I repeat here once again the three Ahadith (Sayings of the Prophet). It is reported that he said :

> "The best of you is the best of you to his family and I am the best of you to my family."

> "Lo many women came to Muhammad's wives complaining against their husbands beating them; those are not the best of you."

> "A male Muslim should never hate a female

> Muslim (wife) because, if he hates some of her manners he is sure to like others."

> "Truly a woman is like a rib. If you try to straighten it, you are sure to break it, but if you leave it as it is, you will enjoy with it while it is a bit bent."

The husband is told to be more patient and should not be angry with her quickly, as she is more emotional; he should therefore be somewhat rational.

> "The most perfect believers are the best in conduct and the best of you are the best of you to their wives."

No husband is to spy on his wife. He should not tell her for example; that: "I shall not come back tonight. I shall go to such and such a place." And he comes at midnight knocking at the door spying on her.

The husband is to maintain his family in its wide and narrow sense of the word (family Husband, wife and children and the Eastern type of joint Family).

He is to provide his wife with all the necessary means of leisure according to his means. He should cut his coat according to his cloth.

He should consort with her and respect her feelings. If she did anything unbecoming, he, is not to reprimand her before visitors or anyone else (especially before their own children).

He should take good care of her personal property and should never spend a penny without her consent.

Both of them are required to preserve personal secrets of the other. Neither of them is to tell people anything of their intimate family life.

He is to allow her to visit her parents. It would be better if he sent her to visit them now and then.

The Messenger of Allah (peace be upon him) told Abdullah b. 'Amr bin al-'Aas, who was fasting daily and spending his nights in prayers: "...Do not do that, fast and break fast (do not fast for some days) and sleep. Truly your, body has rights, on you, your eyes and your wife has (her legal) rights on you .... Give each its rights."

Ownership

Islam fully acknowledges the woman's right of an independent ownership in her money, real estate or on any other properties. This right does not undergo any changes whether she is single or married; whether she acquired the property before marriage or after it. She retains her full rights upon her property whether selling, buying it or other wise.

A woman used to be an object of inheritance. This went on, in some cultures, as late as the nineteenth century, while Islam gave her the right of inheritance 1,400 years ago. She has the full right on her share of inheritance, it is completely hers. Neither her father, husband, mother or anyone else could make any claim on her share of an inheritance. It is hers.

The Holy Quran says:

> "Unto men of the family belongs a share of that which parents and near kindred leave, and unto women a share of that which parents and near kindred leave :-whether it be a little or much a determined share."
>
> (Qur'an 4: 7)

Her share of inheritance is governed by certain factors, whether there are sons and daughters, or the only child in the family etc. etc.

We shall appreciate this more if we remember that as late as the twelfth century a wife was sold in some cultures soon after the death of her husband. Her luck was not even better in Arabia, because she did not inherit anything from her parents or her husband.

Her Maiden Name

Over and above all this, she must retain her full identity: her maiden name. Suppose a Fatima Mohammad ar-Riyamy marries a Khalfan Moosa an-Na'asaany. She never changes her name and becomes a Mrs. Na'asaany. No and never. Her doing so (change of name) is regarded by some of the scholars as completely un-Islamic, that is a sin.

The wife retains her identity while she is with her husband, and when he dies or divorces her and she marries another man there is no such nuisance of rechanging of names for the third or fourth times. Her first maiden (father's) name is hers till she dies.

Going back into history we find that nearly all Christian women lose their maiden names soon after marriage as she has to sign her maiden name for the last time in the Church register after the wedding ceremonies. It was only, of all that I know, Lucy Stone, one of the most famous speakers on the movement to emancipate women, that retained her maiden name as a protest against the unequal laws applicable to married women. She became known as Mrs. Stone and not as Mrs. Blackwell.

It is also said that some of the Slavonic tribes gave the woman a choice of whether to retain her maiden name or change it to that of her husband's.

Political Rights

Throughout the history of Islam, we find a Muslim woman is given full political rights. Women took part in serious discussions and argued even with the Messenger of Allah himself (may Allah give him peace). Through our reading of the following verses of the Holy Qur'an we know how Islam gave her political rights :

> "Allah has indeed heard (and accepted) the
> statement of the woman who pleads with thee

> concerning her husband and carries her complaint (in prayer) to Allah, and Allah (always) hears the arguments between both sides among you: for Allah hears and sees (all things). (58 :1)
>
> "O ye who believe, when there come to you believing women refugees, examine (and test) them Allah knows best as to their faith: if ye ascertain that they are Believers then send them not back to the Unbelievers. They are not lawful (wives) for the Unbelievers, nor are the (Unbelievers) lawful (husbands) for them. But pay the Unbelievers what they have spent (on the dower....)."
> (60: 10 see also 66: 11)

It is reported the Caliph 'Umar said what it meant: "We never paid any attention to whatever was said by a woman before Islam, nor did we ask her any advice. It was only the teaching of Islam that gave her full rights as reasonable being."

> "I was once thinking and pondering over something important when my wife suggested that I had better do this and that. I told her to stop that as it was none of her business.'
>
> "She told me: 'What is wrong with you O Ibn al-Khattaab? You do not want to be given any advice while your daughter argues with the Prophet till he becomes angry.'
>
> 'I went straight to Hafsa and asked her: 'Tell me; daughter; what is it that you discuss with the Apostle till you make him angry?'
>
> She responded, "Yes, father ! All his wives do. It is natural. (He sometimes remains angry for the whole day because of our arguments with him)".

Caliph 'Umar was once discussing with Muslims in a Mosque (as it is not only a place of worship, but also the Parliament, the Court, the Army Headquarters, the Muslim Government itself) certain problems. A woman corrected him and made him declare before the public: "The woman is right and 'Umar is wrong."

One might argue pointing out that there is a Prophet's saying which mean that no country will prosper if it were led by a woman. It has nothing to do with the dignity of women, neither does it hinder her rights. It is rather, due to the natural differences in the biological and psychological set up of the two sexes.

According to Islamic Law the Head of the State is not just a figure head. He is the centre of all activities. He is the chief justice. He must lead people in prayers, especially Friday prayers (Juma) and on religious festivities. He leads people in Jihaad (religious wars) against non-Muslims for the well being of humanity).

During the monthly periods and during pregnancy, women generally undergo frequent psychological changes; let alone the monthly changes of her hormones (which generally happens twice a month) the kind which makes a woman become more emotional than rational.

Health

Had mothers brought up their children themselves and without the help of nannies, maids or baby-sitters, I am sure that most of the mental hospitals, psychological clinics, would have to close down because there would have not been cases that needed their utmost care. The psychotherapists would have to find some other jobs to do.

A child needs maternal care more than anything else especially during his early infant stage if we really need a good and mentally healthy society. And that is why Islam regarded the woman's role in a society as that of a mother and a wife, which is the most essential one in any healthy, society. The society whose members are upright, complex free and carefully reared members.

Hence the best jobs for a woman are those pertaining to Health and Education. I said, "the best" and I did not say "the only". She can do good in any other field as well, but these are the two fields which satisfy her nature more; therefore, she can contribute better to the well being of humanity in general. Not only that, but also she learns more about human nature.

Islam does not restrict a society from benefiting from any exceptionally talented woman in any field.

Participation in Many Affairs

Abu Jahal was torturing Sumayya at the point of death forcing her to abuse Prophet Muhammad and Allah and praise the gods of Quraish Tribe: He told her if she did not do what he asked her she won't see the evening of that day any more as she was going to, die before sunset. Sumayya answered him in a very low and separated and interrupted voice: "Fie to you and your gods and misfortune, befell on you. Is their anything better for me than death that will release me from seeing this ugly face of yours?" Her words and the unexpected outburst of laughter from both 'Utba and Shaiba bin Rabii'a made Abu Jahal so furious that he could control himself no longer. He thrust her with a lance. She became the first martyr in Islam.

We have seen in the Introduction that two members (Nusaiba and Asma'a) out of the 75 Yathrib (Medina) delegation to ask the Prophet (peace be upon him) to migrate to Medina were women. We shall appreciate it more if we remember that these things had happened during the sixth and seventh centuries (of the Christian Era) at the time when in other parts of the world (in Europe) conferences were being held to discuss if a woman was human or not, whether she was with or without a soul and whether she was to worship god or otherwise.

We see Muslim women taking part in Jihad (the religious wars against non-Muslims for the well being of humanity) during the period of the Apostle of Allah (S.A.W.) and after. Their main task was in the following fields: Ambulance, mending and making clothes for the army, preparing food for them, giving them water, nursing and all other essential needs.

Aisha bint Abu Bakar and 'Umme 'Aiman al-Habashiyya and some other Muslim ladies took part in the battle of Uhud. They were giving water to the soldiers, taking care of the wounded and consoling them.

When the Prophet (peace be upon him) was wounded it was. Aisha who ran looking for straws and old mats. She burnt them and took the ash to heal wounds of the Messenger of Allah.

Nusaiba led a women's delegation to the Apostle of Allah asking him to give them permission to take part in the Jihad as men do. He asked them: "What can you (women) do, O Nusaiba?" She responded:, "We can mend clothes, take care of the injured and 'wounded by tending and comforting them, cure the sick and, give water to all."

She even took part in the actual fighting, to protect the Prophet.

In the battle of the confederates, Safia bint 'Abd Al-Muttalib (Hamza's sister) killed one of the Jews who were spying for the enemy of Islam,

Zainab the daughter of the Holy Prophet (peace be upon him) mediated or asked her father to protect Abul 'Aas bin ar-Rabi" (at the time when he was still an infidel) from Abul Baseer and it was granted after he consulted Muslims. No sooner had this stroke of kindness fell on Abul 'Aas heart and he embraced Islam.

Safia (Zubair bin Al-Awwam's mother) was one of those who took part in the Khybar battle. She was afraid for her son Zubair being killed. The Prophet told her that Zubair was going to kill his foe.

In the battle of Yarmouk some Muslim ladies were taken as war prisoners. They wanted to fight for their freedom. They had no weapons with them, They fought with ordinary poles, sticks and pegs from the tents. The freedom battle was led by Khawla bint al-Azwar.

The Muslim woman played a very important role in Islam. Her life was not confined to the house. No, she went out taking part in different walks of life under the banner of Sharia protecting her chastity, and not forgetting her primary role in life is that of wife and mother.

Islam always benefits from the exceptionally talented Muslim woman in any field;

Ali Yahya Mitammar in his book *al-Abadhiyya fi Mawkibit Taarikh* (Ibadhi through History) mentioned many Muslim women of North Africa who played very important role in shaping Islam. You could find this in a chapter heading; al-Mar-atul Muslimatu fi Libya (Muslim Woman in Libya).

Let us quote just one example from Mu-ammar:

> "(7) Ummu Yahya; the pious, highly educated and most able teacher lived at, Amsiyin between Jailaat and Timjaarah, somewhere in Jebel Nafusa (Libya).
>
> She felt that girls education was not complete if she learnt in boys' schools. She thought that had she been able to open a girls' school, that would have provided opportunities for girls to study upto the final stages of education She opened a girls school and opened also what is now called 'A Girls' Hostel' for those girls who live in far different places. She directed her students into a variety of walks of life. She found employment for some, and arranged marriage for others, and further studies for those who wanted to go on with their studies.

Let us sum up with what Dr. Inamullah said in his articles: The Holy Prophet: A Blessing for the Teeming Millions:

> "He (the Prophet) came to grant woman her rightful place in the society of man, raising her above the position of goods and chattels and granting her a respectful entity and a personality to herself. She was considered an independent social and economic unit functioning in her own individual right, if she so desired. For the first time she was given the right to education, the right to hold property in her own name, the right of inheritances and above all, the right to vote, and pray. What is the right to vote, but to have the legal right for a free expression of opinion or choice. Human history fails to give that place of pride which the Holy Prophet gave to woman. His words: 'Paradise lies at the feet of thy mother' are eternal, a sparkling and glowing tribute to the status of woman."

The Inheritance

The chapter of the Qur'an called 'The Woman' (al-Nisa) details in a just manner the share of inheritance that is due to each individual, male and female. According to this chapter, women are not only no longer allowed to be inherited like chattels but, as individuals, they have a legal right to inheritance. 'Men shall have a share in what their parents and kinsmen leave; and women shall have a share in what their parents and kins men leave; whether it be little or much, it is legally theirs'.

This verse was revealed when an Ansari lady came to the Prophet and complained that after her husband's death she and her daughter were prevented from inheriting any of his property. Her husband's brother justified the action by stating that, 'Women do not mount horses, do not endanger themselves and go .into battle', therefore they could not be allowed to inherit.

Before Islam, women were not only deprived of their right to inheritance, but also had no impact over their own destiny, which was a matter between the men of the husband's clan or her own relatives. During the Jahiliyya, when a man lost his father, brother, or son, and that person left a widow, the heir, taking advantage of the fact that her dowry was paid by the dead man, rushed to the widow, covered her with his cloak, thus claiming (unjustly) to himself the sole right to marry her. When he married her, he denied her of her right to the part of the inheritance constituted by the dowry. But if he decided, for one reason or another, not to have her as a wife, he could then ask another person to marry her in return he would take (for himself) her dowry. However, if the widow (at the time of her husband's death) managed to get to her own clan before the arrival of the heir, he would lose his rights over her in favour of the males of her own clan. New laws regarding women challenged the social structure of a society that had given males the upper hand over females in matters related to inheritance. Therefore, it was inevitable that it would create an uproar among sections of the male population who felt threatened by them and questioned the validity of granting women a share in the inheritance. So, they decided to ignore these laws and continued to apply the customs of the Jahiliyya, hoping that as time went by the Prophet would change them. But the matter was brought to the surface by women themselves who continued to suffer from the Jahiliyya mentality.

For pre-Islamic Arabian society, it was outrageous to allow fatherless children who could not fight or earn a living to have shares in the inheritance. Therefore, they were denied any rights to inheritance. Moreover, they were mistreated and not looked after well, especially young girls who were also the object of sexual abuse. For example, the guardian very often decided to marry the prettiest ones thus securing two things for himself. (1) controlling their share of inheritance; (2) setting away from or escaping: paying a dowry for them. If a fatherless girl happened to be ugly or not pretty enough to persuade him to marry her he would use her ugliness, to oppose any marriage for her. In doing so, he did not have to pay her share of inheritance. If a fatherless girl was ugly, her guardian did not give her her share. He forced her not to marry and waited for her to pass away so that he would assume control over her inheritance. Islam, would not tolerate such inhumane practices, with its egalitarian message which aimed at redressing the injustice of society. It began by affirming the legal right of fatherless children to have a share in their own inheritance and ended by cautioning against depriving them of their due.

Although Islam granted woman the right to inheritance, her share is by no means fair and equal to that given to man. The critics refer to the verse that allows the brother to take twice as much as the share of their sisters. Therefore, they view this as detrimental to the dignity of women. By giving women half the share of men, they say, there is a clear implication that women are inferior to men. This argument has been used by both Muslims and non-Muslims. But it is based on a fallacy. If it happens for one reason or another that one sex receives a greater or lesser share than the other, this does not mean that the recipient of the lesser share is regarded as inferior. The whole issue of inheritance in Islam depends entirely on the social and economic context, and the role or function of a particular sex within it. If this crucial contextual factor is borne in mind, a proper understanding of the verses related to inheritance in the Qur'an would ensue.

The Qur'an has ensured that women could get their shares of inheritance not only as daughters, but also as mothers and wives. The fact that women have been given half the share of male heirs has to be looked at within its social and economic framework. In Islam the wife is to be cared for by her husband, even if she is wealthy enough to maintain herself. By law she is entitled to claim maintenance from her husband. At the same time she is not obliged to spend any of her wealth on the household.

In addition a Muslim woman receives at the time of her

marriage a considerable sum of money. This money, which the husband is obliged to pay, constitutes her dowry, or Mahr, which belongs to her alone. She is free to use, spend or invest it in any way she likes. Therefore, as a wife she adds to whatever she receives through inheritance in her capacity as daughter and that, too, without any legal commitment to support either herself or her children.

The position of women is secure as far as inheritance is concerned. Although women have been given half the share of men, their financial situation in the long term is guaranteed. This is due to the fact that the marriage contract gives her the right to ask for Mahr as well as claim maintenance, both of which entail no legal commitment to anybody including herself.

But it may be objected, what about women who cannot marry for one reason or another? What about the ones who cannot work and earn a living, especially in the rural areas where women have been denied the chance to gain a decent education? How would they live and maintain themselves?

The Quranic injunctions make it clear that male relatives, especially brothers, have the obligation to care for women and meet their financial needs. At the moment, in most Muslim countries this issue has been left to the individual conscience, which has led to many cases of abuse and desertion. Therefore, in order to secure and protect these women, governments need to legislate and make it legally binding on those male relatives to pay for the upkeep of their needy women.

The Qur'an makes it clear that a person is entitled to make a will. Indeed, it is highly recommended by the Prophet that a person should prepare a will as early as possible and not wait until it is too late. Contrary to the misconception held by large sections of the Muslim public that a person has no right to make a will, both the Qur'an and the Sunnah encourage people to do so. There are even some misguided jurists who argue, contrary to clear principles in the Qur'an, that Islam does not recommend the making of wills. This negative attitude advocated by a small band of jurists has confused ordinary Muslim people and has led many to abandon the idea of making wills.

The Qur'an, on the other hand, has specifically asked for the distant relatives, the needy people and the orphans to be treated kindly and to be helped if they are present at the time of the division of inheritance:

> If relatives, orphans, or needy men are present at the division of an inheritance, give them, too, a share of it, and speak to them in kind words.

So, if the Quran is so kind even to distant relatives and needy people by virtue of the fact that it encourages people to give them some share of the inheritance, we see no problem, in keeping with this spirit of Divine Justice, that a bequest be made in favour of a needy person, particularly if this person is a close member of the family. The point here is emphasised that if parents think that their daughter is unable to get married for whatever reason and she is in a disadvantaged position, they can write a will in her favour in order to secure her future. This accords with the spirit of the Qur'an and the Sunnah.

The position of Muslim women as far as inheritance is concerned is secure and guaranteed by the Islamic Law. But in practice this is not the case. Constantly, the Divine instructions concerning women's rights to inheritance are violated and overlooked by Muslim societies. Social, political, economic and cultural factors play a major role in determining who does and who does not take a share. In such situations the weak have always been kept at bay when it comes to their right to inheritance. This takes place in both the cities as well as the rural areas.

Very often, strong social pressure is applied on women to renounce their shares for the benefit of the immediate male members of the family. This is particularly the case when women are well off or married to wealthy men. Their due is automatically written off and transferred to their male relatives. Whether they like it or not they are all too often forced to accept the loss of their shares; if they refuse, they are accused of being selfish, greedy, inconsiderate and irresponsible.

Often this has led to tension, friction and conflict of interests among the members of the family, shattering the whole concept of caring and sharing which lies at the heart of the Islamic faith. Here are a few examples which illustrate the evident disregard for the Divine decrees regarding women's right to inheritance.

The Islamic concept of broad and equitable shares which take into consideration the interests of all persons concerned has been transferred into a prerogative for males, outrageously disregarding the Divine Will. There is no doubt about the fact that in most parts of the Muslim world the Islamic Law concerning women's rights to inheritance is not in operation; instead it is the social and cultural rules which dominate. It is crucial that something has to be done to rectify this situation, and women themselves have an essential role to play.

Eight

Rights by Law

One of the objections levelled against the Law of Evidence in Islam is that it equates the evidence of two women to that of one man. This is insulting to the woman and negation of equity to her.

There is no doubt about it that Islam has, in many affairs, made a distinction between the evidence of man and woman. But taking it as an insult to the woman is unjustified and against the teachings of Islam. Islam has not arbitrarily made this distinction. The reasons for it are to be found in woman's nature, temperament and her sphere of action. To appreciate this attitude of Islam in this particular regard one has to understand fully the Islamic point of view in some detail.

Islam has classified evidence under three heads: Evidence in Divine Limits and Qisas. Evidence in matters relating to rights and dealings. Evidence in matter exclusive to her and her sex.

Evidence in Divine Limits

To enforce a divine limit on somebody or for the purpose of Qisas evidence of two men is essential. However, in a case of fornication, four men witnesses are needed without which the allegation of illicit sex shall not be established and the prescribed limit cannot be enforced. The Quran has mentioned the number of witnesses in a case of fornication in the following verse :

> If any of your women are guilty of lewdness,
> take the evidence of four reliable witnesses
> from amongst you against them. [76]
>
> —Al Quran IV: 15

At another place it has been said :

> And those who launch a charge against chaste women and produce not four witnesses (to support their allegations), - flog them with eighty stripes. [77] —Al Quran XXIV : 4

In these verses (four men from amongst you, and four male witnesses) are the words showing that for the establishment of the charge of fornication evidence of four men is essential.

That means that in matters relating to the divine limits and Qisas only men are considered reliable as witnesses. Evidence of woman shall not be accepted. The well known tabi'i, Imam Zahiri says that during the period of the Prophet S.W.W. and Abu Bakr and 'Umar R.A.A. this was the principle in practice. He says :

> From the time of the Prophet S.W.W. and then first two caliphs immediately following him (Shaikhain-Abu Bakr and 'Umar R.A.A.) the Sunnah or the principle in practice has been that in matters relating to the divine limits and Qisas the evidence of women has not been acceptable.

Islam has provided divine limits and Qisas for the protection of life, property and honour and dignity of man. For deliberate murder of some body the murderer has to pay with his own life in Qisas. Unmarried person implicating himself in fornication has to be flogged. The married person is to be stoned to death for illicit sex.

Theft if definitely established deprives the thief of his hand, it has to be smitten. And similarly there are punishments for slander and drinking. The crimes for which Islam has prescribed limits or ordained Qisas. are so serious in nature that even if man survives their perpetration, his honour and prestige in society are shamefully dragged into mire. For these crimes nonacceptance of the evidence of women is apparently because of their peculiar nature and importance. Woman is basically the organizer and manager of her home. She has an intellect and temperament of her own and is brought up and educated and trained in a particular (purely domestic) atmosphere. She seldom comes in contact with those conditions and causes responsible for these heinous crimes. Therefore, about them her knowledge and observations cannot be so perfect as that of man who is mostly in the world outside. Again, for a woman, due to her mild temper and greater sensitivity, it is not easy to keep in mind all the major and minor details of the individual and collective crimes of murder, theft, robbery and those related to sex (including rape), and put them up before the court exactly (without any omissions or additions). Her statement relating to these matters cannot satisfy the court as does that of man, firm and strong. The aspect of uncertainties and wavering shall dominate in her statement. Islam insists that the limits should not be enforced without firmly establishing the crime and no effort should be spared in saving the accused from the punishment. The Prophet S.A.W. is reported to have said :

Keep away enforcement of limits from the believers as far as possible.

In another tradition it has been said :

In the presence of doubts try to avoid enforcement of limits.

There may be some women whose observation can be regarded reliable even in the most formidable forms of murder, theft, robbery and criminal assault on women, and they may be capable of presenting their observations accurately before the court. But the sex as a whole is not suited to this job (weak nerves, sentimentality, careless observation and taking of mental notes). Apparently pronouncing judgement on any particular sex, a few exceptional individuals cannot make the rule. A considerable majority or bulk of a kind (woman kind) has to recommend itself as capable and competent.

Evidence in Rights and Dealings

Barring limits and Qisas in matters concerning rights and dealings, woman's evidence shall be accepted. One reason for that is the exclusive importance of the limits and Qisas, not attached to other matters. Secondly, they are related to every day life. Not withstanding her limited sphere of activity, her home, she comes in contact with these day to day common happenings around her. However, in face of her peculiar circumstances and also due to her frailties, two precautions had to be taken. Firstly, no case should be decided on the evidence of woman alone, but with the evidence of two men or one man and two women. The reason put forth by the Quran for replacement one man by two women is this that it is possible for a woman to forget the details of some incident and in that case the other may remind her companion.

Allah says:

> And get two witnesses out of your own men. And if there are not two men, then a man and two women such as ye choose, for witnesses, so that if one of them errs, the other can remind her. [78]
>
> —Al Quran 11 : 282

The verse may give an erroneous idea that women witnesses are to be accepted only in case men are not available. But this is far from the fact. It simply means that for evidence either, there should be two men or one man and two women. Where woman is acceptable as a witness, even in the presence of men, one man and two women can be called for evidence. It has also been inferred as an argument that the women shall not be separated, making statements in isolation. They will appear before the court together so that if one forgets any fact or some important detail, the other may remind her.

The verse under reference occurs in connection with the rules and regulations and ordainments of debts so the majority of the Imams of jurisprudence have consensus on it that in matters relating to debts and in other dealings the evidence of women shall be accepted.

According to the Hanafite school of Fiqh, the evidence of one man and two women shall not be accepted only in matters relating to Hudood and Qisas. With this exception all other matters like, trade, debt, financial dealings, temporary loan of articles, monopoly, security, nikah, attorneyship, divorce, legacy, inheritance and other matters relating to rights and dealings, their evidence shall be accepted.

The argument brought forward in its support is this that there are three essentials for evidence. Firstly, accurate observation of the incident. Secondly, the observation should be clearly and carefully kept in mind. And thirdly and finally to state these observations just as they are, neither less nor more. The infirmity of woman as stated by the Quran is that she can forget the details and therefore, the corrective provided is two women together instead of one. So barring limits prescribed by Allah and Qisas or retaliatory punishments, in all other matters concerning human activities, woman's evidence shall be accepted.

At this juncture a question can be raised that taking the evidence of two women equivalent to that of one man, in matters that can be decided on the evidence of two men, that of four women should also be decisive. The jurists have answered it on the ground that though our intellect accepts it as reasonable, but if it is permitted, the movement of women outside their homes would be much enhanced, whereas it is the considered plan of Shari'ah that their movement outside their houses should not be too fréquent and free. (Perfect freedom of such frequent and unrestricted movements gives rise to evils and corruptions too dangerous to be allowed in Muslim society. They are before us in such a formidable form).

Evidence for Themselves

The Jurists are unanimous on the issue that the evidence of women is sufficient in all matters relating to themselves, such as the evidence of the new born showing signs of life at birth, since in case of live-birth, there will be funeral prayer for him and all other matters relating to inheritance which ceases in case of a still birth, or evidence relating to a girl coming of age (majority in the juristic sense -commencement of the menstruation) or confirmation of a woman's virginity or otherwise, or evidence in connection with the genital defects and diseases peculiar to women. All these matters have a bearing on nikah and related matters.

In this connection Imam Zahri says:

> The Sunnah or the usual practice has been that the evidence of woman (alone) is permitted in matters with which none else (men) can be conversant (due to strict restrictions), namely the condition of the babe at the time of delivery, (living or still-birth, or the physical defects of the female genitalia or development of secondary sex characters at puberty).

'Abdullah ibn 'Umar, Sa'eed bin Musayyib and 'Urwah bin Zubair's R.A.A. sayings are available on this issue. It is reported about 'Ahi R.A.A. that he decided a case on the evidence of a mid-wife. 'umar R.A.A. is also reported to have accepted the evidence of a mid-wife about a live- birth.

The jurists are at variance about the number of women whose evidence is essential in matters relating exclusively to women. Generally four is the number accepted for such evidence to be effective and conclusive. Imam Malik and Ibn-e-Abi Laila say that decisions can be made on the evidence of two women only. Imam Thauri and the Hanafite school regard the isolated evidence of one woman sufficient for legal purposes.

The Hanafite school has offered two arguments in support of their opinion. Firstly that the number has not been touched upon in the report (quoted above), and hence one woman's evidence should suffice. The second argument is that the exclusive evidence of women is considered enough in matters related to women alone, and men's evidence was not deemed necessary for the simple reason that men's observations or examination of the private parts of a woman is more undesirable than the same undertaken by women. (Difference of the degree of undesirability only). It can be asserted on this basis that observation and examination by more than one woman involves greater degree of undesirability. But in spite of that the precaution demands that there should be more than one-two or three -women for furnishing evidence.

Equal for Equal

Qisas or the law of equality (equal for equal) pertains to life as well as injuries and wounds. Qisas for life is that any one murdering an innocent person the murderer shall forfeit his life and be killed in return for that murder. That for wounds and other injuries is that if somebody inflicts a wound on some one or injures some organ of his body, the injured or wounded person shall be avenged accordingly. This law of Qisas is meant for providing protection to the life and limb of man. The question arises whether the law is applicable to man and woman alike or there is some discrimination where woman is the offender. The question has raged in our Fiqh since long. And lately with the voices raised in support of the rights of woman, it has once again surfaced to engage our attention. Here we shall try to present only the needful details of the problem, the most acceptable and preferred by the generality of the jurists, being brought forward.

The Quran has ordained Qisas in the following words :

> Oyé who believe! The Law of equality is prescribed
>
> to you in cases of murder: [70]—Al Quran 11 : 178

And the underlying wisdom has been stated thus:

> In the Law of Equality there is (saving of) life to ye men of Understanding. [71] —Al Quran 11 : 179.

With reference to the Torah it has been said :

> We ordained therein for them "Life for life." [72] —Al Quran V : 45

Under this law if a man murders a woman the man shall pay for it with his life. And if a woman murders a man, a woman shall be put to death for her crime. The Hadith supports it. It has been expressly said in a report from the Prophet S.A.W. :

> If a man were to murder a woman, he shall be killed for his crime.

This is further supported by other reports. A report of Sihah-Sitta (the six most reliably correct Hadith collections — Bukhari, Muslim, Abu Da'ood, Tirmizi, Ibn Majah and Nisai), says that a Jew, to snatch her jewellery, crushed the head of an Ansari girl and threw her dead body into a hole in the ground. In her last moments she was brought to the Prophet S.A.W. When the probable murderers were named she denied by just shaking her head. But when that particular Jew was named within her hearing she confirmed it by a nod (of assent). When the accused Jew was questioned about it, after some resistance he broke down and confessed his guilt. And so he too was stoned to death in Qisas (equal for equal). Imam Navavi says : So many issues arise from this report :

One of them is that man shall be put to death in return for the murder of woman. There is consensus on this issue of all those that count.

In a lengthy report quoted by Abu Da'ood, it has been said:

> The blood money of murder by a woman shall fall due to her 'usbah. But in case she is murdered her blood money will have to be distributed among them all without any distinction of As'habul-Faruz and 'Usbah. And if they decide on Qisas they would be permitted to take the life of the murderer of their related lady.

Here in the text of the report "they can take the life of their murderer" means the murderer of their kins woman. Nisa'i and Ibn Majah have reported it with the words "her murderer". That makes it amply manifest that a man shall be put to death in return for the murder of a woman. In calling the woman's murderer that of her relatives indicates that the legal position that he is not only the murderer of the woman but that of all her inheritors. They would be in their rights legally to have him put to death for his crime or accept blood money in lieu of it or even consent to forgive him.

The great stalwart among the Tabi'een, Sa'eed bin Musayyib says:

> Man shall be put to death for the woman, if he is found guilty of her murder.

Imam Bukhari says:

> The learned men have said that the man shall be put to death for the murder of a woman.

And this is the opinion of the four most outstanding Imams of jurisprudence from the point of view of their following, Imam Abu Haneefah, Imam Malik, Imam Shafi'i, Imam Ahmad R.A. and other great erudites of the Muslim Ummah.

Allamah Ibn Abdul Bar says that there is consensus on it that man shall pay for his crime against a woman, worth his life and the woman shall likewise be put to death if she has taken his life. Among the companions 'Ali R.A.A. and among the tabi'een Hasan Basri R.A. are said to be of the opinion that if man murders a woman and her inheritors want him to be put to death they can do so after payment of half the blood money since a woman's blood money is half that of man. If they do not pay half the blood money, they will get the blood money of the woman. But this does not stand confirmed from 'Ali R.A.A. As a matter of fact this is the opinion of 'Uthman-al-Labatti, a jurist of Basrah. We are also told that Hasan Basri and 'Ata R.A. are also of the opinion held by the majority.

That the blood money of woman is half that of man is no strong argument and hence man will be liable to Qisas or forfeiting his life, when half the blood money has been paid to him since the punishment for Qazaf or slander is the same for both. The woman calumminating a man with involvement in fornication shall be liable to the same punishment as for the man slandering a woman. Man shall not be the recipient of any amount as return before being put to death. No discrimination is made between the murderer and the murdered on the basis of their positions. That is why an entire body of men joining hands in the murder of an individual, shall all be put to death for their participation in the crime.

Imam Shaukani says' that the purpose and underlying wisdom of Qisas also supports the opinion of the majority of the jurists. The wisdom behind Qisas is to prevent shedding of blood of man and oppression and excesses may not torment him. If the man is not put to death as Qisas for a woman, for several reasons is to deprive her of her share in inheritance. The person who does not want to give her anything from inheritance may very likely murder her and thus getting her out of the way. The other reason may be the sense of shame and degradation of the days of Jahiliyah which may prompt him to murder a daughter, particularly incase of a minor slip on her part may be made the excuse for it. Female offspring was buried alive during the period of Jahiliyah for this reason alone is a shame and disgrace. The third very strong reason is her frailty. The intending murderer does not expect the same resistance from her as from man. Therefore, any leave or relaxation in Qisas will enhance oppression and tyranny and taking her life shall become an easy job.

Life for a Woman

These details reveal that there is consensus of the ummah or at least the four well known imams of Fiqh and the majority of the jurists are unanimous on the issue that a woman shall be put to death for taking the life of a man and vice versa. Now the question that remains is whether the punishment shall be enforced even if the murderer and the murdered are both women. The answer to this query is clear enough. When a man can be put to death for the murder of a woman why a woman cannot be put to death for the murder of a woman. The Quran is explicit about it:

And woman shall be put to death for woman.
[73] —Al Quran 11 : 178

So there is no contention on this point among the jurist that a female murderer can be put to death for taking the life of another woman. The statement of the Quran is general and the Hanafite Fiqh has also reasoned on its basis that a free woman murdering a slave girl shall also pay for it with her life.

Punishment for Injuries

Let us now take up the punishment for the physical injuries to a woman. It also takes the same forms discussed earlier under loss of life: A woman shall pay for her crime against man. Man shall be put to death for the murder of a woman. A woman shall be liable to punishment for any crime against a woman.

The following Quranic verse has ordained Qisas :

> We ordained therein for them 'Life for Life, eye for eye, nose for nose, ear for ear, tooth for tooth, and wounds equal for equal.' But if any one remits the retaliation by way of charity; it is an act of atonement for himself., And if any fail to judge by what Allah hath revealed, they are wrong-doers. [74]—Al Quran : 45

The question arises whether in case of men and women injuring one other, like man taking the life of woman or vice versa are put to death, the injuries, wounds and other types of damage shall be avenged or there is some difference between the two (life and injuries).

'Abdullah Ibn Abbas R.A.A. says that the Arabs did not inflict capital punishment on woman in Qisas for murder committed by her. They punished woman for a crime against woman and a man for murder of an individual of his own sex. In the verse above it was pointed out that Muslim man and woman if they are free (not bonded) are peers or equal in status. One taking the life of another intentionally or causing a damage of a lesser degree (than murder), shall have to pay for it on the basis of equality.

Imam Navavi says that the majority among the companions, tabi'een and latter day 'ulama reasoned from the verse that the ordainment of Qisas shall be enforced among the men and women also and murderers of each other shall pay with their lives. And physical injuries shall be avenged accordingly in a just measure. For example, a man fracturing the hand of a woman or vice versa, the hand of the culprit shall be fractured likewise. But in case of an injury in which avenging on the basis of equality is not possible, compensation will have to be allowed for it. Anas R.A.A. reports that his paternal aunt, Rubayyi broke a tooth of an Ansari girl. Her people wanted her to be forgiven or compensation demanded of her. But the family of the Ansari girl appeared bent on being avenged. When the case was brought before the Prophet S.A.W., he ordered Qisas (tooth for tooth). The uncle of Anas, brother of Rubayyi' said, "O Messenger of Allah ! By Allah Rubayyi's tooth shall not be broken." Now he had outspokenly opposed the decision of the Prophet but due to his faith in Allah's mercy and confidence in himself that he would ultimately prevail upon the parents of the complainant to remit retaliation or accept *diyat* (compensation). The Messenger of Allah S.A.W. said to Anas that the Book of Allah ordains equal for equal which cannot go unavenged. A little later the party insisting on Qisas consented to accept diyat instead. Seeing this change in their attitude the Apostle of Allah remarked that there were slaves of Allah who, if they take an oath with trust in Allah, He proves them true.

This is a report carried by Bukhari and others which goes to prove that a woman injuring another must pay in the form of Qisas. The report by Muslim tells us that sister of Rubayyi', Umme-Harithah wounded a certain person. When the case was brought to the notice of the Prophet S.A.W., he said, "She will have to pay for the injuries." At this Rubayyi's mother intervened saying, "Shall umm-e-Harithah be subjected to retaliation ? By Allah ! It will never come to pass." The Prophet said to her, "Allah be glorified ! What manner of talk is that ! The Book of Allah has ordained Qisas." But the people of the wounded person later accepted diyat. The Apostle of Allah at this change in the situation remarked that there were slaves of Allah who, when they swear in the name of Allah, are not disappointed.

Imam Navavi says the report reveals several things. One of them that is proved by it is that there will certainly be Qisas or retaliatory punishment between man and woman if occasion arises for it.

Now we are presenting here some sayings of the companions R.A.A. and Tabi'een R.A., which go to prove that woman has to pay for her crime against man and vice versa.

Imam Bukhari says that 'Umar R.A.A. is reported to have said:

> If a woman murders a man intentionally or in lesser degree causes some hurt to him, she will be called to pay it with her life or retaliatory punishment equal for equal.

When woman will have to suffer for her crime, man is all the more liable to such retaliatory action. And we find 'Umar R.A.A. saying on another occasion :

> The wounds of man and woman hurt equally.

'Umar bin Abdul Aziz R.A. says :

> The ordainment of Qisas shall be enforced between woman and men, even in the matter of life.

Abu Zanad says about seven well-known jurists of the period of Tabi'een and such other 'Ulama and jurists :

Women will have to pay for the crimes against man, eye for eye, ear for ear and various types of wounds equal for equal. (In a similar manner man will have to pay for his crimes against woman) and if man murders her he will be put to death.

Imam Malik reasoning from the verse quoted above (Q.V : 45) says:

> The ordainment of Qisas as it is applicable to cases between men and men, so also it is binding on men and women in their crimes (of one against the other sex).

Allamah Ibn Qudamah Hanbali says that the persons (men and women) between whom Qisas is applicable to the matter of life, retaliatory punishments for lesser damage, physical injuries, will also be enforced. And this is also the opinion of Imam Malik, Imam Thauri, Imam Shafi'i, Is'haq bin Rahuwaih, Abu Thaur and Imam Ahmad. Under this principle since for the life of man, woman is put to death and for the life of woman, man is put to death, so if they cause injury to each other, they will pay for it on the principle of equal for equal.

According to Hanafite school of jurisprudence, retaliatory capital punishment for the lives of men and women is permitted in case of wilful murder of one by the other, but it ceases where lesser damage, injuries and hurts of various kinds come in between them. For example man murdering a woman or vice versa shall be put to death for their crimes. But if a man smites the the hand of a woman or the other way round, none of them in Hanafite jurisprudence shall be punished with like for like, but will have to pay diyat for it. Murder shall be the cause of loss of life to the man as well as to the woman, loss of life being common between them, and so retaliatory action or Qisas is justified. But the matter of body organs is different. They are in the nature of property. Property is also meant for the protection of life. And body organs are also meant for this purpose (protection of life). Qisas relating to them can be permitted only when their value is the same. The Shari'ah has evaluated woman's organs a little lower than those of man. (We shall take it up later). When there is a difference in their value, there shall be no Qisas or retaliatory action for one against the other.

The ordainment of Qisas in Surah Ma'idah (Q. V : 45) is not absolute. It is accepted on all hands that there is no Qisas for a Harbi and Muslim (a citizen of a country at war with the Islamic state is Harbi and one temporarily offered refuge is Mustamin). When they have been exempted from the coverage of the verse, the women can also be granted immunity on the authority of this Hadith.

If it is asserted that the hands of men differ in length and so they differ also in applying energy and power of grip, but there is no consideration in the application of the ordainment of Qisas. Measured by this yardstick no distinction should be made between man and woman on the difference of size of their hands, etc. The argument offered against this reasoning is that since difference between the diyat of man and woman has been recognized, it will have to be taken into account. But the difference between the hands of one man and another cannot be given any consideration since there is no rule for it. So for all practical purposes they will be regarded equal.

One of the objections raised is this also that if equality of diyat between man and woman is not made the basis of comparison in the matter of Qisas of limbs and organs, it would not be wrong to punish woman as a retaliatory measure for crime committed against man, since diyat of man's organs is greater than those of woman. Why Qisas for something more valuable cannot be imposed on a comparatively cheaper object ? For example, if a woman smites the hand of a man, it would be right to have her hand cut off since diyat of man's hand is not only on a par with woman's hand but greater, although Hanafite Fiqh does not regard it justifiable.

The well-known opinion and usage of the Hanafite Fiqh is also this. However, there is also in this school an opinion permitting it. According to it, if the woman were to smite the hand of man, her hand too can be cut off as a measure of equal for equal. If this opinion is accepted the objection vanishes.

Concerning the wounds of head and face, there is an opinion in Hanafite Fiqh that Qisas between man and woman cannot be allowed in such cases since equality must exist for Qisas in value and utility, and it does not factually exist between man and woman. But there is a different opinion also in this regard which permits Qisas between man and woman since there is some difference between the Qisas of limbs and organs compared with that for wounds. Cutting off limbs and organs ends their utility and the defect abides. But wounds inflicted on the face, though causing deformity and defect, do not affect utility. And on this point man and woman are at the same footing.

The wounds of the face are not alone in causing disfigurement. The loss of limbs and other organs also causes deformity and defects. When on the basis of disfigurement due to facial wounds Qisas is justified, the damage to limbs and other organs too deserves the same consideration and treatment. Apart from the point of utility if consideration is given to the aspect of defect the opinion of Hanafite Fiqh necessitates further thought and discussion. In this matter the opinions of other Imams of the well-known and recognized schools of Fiqh and that of the majority of jurists appears to be stronger — that in the Qisas for organs and limbs, there is no distinction between man and woman.

Monetary Compensation

The Monetary compensation for wilful murder of lesser harm in the form of physical damage imposed by the Shari'ah is known as 'Diyat' (Blood Money). One of the objections raised against the Law of Diyat in Islam is also this that here too as in other fields of activity, it has failed to maintain equality between the sexes. The objection, however, does not hold water.

This is a juristical discussion and individuals and schools of thought differ in their opinions. Below we are going to furnish some details and an analysis of the issue under attack.

According to the Hanafite Fiqh, diyat of woman is half that of man whether it be for loss of life or damage to limbs and organs.

This is also the opinion of Imam Shafi'i, Sufyan Thauri, Imam Laith and Abu Thaur. The argument brought forward in support of it is that according to Mu'az bin Jabal R.A.A. the Prophet S.A.W. said :

> The diyat of woman is half that of man.

This report is not based on strong authority.

However 'Ali R.A.A. says:

> The Diyat for the injuries of woman is half of those of man, whether they (her injuries) are extensive or limited.

Ibrahim Nakha'j reports from 'Umar and 'Ali R.A.A. both

> The diyat of woman is half that of man whether it pertains to loss of life or a physical damage of lesser degree.
>
> And this opinion is also said to be that of 'Abdullah Ibn 'Umar and Abdullah Ibn Abbas R.A.A. Hafiz Ibn Hajar, however, informs us that he failed to find this opinion of these two companions.

The question arises why woman's diyat should be half that of man ? The answer offered is that since man is the bread-winner of the family and bears the financial burden, his death causes greater loss to his family than that in the event of woman's death. Therefore, his diyat has been fixed twice that of the woman. Allamah Rasheed Raza Misri says:

> The basic consideration in this matter is that due to man's death the family is deprived of greater benefits than their deprivation through the death of woman. So on the grounds governing man's share in the inheritance his diyat has also been kept double that of woman.

Another thing that has been brought in support of it is that according to the Islamic Law it is the man who has been declared fit for holding positions of authority like Imamat (leadership) of prayer and Hajj as also heading the Islamic state and positions for the collective responsibilities like military services and guarding the frontiers. In purely mundane affairs also, the industries and professions essential for the survival of man, he has a much larger share. So man's loss of life extends further, causing damage to the society in addition to his own family, in a much bigger way than that caused by woman's loss of life. Naturally his diyat has been fixed double that of the woman.

Undoubtedly these arguments carry weight. But the ordainments of the Shari'ah do not stand on reasoning alone. Strong and convincing arguments of the Quran and the Sunnah are needed to confirm an issue. The reports from the Prophet S.A.W. and sayings of the companions that have been presented in support of this issue, as stated earlier, are not strong enough.

According to Imam Malik and Imam Ahmad and others, there is no difference between man's and woman's diyat upto one third. However, after one third, woman's diyat becomes half of that of man. It finds support in the report by 'Abdullah Ibn 'Umro bin-al-'As. He reports the Prophet S.A.W. to have said :

> Woman's diyat is equal to that of man until it (her diyat) becomes one third.

This report is not strong in the matter of authority.

In support of this *maslak* (way or code of conduct) the following words of Zaid bin Thabit R.A.A. are put forth. He says :

> The diyat of man and woman is the same up to a certain limit. After crossing that limit it will become half that of man.

A more or less similar report has come down to us from 'Umar R.A.A.

Sa'eed bin Musayyib R.A. says that up to the limit of one third, the diyat of man and woman will be equal whether it pertains to a finger, a tooth, a wound on the body, or a head injury; beyond that the woman's diyat becomes half that of man.

Imam Malik R.A. says that Imam Zahiri R.A. and 'Urwah bin Zubair R.A.A. also hold the same view as that of Sa'eed bin Musayyib R.A.

It is said that this is also the opinion of the majority of the jurists of Madinah, the outstanding jurists among the Tabi'een, the seven well-known jurists, 'Umar bin Abdul Aziz R.A., Imam Laith and Qatadah.

Qazi Ibn Rushd is a Malekite. He opines on these arguments : The first of these groups-Malik and others have reposed their confidence in merely some Mursal reports.

This much about their supporting authority. Now, let us take them up at the intellectual level. A very pertinent question arises: what is the wisdom (reason) behind the statement that up to a certain limit man and woman are made to stand at the same level but after one third (limit) the woman's diyat becomes half that of man ? The answer given to this question is that if one third also is halved it becomes very small and cannot compensate the loss incurred by the woman. So upto one third it was kept on a par with man, but after crossing that limit reduced to half that of man.

If the reports quoted above are accepted as in order and reliable, this answer appears reasonable enough. But another question crops up and it is this that the injuries and wounds for which the woman receives one third diyat, for much more serious injuries it gets reduced to less than one third, whereas common sense demands that proportionate to the damage caused to her, she must be allowed enhanced compensation. So we find that according to the report of Mu'atta, the following discussion on this issue took place between Rabi'ah bin 'Abdur Rahman R.A. and Sa'eed bin Musayyib R.A.:

Rabi'ah : "Sir, tell me about the diyat of one finger of a woman."

Sa'eed bin Musayyib: "Ten camels."

Rabi'ah : "And that of two fingers?"

Sa'eed bin Musayyib : "Twenty camels."

Rabi'ah : "And what about three?"

Sa'eed bin Musayyib : "Thirty camels."

Rabi'ah : "What do you say about four fingers?"

Sa'eed bin Musayyib : "Twenty camels only since the diyat of the life of man (with his entire body) is a hundred camels. The diyat of woman exceeding one third, became half according to him."

Rabi'ah : "When the woman suffers pain and trouble due to greater loss (damage) will diyat in that situation come down?"

Sa'eed bin Musayyib : "Are you an Iraqi that you are given to belief in reasoning in every thing, even where an injunction (Sunnah) comes in ? Guess work against definite ordainment!"

Rabi'ah : "No. I am a student and anxious to learn about the nature of the issue."

Sa'eed bin Musayyib : "My son ! This is the Sunnah."

Among the latter day jurists Imam Shaukani held this opinion that after a third amount of diyat, woman's share becomes half that of man. But he is conscious of the weight of the objection that in this way after a third, woman's diyat gets much reduced when common sense demands that it should be enhanced. According to him up to one third, the diyat of man and woman are equal. Only in the excess after one third, it will become half. For example, where man will be entitled to forty camels, woman's diyat shall be thirty five camels. He says that the report of 'Abdullah bin Umro bin-Al-As, that is put forth there, is no deterrent to construe it this way. As for that of Sa'eed bin Musayyib, it is a Mursal report and hence, unacceptable. And this is not all. He writes that it is necessary to construe the Hadith like this :

So that man may not find himself lost in a narrow gorge against all that justice and equity, reason and conjecture demand.

Other Contentions

There are differences of opinion and contentions based on reason. Those who hold the opinion that after the limit of a third, woman's diyat becomes half, have this contention among themselves whether one third is that, one third as such forms a part of it or not. One opinion is that before reaching one third, man and woman will have equal diyat. But as soon as it attains that value, one third, it shall become half. The other opinion is that it becomes one third. Ibn Qudamah a Hambalite, has preferred this opinion. He says that the words of the report "until it reaches one third" tell us that the equality of man and woman is limited to less than one third.

Some of these learned men do not believe in the equality of diyat of man and woman even up to one third. 'Abdullah Ibn Mas'ood R.A.A. says that in the diyat of tooth and '*muzihah*' (a wound exposing the under lying bone), man and woman will be equal, but after that woman's diyat shall become half that of man.

A tradition of the Prophet S.A.W. says that the diyat of a tooth is five camels. And this is also the diyat of 'muzihah', namely five camels. That means up to five camels, there shall be no difference in the diyat of man and woman. After that the diyat of woman shall become half that of man. This also is said to be the opinion of Qazi

Shuraih. There is one opinion to this effect that up to 15 camels the diyat of woman shall be equal to that of man and half after that.

As against this Hasan Basri R.A. says that upto half (fifty camels) man and woman shall be equal in the matter of diyat. After that, woman's diyat shall be half that of man.

More or less the same opinion we come upon among the learned men of the latter days. Allamah 'Abdur-Ra'uf Manavi, a Shafi'ite, says that upto one third the diyat of organs and limbs of woman is like that of man. But when it becomes half, the woman's diyat shall be half that of man.

Exactly the same thing has been said by Allamah Muhammad bin 'Abdul-Hadi Sindhi who subscribes to Hanafite jurisprudence.

In this way that majority of the jurists though unanimous on it that woman's diyat shall be only half that of man, differ widely in details. Every diyat of woman, big or small, shall be half that of man or half of that excess over one third of the total diyat when it becomes half? And there are other contentions too besides these. The reason is to be found in the fact that there is no definite instruction in the Quran to this effect. The traditions of the Prophet S.A.W. brought forward in this connection are not strong enough in authority on whose basis there could be some decisive derivation that could remove all doubts, and end contentions once for all. The sayings of the companions and their followers (*tabi'een*) are not also in harmony and are differing widely in details. And that naturally caused greater differences among the jurists. There is room for all these opinions and any one of them can be given preference also. And keeping all these contentions and discussions, further thought can also be given to them.

We also come upon yet another opinion, that of Asam and the exegetist, lbn-e-'Atiyah. He says that the diyat of man and woman is the same. He reasons for it from the Quranic verse :

And who ever kills a believer by mistake, it is

> ordained that he should free a believing slave
> and pay blood money to the deceased from it.
> [75] —Al Quran IV: 92

There is consensus of opinion that in this Quranic verse the murder of both man and woman is meant and so their diyat should also be the same.

Allamah Rasheed Raza Misri says that the Quran has mentioned diyat absolutely without any specification of man or woman. The word has been used in a general sense. It demands that to whatever quantum of diyat the heirs of the murdered person agree would be in order and acceptable, no matter whether it is too low or too high in the estimate of the opposite party. But the Sunnah has put a limit on it, keeping the diyat of a free Muslim who is not guilty of any crime to forfeit his blood, is a hundred camels, or their value in cash. And that of a woman is half that (fifty camels or their market price in the form, of cash). After that he goes on to say :

The Quranic verse makes it clear that there is no discrimination here between man and woman. Undoubtedly the well known jurists have not adopted the opinion that the diyat of man and woman is the same, and as such it is an isolated and rare opinion.

Part - Four

Family

Nine

Family as an Institution

In our society, the importance of the large-scale ideological and economic factors in the everyday life situation of the individual, and the way in which this ideology has opened up the possibility of divergent adaptations and a new household economy. Moreover, the burden that economic changes place on adult males (who still are the main providers in most families), as well as career married women, has increased. This has complicated and intensified the tradition of child-rearing, cooking, washing, cleaning the house, taking care of the family and social networks, as well as the time spent on purchasing goods and supervising children after school. The large-scale economic reforms, and the new household economy, have affected the life of family members in different ways. The form and the rituals of household activities in everyday life are central themes in the following section.

The economic crises of the Islamic state and the new ideological demands have incurred cumulative and overlapping perspectives. This has left a narrow range of options for young and ambitious couples, forcing them to seek opportunities outside the home country, as exemplified by Mahry's extended family. Marriage and higher education has traditionally served as a passage for social and economic independence, although it has often been the case that newly-weds stay in the house of the wife's or husband's father for a while, before establishing an independent household. For ten years Halimeh, a 44-year-old female school teacher, shared a residence with her sister-in-law before she and her husband could save enough money to buy one of the two-room flats offered to school employees.

Marriage has always been an economic security for the wife, and the husband is traditionally responsible for the economic security of the family. The reality of the current socio-economic situation for the average lower and middle-class category, is such that extra economic support is necessary, either from the wife-particularly in the case of young married couples-or from parents.

A young family's economic independence and higher social status, such as in the case of Mahry and her siblings, depends upon occupation and further education. Mahry and her family had less chance of obtaining higher education because of the increased number of applicants, and also because of new Islamic ideological criteria for the selection of religiously active candidates. A new mode of adaptation, and a new economic niche, has emerged for family members who are able to take on additional roles.

As a result of constant price increases on household goods, the consequences of these economic niches have affected males and females differently. Managing the household economy is difficult in lower and middle-class families, even when the breadwinner (often the man), has previous work experience, or higher education. Families are dependent on a single income from employment in the public sector, such as teacher or office work jobs.

Grown-up children, despite their higher education, are economically dependent on their parents, who returned home from abroad during the Iranian revolution in 1978. This dependency may be permanent for some, thus placing a burden on the parents. In post-revolutionary Iran, large numbers of urban middle and higher-class Iranians left home.

Distinctive Domestic Structures

Two distinctive, significant and completely new household structures emerged in post-revolutionary Iran. These were: (a) the extended household composed of parents and married children who shared a residence, and (b) the households consisting of elderly couples who remained in Iran, while their children left home and took permanent residence abroad. The former household composition is common among families where a majority of the members stayed in Iran, and only a few moved abroad. The latter household composition consisted of elderly couples who voluntarily lived alone at home, visiting their children only once in a while abroad. These are often better-off couples, contrasting dramatically with the lower and middle-class extended household, where parents accommodate a married daughter or son and their families.

To maintain the economy of daily life many young educated men started a business of their own, or with other male relatives. The inevitable solution for lower and middle-class families was to have two members of the family in employment. Alternatively the breadwinner of the family would take two jobs, one in the official sector and another in the private sector. In the case of Mahry, close and distant male relatives were employed as civil servants, teachers, low-ranking army officers, social health personnel, etc. Due to the high cost of living they worked in their spare time as independent taxi drivers, as salesmen buying and selling land, as dealers in foreign currencies or rationed goods, or as shop assistants. In comparison, women were either housewives or, as is the case among a few middle-aged women, they were employed as nursery teachers, computer assistants, students, social health workers or, like Mahry, they worked with sewing and embroidery.

Most of the young families in the community, either rented rooms that cost them half of their salary as state employees, or they shared a residence with their parents or a close relative in order to save money. Many were also dependent on others for economic support, directly or indirectly, in the form of cash, household subsistence, and goods. Such socio-economic insecurity, along with the poor educational opportunities for themselves and the problems facing their children, as well as the general political harassment, has led many of these middle-class families to join the flow of migrants of the 1980s.

Household work is not only a distinctive personalised domain, but is also a part of the larger economic and post- revolutionary ideological development, as well as being a focus of change. Domestic work in post-revolutionary Iran involved a series of new tasks and more intensive work schedules for women.

Adaptability of household members to changing conditions depended on the availability of facilities and resources. A married woman explained that due to the intensive work schedule and, for example, the lack of communal facilities, she had to do the laundry at night when water was more easily available, and the shopping before sunrise so as to be able to prepare the mid-day meal for the family. This example illustrates how the mode of work among women mainly concerned with 'domestic' tasks has intensified due to broader political and economic conditions. One could hardly escape the daily observation of lower and middle-class women (often mothers), accompanied by small children, waiting impatiently for several hours in queues, in order to purchase hygienic supplies of milk, foods, and other 'domestic' items, at a more reasonable price than in the open market. Commonly they were worried about the daily household routines; for example, one waiting in such a queue told how worried she was at being delayed in preparing the noon meal for her husband and children coming home from work and school.

Foreign goods, such as electrical appliances, were very expensive and considered as luxury items by lower middle-class families. Moreover, these items provided a new form of enterprise for well-off families. Being able to sell foreign goods in the home market greatly boosted the income of such well-off families. The extended household has to some extent solved the problem of married children who are not able to establish an independent household without economic support from their parents.

High prices of household equipment and house rent made it impossible for young families with average economic means to establish an economically independent household. However, such an intensive relation and extended household dependency has increased family conflicts dramatically, particularly in already controversial relationships such as between daughter-in-law and mother-in-law.

Career Options

Career options are limited for young members of lower-class families. Petty trading seems to be an acceptable strategy for boys. Wheeler-dealers, and street vendors, are two forms of economic activity adopted by recent school-leavers. Bazar-e azad activity has opened a series of channels through which household items rationed by the state flow into the black market. Such enterprises, and the extra income earned, are often considered insecure, illegal, not quite respectable and even immoral. Middlemen, such as wheeler-dealers, after spending long hours in queues, buying goods such as cigarettes and eggs from the co-operatives shops, and then selling them at black-market prices. This type of occupation may serve as a source of income for young and middle-aged male members of low-income families. For families with low incomes, daily petty trading is not a permanent enterprise.

Self-employment yields more income than a low-paid permanent job. Establishing a business requires both economic and social capital, without which it is difficult to obtain goods to sell, or to rent a shop. When renting a shop a deposit is paid. The price has increased with inflation from around 50 thousand tomans in 1979 to an average of one million tomans in 1990. This means that it is virtually impossible to establish a permanent business. It also means that large profits can be made from letting shops, houses, flats and rooms. Those who have parents with a large capital may set up a small business.

While the father is still alive, they will be allowed to enter the family business as part of their eventual inheritance. The street-corner traders sell items such as dollars, cigarettes, rationed foods, and stockings. Dast-forosh is an enterprise open to even those with little capital, and is often a second source of income for individuals such as a grown-up son, or a head of a household. Any form of self-employment to supplement the limited household income, is justified on the grounds that multiple sources of income are necessary. Since a single-income job in the public sector cannot meet all of the household's real expenditures, the idea of a second job has become widely accepted.

Resourceful entrepreneurs will be able to provide for family consumption, as well as accumulate considerable wealth. In contrast, permanent business activities are generally open only to better-off middle-class merchants and craftsmen, and other traditionally independent producers and distributors. These are often co-operative family businesses jointly owned by close male relatives, such as a father and his sons, brothers, cousins and in-laws. This contrasts with the petty trader who sets up his business independently. Recently, because of restrictions, male shopkeepers are forbidden to sell female lingerie, or to open female hair-dressing salons.

As a consequence, female shopkeepers and co-partnership with a female relative has increased. The open market makes non-rationed items available to the public, such as electrical appliances, clothing, and domestic goods, as well as scarce medicines. The scarcity and long queues have forced many people to purchase items in the black market.

The rise in prices of local commodities may be explained by: (a) the government extra export policy for earning foreign currencies; (b) the rise in the exchange rate for dollars; and (c) the two devaluations of the rial. Devaluation of Iranian currency has been of particular importance for the family household economy, since family incomes are in the form of rials. Subsequently they are the hardest hit by inflation, exchange rates, and the black market policy of the state.

Broad structural and economical changes, such as the rationing system for the distribution of goods, has encouraged the development of a new transactional pseudo-occupation niche. Some of these new enterprises are considered immoral, in terms of their transactional and insecure nature. Self-employment and free-enterprise activities are considered to offer greater opportunities for meeting the daily increases of expenditures. Government employees, who are particularly well educated, and with fixed low wages, have become very disappointed with the monthly income of their permanent jobs. It is not adequate to cover their household expenses, such as rent. The difference in the earnings of these well-qualified government employees, and those whose main source of income is selling dollars in the black market, has marginalised the former category both socially and economically.

Wages for average civil servants and employees in official sectors, such as education, have remained relatively the same as they were before the revolution. According to a study by Behdad, in 1980 there had been an increase in the official minimum wage and a change in the rate of income tax to 12 per cent.

Most workers were affected by the new law stipulating minimum wages, the exception being urban workers in large firms. It must be keep in mind that family economic viability in post-revolutionary Iran is a problem for most government employees, hence the interest in free business and double waged jobs.

The most profitable enterprises involve trading in foreign currencies and goods, such as dollars, pounds, gold, household items and land, and money lending. Thus, the families that had invested capital in such commodities as land, houses, cars, gold, shops, etc., prior to the outbreak of the war between Iran and Iraq in 1980 are now in position. Expansion of the black market has an advantage as it further benefited those who have access to foreign currencies, imported goods, and are able to travel abroad frequently.

Land ownership has always been an important source of local identity and power in Iran. After the revolution, long-term investment in land has more than ever become an important form of capital, as well as a strategy for rapidly accumulating wealth. The dramatic rise in land prices since 1980 has applied even to the purchase of the isolated land outside the city limit, which is not even supplied with electricity and water.

Rapid Social Mobility

An example of rapid social mobility through land ownership is the case of an educated civil engineer. He qualified in England in the 1970s. He and his family returned to Iran shortly after the Iranian revolution in 1980. He started to work for his former employer, where he had previously been employed in a junior position. Due to his high foreign qualification he was soon offered jobs in different cities, including one in a province where he received high wages due to the difficult geographical conditions. Shortly after he returned home from England he bought a piece of land at a low price. The land was on the non-residential periphery of a town without electricity and water supplies. It cost him 60 tomans per square metre in 1980. However, inflation increased its value to 5,000/6,000 tomans per square metre in 1989.

In the long term ownership of land is highly beneficial, the rapid increase in value making it a secure investment. The demand for land has particularly increased as a result of demographic changes. These can be explained as follows: (a) rapid population growth; (b) the continuous migration from small towns and nearby villages to large towns. The rapid expansion of towns toward the city limits increased the value of cheap and isolated land from 20-60 tomans per square metre in 1979, to 6,000 tomans per square metre in 1989-90. Such land could not, however, be used for building a house until it had been included within the town's official boundaries.

The profit from land ownership was greater than from the ownership of fruit gardens, the latter providing only a small annual income for urban middle-class and business families. This was the common enterprise that led to the serious destruction of the famous orchard land in Shiraz. The grape and apple farms changed into building sites, thereby bringing a high profit to their owners. It would be interesting to evaluate the impact on agricultural production.

Land confiscated during the revolution has been sold cheap to religio-politically privileged community members, such as war veterans, employees of the Islamic institution for rehabilitation, and to families of martyrs or hostages. In recent years government supporters have been favoured for the redistribution of economic and social opportunities, such as obtaining employment, education, rationed goods and land. Special allocations have been given as the rewards for their support. Thus, economic advancement has been possible not only for those who have accumulated capital under the former regime, but also for those who have gained high status as first-class citizens in the Islamic regime, whatever their class background may have been.

Gifts of gold signify sets of kinship relations and are part of large chains of acts distinguishing close relatives, high-ranking guests and close friends. The value of gold is both an objective and a subjective cultural phenomenon, and concerns the relations between people on various levels. Gold has always been associated with prestige and high status and is often exchanged as valuable gifts among Iranians. There is a strong tendency for women to own some gold, receiving and giving in accordance with expectations. The saving and management roles women play within the family in this context is considered to be related to their orientation toward the future. Gold functions for women both as prestigious ornaments, and as a status symbol. Gifts of gold signify a 'proper' bride and provide capital for the family and her husband.

While purchasing land has remained the principal investment and economic transaction for men, gold has played a similar role for women. The constant rise in the value of gold, along with inflation, has meant that its importance not only as solid capital, but also as a status symbol, has grown.

The common strategy is to buy as many articles of gold as possible when the prices are low, and then sell or exchange these items when the prices have gone up. Accumulation of gold is considered a wise policy, both from the point of view of the individual and the family.

Gold is a significant gift requested by the bride. The amount to be received is often agreed upon at the time of engagement. Gold jewellery, or a number of gold coins, may be agreed upon as being a part of, or the entire *mahryeh*. The increasing tendency among middle-class brides to have mahryeh in gold coins than rials is because gold is more stable in price and more likely to rise in value than fall. The quantity of gold received as wedding presents depends on how wealthy the relatives are, and the number of guests. Such gifts may also be given on other significant occasions, such as at the birth of a child, during the first pregnancy, upon obtaining a higher degree, or on the Iranian New Year in March.

The young married women were considered inexperienced, and were constantly advised by their mothers and sisters about future relations with their husbands and their families. Planning a secure future, the mothers advise their daughters to buy gold instead of toys and decorative items, and to be concerned about the future. Such issues have become important lessons given by mothers to their married daughters. The importance of the gift of gold as capital is revealed at times of family crises. It is increasingly common for married women to give their savings to their desperate husbands to start a business or purchase property. Such a form of economic support brings extra recognition and respectability for the wife. The husband is often willing in return to register part, or whole, of the purchased property in her name.

On one occasion Farideh, a 30-year-old married housewife, proudly exclaimed how she sold all of her wedding jewellery and the children's gold to give tomans to her husband, so he could purchase a piece of land that was especially offered to him at his place of work. Her husband in return registered the land in her name. Another situation in which a woman's gold reserves may be vitally important to the whole family is exemplified by Mahtab, an elderly mother with a family of ten, who was forced to seek shelter in Shiraz during the Iraqi bombardment of Abadan in 1981. The only property they could bring with them was her gold (one kilogram). Soon she decided to sell it, despite the market rate being low, because she considered it important to provide the necessary clothing and accommodation for her daughters, and to protect the family. The only thing she had been reluctant to sell was a ring that had once belonged to her mother.

A third example is that of a 55-year-old woman, who sold all of her gold jewellery and borrowed money from her oldest daughter, in order to visit two of her children living in Norway. To her the value of the visit was worth more than her gold. She thought, what would be the use of saving when she might never again have the chance to see her children and grandchildren?

The distance, and the high cost of the journey, signified the importance of the visit and, and as she put it, 'it may be the only chance in my lifetime'. She had to insist on the importance of such a visit since her old husband thought that it was more important to take care of the house, and was thus reluctant to give her any financial support. Finally she alone provided the money for her journey to visit her children. She frequently talked about this as an event to gain respect.

A fourth example is that of a couple educated abroad, who had recently returned home and needed to pay for the transport of their household goods from Germany to Iran. The wife, Shahla, decided to sell her own gold, as well as her daughter's, to pay the required sum. She considered the household items to be of equal value to the gold since these were enormously expensive and scarce in Iran. Her mother, Mahtab, proudly returned to this case, telling others how her daughter managed her family life, thus presenting her daughter as a good wife to a good husband.

Honourable Identity

Contributions to the family economy in times of crises would allow the wife to emphasise her honourable identity and enable her to negotiate with her husband. The latter may, as noted, often agree to reward his supportive wife by registering some property in her name.

Some women insist on keeping some of the gifts of gold received through their own lineage by transferring it to their daughters or daughters-in-law, or to their mother's lineage (sister's daughter). Such a form of gold exchange signifies sets of kinship relations in which the wife competes with the husband's for support. Thus, women often adopt far-sighted perspectives on the value of gold, a view that their husbands may not necessarily share, but from which they often benefit.

Dowry consists of household goods that the bride will bring to her husband's house. Mahr is a sum of money or valuable items such as gold and land that the husband pledges to pay the bride upon marriage. This amount will be written as a legal document for the bride's security, and may become a legal debt upon the bride's request. These two forms of payment play important roles in the dynamics of the marital relation, giving a woman a high degree of security and also a deterrent for a divorce.

It is generally assumed that the larger the dowry (i.e. consisting of kitchen utensils, carpets, bedroom furniture, etc.), the greater is the respect shown to the daughter and, thus, the greater is the prestige gained in the eyes of the husband's female relatives. Due to the open market prices of dowry items people purchase presents through the newly established Islamic state marriage institution, which offers a few items for those newly wed. These might include items such as a stove, a machine-made carpet, and an oil heater. Two or three items were sold to each newly married couple in 1989.

The better the daughter's education, job and appearance, the less pressure is placed on the parents to provide an expensive dowry. This point of view was expressed by at least ten of the working women, aged between 30-45, including 4 teachers (1 nursery, 2 school, 1 university), 3 hairdressers, 1 social worker, 1 accountant, 1 office worker. Of these two had resigned, one of whom was Narges, a 40-year-old woman and former accountant, the other being a teacher who had several times taken leave to avoid the political stress associated with her working conditions.

Working women have often purchased household goods either through the co-operative institution where they worked, or when such goods were available at a special price. Six of them had been working before marriage. As part of their dowry they brought these goods to their husband's house without putting economic pressure on their parents. The average parent, with several marriageable children, may find themselves in serious economic difficulties, unable to provide a dowry for their daughters. However, some parents, in order to reduce these expectations, will give a little dowry to the daughter and in return agree for a simple wedding party and a smaller gift of gold.

In order to reduce the expenses of the groom, a one-day celebration for the two phases of the wedding is the most usual form of marriage. The first phase of the wedding party starts with the *aqad* ceremony, in which the Muslim marriage contract will be written. At that time the close relatives of the bride and the groom are invited, and a warm meal will be served at the expense of the bride's family. In the afternoon the second phase of the celebration, known as the wedding party, will be held. Then dinner will be served to a large number of guests, including distant relatives, friends and close neighbours. This part will be held at the expense of the groom. The wedding marks a recognition of the Muslim marriage contract. It is seldom the case that a bride moves to live with her husband before the second phase of the marriage celebration.

Devaluation of the rial brought a series of dramatic changes to families and the household economy. The reduced value of rials provided grounds for parents of brides to request higher *mahr*, to guarantee more security for women at the time of divorce. The average mahr requested by the bride's family increased from a few hundred thousands before the revolution, to 3 million for the average middle-class family in 1989, and to 10 million in 1994. Knowing the existence of such a threat causes the girl's family to request a higher amount of mahr.

In the past, the mahr was so low that initiating a divorce today has been easy for some husbands, being only a matter of paying an insignificant amount of cash to the wife. The predicament of a woman facing divorce due to low mahr, can be illustrated in the case of Narges. In 1970, when she married, her mahr was 100,000 tomans; (a high sum at that time). When she divorced in 1989 the average mahr was 3-5 million tomans; among the better educated and well-off families. Her husband thought it was an easy matter simply to give her the total amount of 100,000 tomans in cash, thus fulfilling the sole legal condition for a restricted third-degree divorce. For the husband this equalled the price of a pair of car tyres.

The high amount of mahr today makes it impossible for husbands to pay it to their wives in case of divorce. However, to women the sum is more a matter of status, providing them with more power and ability to negotiate with the husband in case of divorce. Family insecurity and the increasing number of divorces on one hand, and the continuous devaluation of rials on the other, induces parents to increase their demands of mahr, thus hoping to guarantee greater security for their daughters in marriage.

Their Status

The legal, moral and social status of woman is not affected in any way if she engages herself in the maintenance and upliftment of the home. Islam, on the one hand, safeguards all her rights by law and on the other, instructs society to render her a kind and fair treatment. Islam creates such an environment that whatever position woman assumes, she holds it with all her dignity and honour. As long as such an encouragement prevails, no change can ever occur in her honour and dignity. There are three prominent positions of woman at home — a daughter, a wife and a mother. Islam bestows great rank and position on her in all her three roles. No one can pull her back from this high position while she remains in the fold of Islam.

As a Mother

Islam assigns the highest rank, after Almighty Allah and His Prophet, to mother. Islam instructs man to give just and fair treatment to both father and mother and commands him for their obedience because both of them confer benevolence on him. But, in the Qur'an and Hadith, reference to the great benevolence of mother occurs more evidently and prominently. The Qur'an says:

> And We have enjoined on man (to be good) to
> his parents: in travail upon travail.

Did his mother bear him,
And in years twain
Was his weaning (hear the command)
'Show gratitude to Me and to your parents:
To Me is (your final) goal. (31:14)

At another place Allah Almighty says:

We have enjoined on man
Kindness to his parents:
In pain did his mother
Bear him, and in pain
Did she give him birth
The carrying of the (child)
To his weaning is
(a period of) thirty months. (46:15)

In all the works of child upbringing like feeding, nursing, education and training, the father participates with mother. But it is only the mother who bears all the pains and troubles of pregnancy and delivery individually. To bear the burden of pregnancy for nine long months, to give birth to a child after a great struggle of life and death and to feed her child out of her own blood and to lead a life of full care and strict precaution in all these stages is not at all an easy task. Father does not undertake all these hardships and does not bear all this pain. Therefore the benevolence and favours of mother on man are more than those of the father.

There are several Hadith which draw our attention towards rendering great service and obedience to mother and to behave politely with her. Some of its precepts are being discussed here.

Prophet Muhammad (peace be upon him) instructed man to give fair and just treatment to both father and mother. But the Prophet stressed the fair treatment more to mother. The Prophet said:

> 'I enjoin man about his mother, I enjoin man about his mother, I enjoin man about his mother, I enjoin man about his mother.

> Hazrat Aisha reported that she enquired: 'O Messenger of God, who has the greatest right on woman?' The Prophet Muhammad, upon whom be peace, replied, 'Her husband (has the greatest right on her)'. She then asked, 'Who has the greatest right on man?' The Prophet replied, 'His mother (has the greatest right on him).'

Some of the people are of the opinion that since mother is weaker than father, hence the Prophet (peace be upon him) instructed man to serve and obey the mother much more than the father. Probably it is also true. However, the fact is, mother confers more benevolence on man than father and therefore she deserves more attention and obedience.

In traditions, disobedience to parents is included in Kaba'ir, i.e. , great sins.

A separate instruction is also given forbidding disobedience to mother which is condemned as an unlawful act. Prophet Muhammad (peace be upon him) said:

Allah has forbidden you to be undutiful to your mothers, to withhold (what you should give) or demand (what you do not deserve), and to bury your daughters alive. Prophet Muhammad (peace be upon him) mentioned sins and said that when his Ummah perpetrates these sins, great difficulties and torment will fall upon them. One of such sins is:

> 'Man would accept the words of his wife and would disobey his mother; would adopt a pleasant behaviour with his friend and the behaviour with his father would be severe.'

In one of the Hadith, disobedience to parents is regarded as one of the signs of the approaching Dooms Day.

The just and fair treatment to mother is regarded as a means of atonement for one's sins and the attainment of Paradise.

Hazrat Aisha states that Hazrat Harsa bin Noman behaved with his mother in a most respectable, pleasant and polite manner. Once Prophet Muhammad (peace be upon him) said:

I saw heaven in my dream where I heard somebody reciting the Qur'an. I asked whose voice was that. I was told that it was the voice of Hazrat Harsa bin Noman. Then the Prophet said that it was the reward of fair treatment to mother.

Hazrat Abdullah bin Amr says that someone confessed to the Prophet that he had committed a great sin. Is there any way of repentance for it? The Prophet asked: Do you have your aunt (maternal)?' The man replied, 'Yes'. The Prophet said: 'Render her just and fair treatment.'

It evidently shows that it is not the service to mother alone but the service to her relatives too, can be one of the means of the expiation for sins.

Service to mother is superior to the service to father. It is next only to the mother that the position of any other person can be determined. Hazrat Abu Hurairah relates that a person questioned Prophet Muhammad (upon whom be peace): Who deserves my polite behaviour most? The Prophet replied: 'Your mother'. The man asked: Who (deserves) the next? The Prophet replied: 'Your mother'. The man enquired for the third time that who deserves the next? The Prophet made the same answer: 'Your mother'. When the man repeated the same question for the fourth time, Prophet Muhammad (peace be upon him) said, 'Your father.'

There is one more Hadith according to which a companion of the Prophet asked him who deserved the greatest right for his decent and just treatment. The Prophet replied: 'Your mother'. The man asked who stands next to her? The Prophet replied: 'Your mother'. The man asked the same question for the third time. The Prophet gave him the same answer again. When he put the same question for the fourth time, the Prophet replied: 'Your father', then whoever stands as much nearer to you in relations deserves as much decent treatment.

Qazi Ayaz states that some people say that both mother and father deserve just and fair treatment. But mother deserves more rights for service. Imam Nawawi says that this opinion is the correct one since most authentic Hadith support it. Haris Muhasbi says that consensus seems to be that in matters of service from children mother has more rights than father.

There are different Traditions on the question whether the polite behaviour with mother should be double or triple? Imam Tahawi says that in this connection those Traditions are more authentic in which it is said that a man should offer kind and mild treatment to mother three times more than what he should offer to his father.

Imam Ahmad says that father should be obeyed, but as far as the fair treatment is concerned, out of the four parts, three belong to mother.

Islam does not stress the legal rights of mother and father alone but also prescribes a kind and decent treatment to them. Islam holds that the legal rights of parents should be observed heartily and with love and devotion and should not be regarded as burden. It also unfolds the fact that apart from the legal rights, one should give as noble and humble treatment to parents as possible and in this treatment again, mother deserves more affectionate treatment. Mother should be offered better behaviour than what is offered to father.

As a Wife

In Islam woman possesses an independent entity of her own. Because of Nikah, neither her personality gets dissolved in the personality of her husband nor does she become his subject or servant. When she holds some new responsibilities after marriage, she becomes the owner of some new rights at the same time. As she cannot refuse these responsibilities, in the same manner her rights cannot be taken away from her.

Now let us see how Islam views the relationship between wife and husband and what legal and moral basis Islam provides for this relationship.

The relation of husband and wife is, in fact, the relation of love, affection and intimacy. The natural love and attraction which God has placed between husband and wife is described in the Holy Qur'an thus:

> And among His Signs
> Is this, that He created
> For you mates from among
> Yourselves, that ye may
> Dwell in tranquility with them
> And He has put love
> And mercy between your (hearts),
> Verily in that are Signs
> For those who reflect (30:21)

What is suggested is that there should be a relation of love, sympathy and affection between husband and wife. It is all their natural urge indeed. If hostility and animosity take the place of love and affection, it is against nature on which Allah Almighty has created them.

There is always a head of any minor or major institution. The structure of the family and the relationship among its members and its problems are more complicated and varied than all the other institutions and their problems. Order and discipline cannot be there in a family in the absence of its head. If there is no head of a family or no one is responsible for a family, it would definitely get disorganised. In Islam, man obtains the position of a head of the family for several reasons. This does not mean that man has acquired unlimited and whole and sole authority on his wife and that she is merely his subject. It actually means that while it is the responsibility of woman to accept her husband as a leader and obey and follow all his 'lawful demands', she also enjoys her rights. It is compulsory and obligatory for a man to perform these rights rather to pay all her dues. Hence the Qur'an says:

Men are the protectors
And maintainers of women, because God
Has given the one more (strength)
Than the other, and because
They support them
From their means
Therefore the righteous women
Are devoutly obedient and guard
In (the husband's) absence
What God would have them guard (4:34)

Again in another place, says the Qur'an:

And women shall have rights
Similar to the rights against them, according
To what is equitable;
But men have a degree
(of advantage) over them
And God is Exalted in Power, Wise.(2:228)

Woman, while accepting the superiority of man in domestic life, gains and enjoys all rights of maintenance allowance, residence, alimony, and education and training and several other rights. If man falls short of performing all these rights of woman, she can secure them through law.

Islam exhorts man not only to discharge the legal rights of his wife but to behave with her decently and justly. Nice treatment with wife is required in every condition. Sometimes man dislikes the face, temperament and habits of his wife, which affects their relationship. In such cases man is instructed to consider the better aspects of his wife because if he dislikes one aspect of hers, there can be then praiseworthy qualities in her. Therefore it is the demand not only of morality and nobility but also of wisdom and sagacity that man should keep farreaching interests before him and should not spoil the cordial relationship with his wife. Sometimes a certain thing appears unpleasant to man, but in it are hidden unaccountable aspects of goodness. In this connection, Islam lays down such a noble and ideal rule that cannot be found anywhere else. Allah Almighty says in the Qur'an.

> On the contrary live with them.
> On a footing of kindness and equity
> If ye take a dislike to them.
> It may be that ye dislike
> A thing, and God brings about
> Through it a great deal of good (4:19)

A lucid elucidation of such a polite behaviour with wife can be found in the sayings of Prophet Muhammad (peace be upon him).

Hazrat Muawiya Qushairi once enquired about the rights of wife of the Prophet (peace be upon him). In reply the Prophet said:

That you should give her food when you eat, clothe her when you clothe yourself, not strike her on the face, and not revile her or turn her out of the house (if separation becomes necessary) but live separately within the house itself (temporarily).

The same Tradition is expressed again in some other words:

> Feed her what you feed yourself with, her clothing should be of the same standard as yours, do not beat or abuse and rebuke her.

First, husband should follow the same standard of eating and drinking, clothing and dressing for his wife which he keeps for himself. It is unjustified if he keeps a high standard of life and compels his wife to subsist on a lower standard. Secondly, in association and relationship with her, his performance should be honourable. He should not treat her harshly or cruelly.

If any action of woman looks unpleasant or disagreeable, Prophet Muhammad (peace be upon him) advised man to endure and to have patience because this unpleasantness may prove temporary. Where some act of hers is unpleasant, some other acts may be pleasing to heart. To express lament and to show hatred and to be enraged at the slightest provocation will spoil mutual affectionate relationships for ever. Hazrat Abu Hurairah relates that Prophet Muhammad (peace be upon him) said:

> A believer must not hate a believing woman; if he dislikes one of her traits, he will be pleased with another.

Sometimes man demonstrates high morals and displays good conduct with others but his behaviour with his wife is reproachable even though his wife who is his life-partner is most deserving of polite and decent behaviour. Hence the man whose behaviour with his wife is just and fair is regarded as the best man. In a Tradition Hazrat Abu Hurairah relates that the Prophet said:

> The believers with perfect faith are those who have the best disposition and the best of you are those who are best to their wives.

In a Tradition, showing courtesy and love to wife and children is regarded as an attribute which completed faith (Iman). Hazrat Aisha related that Prophet Muhammad (peace be upon him) said:

> Among the believers, the man whose moral is best, has the perfect faith and who behave with his wife and children with more love and affection.

In another Tradition Hazrat Aisha relates that Prophet Muhammad, upon whom be peace, said:

> The best of you is he who is the best to his family, and I am the best among you to my family.

Islam regards the standard of relationship between husband and wife free from contention and strife as commendable. Wife should try to keep her husband delighted and contended, to obey him in rightful works and to safeguard his honour and dignity and wealth and property. On the other hand, husband should consider such a chaste and virtuous wife to be an excellent asset of life and should offer more decent and polite behaviour to her.

Hazrat Abu Hurairah says that Prophet Muhammad (peace be upon him) was asked about the attributes of a virtuous and righteous woman. The Prophet said:

> 'The one who pleases (her husband) when he looks at her, obeys him when he gives a command, and does not go against his wishes regarding her person, or property by doing anything of which he disapproves.'

Hazrat Abu Amama relates that Prophet Muhammad (peace be upon him) said:

> 'After fear of God, a believer gains nothing better for him than a good wife who obeys him if he gives her a command, pleases him if he looks at her, is true to him if he adjures her to do something, and is sincere towards him regarding her person and his property if he is absent.'

Hazrat Abdullah b. Umar b. Aas says that the Prophet said:

> 'The whole world is to be enjoyed, but the best thing in the world is a good wife.'

Hazrat Omar asked Prophet Muhammad (peace be upon him) that Allah Almighty forbids to store gold and silver, what type of wealth, then, we should keep with us? Prophet Muhammad (peace be upon him) said:

> 'Each one of you must possess with you, a thankful heart, a God-remembering tongue, a (Muslim) believing wife who assists him in the works for Akhirah (eternal life).'

It is quite evident from the above Traditions what type of

relationship Islam wants to promote between husband and wife. If such a type of relationship exists between them, both of them will be assistant and well-wisher of each other, their life will be pleasant and ideal and all the unpleasant problems of rights and demands which cause disturbance and destroy the domestic life would never occur in their life.

As a Daughter

Before the proclamation of the Prophethood of Prophet Muhammad (peace be upon him), parents were much proud of their sons and they were supposed to be their great asset, because they gave more strength to their tribe and they were assistant in their great exertion in the field of finance. But daughters were considered to be burden on them and they were supposed to be the cause of ignominy or disgrace and on their very mention their heads dropped in shame. The Qur'an portrays a very graphic picture of the feelings of a parent on the birth of his daughter at that time.

> When news is brought to one of them of the
> Birth of a female (child), his face
> Darkens, and he is filled
> With inward grief!
> With shame does he hide
>
> Himself from his people, because of the bad news
>
> He has had Shall he retain it
>
> On (sufferance and) contempt, or bury it
>
> In the dust. (16:58-59)

One of the results of these obnoxious feelings for daughter was that some tribes used to bury their daughters alive. The Qur'an vehemently criticised the murdering of children and regarded it a capital offence and put an end to this abhorrent practice once and for all. The Qur'an says that on the Last Day, one would have to answer for the hard-heartedness to God. The Qur'an says:

When the female (infant)
Buried alive, is
Questioned
For what crime
She was killed (81:8-9)

Islam inculcated totally different feelings for girls in place of their barbarous and brutal feelings.

The first and foremost that Islam says is that it is the will and wish of God that favoured some with children and to some He debarred and to some He gave only sons and to some He favoured with daughters alone and to some He blessed with both sons and daughters. None of this case is a cause of honour or disgrace or cause of dishonour or ignominy. All this is a natural phenomenon representing as it does the boundless knowledge and wisdom of God. Those who consider it a standard of dignity or ignominy are cavilling at His wisdom. The Qur'an says:

To God belongs the dominion of the heavens
And the earth. He creates what He wills
(And plans). He bestows (children) male or
Female according to His will (and plan)
Or He bestows both males
And females and He leaves
Barren whom He will
For He is full of knowledge and power.
(42:49-50)

There is exhortation in Islam for the proper nourishment and sustenance of daughters. It is regarded as a good deed and a means for the attainment of Heaven. Hazrat Aisha relates that Prophet Muhammad (peace be upon him) said:

'Whoever is in charge of (put to test by)

three daughters and treats them generously,

then they will act as a shield for him

from the (Hell) Fire.'

In Traditions, the upbringing and nourishment of two or three daughters or sisters or even one daughter or sister is referred to as a means for entering Heaven. From this the reward or requital to the person who brings up more than three daughters or sisters can be well realised. Hazrat Itba bin Aamir relates that Prophet Muhammad (peace be upon him) said:

> 'Whoever has three daughters, and bears with the miseries in their connection, feeds and clothes them with the earnings of his labour, they will become a curtain on the fire of hell, for him.'

Hazrat Abu Sayeed Khudri relates that Prophet Muhammad (peace be upon him) said:

> 'Whoever amongst you has three daughters,
>
> or three sisters, and he treats them gently,
>
> he will surely enter heaven.'

Hazrat Abu Sayeed relates one more Hadith that Prophet Muhammad, upon whom be peace, said:

> 'Whoever has three daughters or three sisters or two daughters or two sisters and he adopts a good company with them and fears Allah about them, He has (place for him in) Heaven.'

Hazrat Anas relates that Prophet Muhammad (peace be upon him) said:

> 'If anyone cares for two girls till they grow up, he and I will come on the day of resurrection thus', and he joined his fingers.'

Hazrat Abu Hurairah relates that Prophet Muhammad (peace be upon him) said:

> Whoever has three daughters and he bears

> with the difficulties and financial problems, in connection with them, Allah will make him enter Heaven, for courtesy towards them.' Abu Hurairah reports that a man enquired if he has two daughters (and bears with the difficulties in connection with them). The Prophet replied, 'Even if he has two daughters (Allah will bless him with Heaven)'. A man asked, if he has one? The Prophet said (He will) even if he has one.'

Hazrat Abdullah bin Abbas relates a similar Hadith that Prophet Muhammad (peace be upon him) said:

> 'If anyone takes care of three girls or the like number of sisters, training them and showing kindness to them till God enriches them, God will guarantee him paradise.'

Hearing such a great reward, a man humbly enquired Prophet Muhammad (peace be upon him) that if anyone renders the same service to two daughters or sisters in the same way does he get the same reward? The Prophet replied, 'Yes, he would get the same reward'. The one who relates the above Hadith says that if the man would have enquired for one daughter or sister, the Prophet would have given the same reply.

It shows that for providing nourishment and giving proper training to one daughter or sister a man deserves a seat in paradise. If he nourishes and brings up more than one daughter or sister, his rank may be raised accordingly.

It is stated in the Hadith that with the good nourishment of daughters, they should also be given good education and training and should also select a good match for the marriage and should continue fair and just treatment with them. Hazrat Abu Sayeed Khudri relates that Prophet Muhammad (peace be upon him) said:

> 'Whoever nourishes three daughters, educates and trains them, gets them married (and afterwards) offers a gentle behaviour to them, for him there is heaven.'

Generally more love and affection is showered on sons in feeding, clothing, education, training and in every respect more preference is accorded to them. This is total injustice and oppression. In Hadith such a treatment is forbidden and condemned.

Hazrat Abdullah bin Abbas relates that Prophet Muhammad (peace be upon him) said:

> 'Whoever has a girl, who has neither buried her alive nor gives a mean treatment to her and not even gives preference to his son over his daughter, God will make him enter Heaven.'

In all these Hadith on the proper nourishment, education training, arrangement of marriage and equal treatment to daughters or sisters, glad tidings is given for liberation from Hell and the attainment of Heaven. One who does not have faith in God and the eternal day and one who gives all importance to the present world alone does not realise the significance of these Traditions. But the very goal of the believer (Momin) is success on the Judgement Day. There is all what he wishes in this goodness for a believer.

With the inducement of the proper care for girls, this conception is also laid down that she is not worthless or valueless as the world considers her, but she is the most valuable boon of nature. The love and affection which she possesses in herself, a boy does not have it.

Hazrat Aqba bin Amir relates that Prophet Muhammad (peace be upon him) said:

> Do not hate girls. They are comforter and much precious.

Such a teaching for a fair and just treatment of girls is an example which is found nowhere. According to Islamic law, if the child does not own any position and does not have any proper means for living, his maintenance is obligatory on his father. In accordance with this rule, the maintenance or allowances for daughters is obligatory on his father till her marriage and in the absence of his father, it is necessary for her nearest relative to ensure her maintenance. After marriage, the responsibility of her maintenance shifts to her husband and on the death of her husband or in case of divorce and if the woman is not self-sufficient in financial matters, the responsibility goes to her children or in case she has no children, the responsibility for her maintenance falls on her nearest relative. This is a legal right and in the Tradition its importance is well emphasised.

Hazrat Suraqua bin Malik relates that Prophet Muhammad (peace be upon him) asked him:

> 'Shall I not show you what is the greatest charity. He said: Messenger of God, certainly show (it). The Prophet said, 'To be grateful to your daughters who (after becoming widow or being divorced) is sent back to you and there is no one save you, her earning man.'

The Companions of the Prophet were so thoughtful about their widows and daughters that it can be well understood from this example that Hazrat Zubair endowed some of his houses. In the details of this endowment the following statement was also included.

Whosoever of his daughters (being divorced or by becoming a widow) would come back to her house, she would stay in it.

Neither she would put it in loss nor would she be put in loss. If she is self-sufficient in respect of finance without depending on her husband, she would not have any right in it. In this way, in the family system of Islam, the legal right of woman are secured.

Ten

Dignity of the House

Islam has promulgated rules and regulations for all actions and deeds, so, it has also set some principles for entering the houses in order to maintain the sanctity of home-life. It is not permissible to enter a house without seeking permission of the head of the family.

In the places not used as residences such as schools, guesthouses, monasteries where there is no restriction to go or in the houses where no one resides, one may enter without seeking permission. If, however, restrictions are imposed on the entry of some persons, they should not go therein. It has been mentioned in the Holy Quran:

> It is no sin for you to enter uninhabited houses wherein is comfort for you. Allah knoweth what ye proclaim and what ye hide.(24:29)

Except the above, it is not permissible to enter the houses without prior permission. It has been said in the Holy Quran:

> O ye who believe! Enter not house other than your own without first announcing your presence and saluting (saying Assalamo Alaikum) to the folk thereof That is better for you that you may be heedful.
>
> (24:27)

If you want to go in the house of another person, you should first ask permission from the head of the house according to the Islamic principles. He may be the owner of the house or residing in it on rent or without rent and the inmates of house may be mahram or ghair mahram or males or females. He must ask permission under all circumstances from the head of the house or from the member of the family whom he has authorised to do so. If he refuses permission to enter, he should go back at once and should not insist or compel. If no one responds to his call he should call out thrice and if no one responds even at the third call, he should return. It is not permissible to enter a house about which it is not certain whether anyone is living there are not. It has been mentioned in the Holy Quran:

> If you find no one therein, still enter not until permission hath been given. And if it be said unto you: Go away again, then go away, for it is purer for you. Allah knoweth what ye do. (24:28)

Supposing there is none in the house, even then you have no right to enter a house which is not meant for general public use. Moreover, if the permission to enter is not granted, it is futile to insist and to enter forcibly in the house. It is a great sin and offence. It is also against moral and ethical principles. So the 'Ulama are of the view:

If the entry is refused one should neither insist for permission to enter nor ask that purdah should be observed. He should also not wait as all these acts are against good etiquettes. He should not knock at the door. The author of *Kashaf* has explained his view while commenting upon the above verse.

Many an Advantage

There are many advantages of seeking permission to enter a house. In the terminology of Hadith it is called Istidhan. It is an obligatory duty in Islam and one must act upon it. No one knows how much harmful it is to himself or to the family if anyone enters the house suddenly. It is just possible that someone may be naked, his glance may suddenly fall on him/her. It is, therefore, proper that no one should enter the house without seeking permission. If a number of married sons and daughters of the same father are residing in a house, it is necessary to seek permission before entering so that the inmates of the house may become alert and recompose themselves. The principle should be observed in entering the female apartment.

The Holy Prophet (peace and blessings of Allah be upon him) instructed his Companions to seek permission before entering a house. Many such events have been mentioned in the Ahadith where the Holy Prophet instructed his Companions to act upon this principle. Hadrat Abu Musa reported that the Holy Prophet (peace and blessings of Allah be upon him) observed:

> Asking of permission is for three times. If you are permitted, well and good, otherwise, you should return. (Riyad as-Salihin)

A person who belonged to Bani 'Amir once went to the Holy Prophet (peace and blessings of Allah be upon him) who was in the house. When he arrived at the door of the house, he said, May I come in? When the Holy Prophet (peace and blessings of Allah be upon him) heard his voice, he said to his servant: Go to the person who is outside and teach him the way to ask permission in accordance with the Shariah. Ask him to say: Assalamo Alaikum! May I come in? That person heard the instructions which the Holy Prophet (peace and blessings of Allah be upon him) was giving to his servant and said: Assalamo Alaikum! May I come in? Thereupon the Holy Prophet (peace and blessings of Allah be upon him) gave him permission and he came in.

Hadrat Kuldah bin Al Hanbul (Allah be pleased with him) said: I went to the Holy Prophet (peace and blessings of Allah be upon him) and entered without saying Assalamo Alaikum. Thereupon he said: Go back and say: Assalamo Alaikum! May I come in?

It is clear from the above Ahadith that the correct way to ask permission is that one should first say Assalamo Alaikum and then ask permission to enter. To seek permission without saying Assalamo Alaikum is not correct. It is also evident from the above Ahadith that one should ask permission thrice and if there is no response even at the third call one should not insist and return.

> In a Hadith the incident of Hadrat Abu Musa has been narrated. He went to Hadrat 'Umar and asked permission thrice. No response came and he came back. Hadrat 'Umar was busy in some work. When he was free he said: Call Hadrat Abu Musa in. When the person went out to call Abu Musa in, the latter had gone. He informed Hadrat 'Umar accordingly. When Hadrat Abu Musa again came to see him on some other occasion he enquired from him: Why did you return on that day. He said: I asked permission thrice and having no response I returned as I heard the Holy Prophet (peace and blessings of Allah be upon him) saying: Should anyone of you seek permission thrice and has no response he should return. (Ibn Kathir)

There is another incident relating to the Holy Prophet (peace and blessings of Allah be upon him). He went to Sa'id bin Ubada and asked permission thrice after saying Assalamo Alaikum. When he had no response he returned. Meanwhile, Hadrat Sa'id came to him running and took him to the house.

Permission Necessary

It is necessary for the visitor to ask permission first so that he could not see any one of the inmates of the house all of a sudden. It has been narrated that once the Holy Prophet (peace and blessings of Allah be upon him) was sitting in the house and scratching his head. Someone came and began to peep in. When the Holy Prophet (peace and blessings of Allah be upon him) knew it, he became very angry and said: Had I known it, I would have had his eyes torn out.

Is he not aware: The visitor, must therefore not stand in front of the door; he should remain at one side.

Hadrat 'Abdullah has reported that whenever the Holy Prophet (peace and blessings of Allah be upon him) went to anyone he stood at one side of the door and said: Assalamo Alaikum! In those days curtains were not hung at the doors of the houses. If it is hung, there is no harm in standing in front of the door; but etiquettes demand that one should not ask permission to enter standing just in front as thus there is every possibility of seeing the inmates of the house.

It has been mentioned in a Hadith that a person came at the door of the Holy Prophet (peace and blessings of Allah be upon him) and asked permission standing in front of the door. The Holy Prophet (peace and blessings of Allah be upon him) beckoned him to stand at one side of the door as the law of seeking permission has been made due to gazing in.

It is forbidden to peep in from fissures of the doors or that of the windows as the very purpose of seeking permission is thus violated. According to a Hadith in Sahihain the Holy Prophet (peace and blessings of Allah be upon him) said:

> If a person peeps in your house without permission, you throw a stone at him so that it hurts out his eye; there is no sin upon you.
>
> (Ibn Kathir)

If he seeks permission to enter after saying Assalamo Alaikum and the inmate of the house asks who is he, he should tell his familiar name. It should not be said: 'It is I', as the person cannot be recognized in this way. The Holy Prophet (peace and blessings of Allah be upon him) does not like that an ambiguous reply should be given.

Once Hadrat Jabir went to the Holy Prophet (peace and blessings of Allah be upon him). He (the Holy Prophet) asked: Who are you? He said: It is I. The Holy Prophet (peace and blessings of

Allah be upon him) disliked the reply and said: What do you mean by this I, I. The Companions of the Holy Prophet (peace and blessings of Allah be upon him) also taught their followers the way to seek permission and exhorted them to act upon it.

The permission to enter the house should also be asked from the *mahram* such as mother and sister, etc. It has been stated in the verse regarding 'Istidhan' that a woman from Ansar came to the Holy Prophet (peace and blessings of Allah be upon him) and said: I am in such a condition that I do not like any one, even my father to see me; but these persons come and go in this state. Thereupon the verse a particular was revealed. Various instances have been narrated in Ahadith from which it is evident that *mahrams* are also required to ask permission as no body knows about the condition in which the women would be sitting. In my opinion one should not enter without permission even if there is only wife in the house as she might be naked and no body likes to be seen in a state of nudeness.

A person asked the Holy Prophet (peace and blessings of Allah be upon him): Is it necessary to seek permission from mother? He said: Yes, permission needs to be sought from mother. He said: I live with her. In other words, she is not required to observe purdah from me .then why is it necessary to ask permission? The Holy Prophet (peace and blessings of Allah be upon him) said: Ask permission from her also. He said: Even if you go to your mother you ask permission. Would you like to see your mother naked? He said: No. He (the Holy Prophet) said: That is why I say that you should seek permission before seeing her.

Hadrat Zainab (Allah be pleased with her) says: Whenever Hadrat 'Abdullah bin Masud (Allah be pleased with him) came in for some need, he first stopped at the door and coughed and then came in. He did not like to come in suddenly. Zainab was the wife of Hadrat 'Abdullah bin Masud.

Hadrat Abu 'Ubaida says: When Hadrat 'Abdullah arrived he asked permission loudly at the door. Hadrat Imam Ahmad bin Hanbul says: When a person enters the house he should cough loudly or strike his shoe with force so that the inmate of the house may know that some one is coming.

The purpose of Assalamo Alaikum for three times is that the inmates of the house may know about the arrival of the visitor. They may become alert at the second and may grant or refuse permission at the third.

Ibn Al-'Arabi is of the view that it is an incumbent act to ask permission before entering the house of others. As regards one's own house, it is not an incumbent duty. If, however, mother and sisters are living there, he should cough and then enter. At the door he should strike his feet so that the women may become aware of his arrival. Sometimes even mother and sister are in a condition that it is not proper to see them.

According to Imam Malik, it is necessary to ask permission before seeing the mother or sister. It was again and again enquired from Hadrat Ibn Mas'ud and Ibn 'Abbas whether it is necessary for the persons to ask permission from the mother and sister residing with him. He said: No one likes to see his mother naked, then why do you insist on this question.

If you ponder over the Islamic rules and regulations you would come to the conclusion that they are not only rules of wisdom and freedom but excellently safeguard modesty.

We are constrained to say that these rules and regulations of entering the houses which have been explained by the Holy Quran and the Ahadith ~ and practically followed by the noble Companions of the Holy Prophet throughout their lives are being overlooked by the Muslims of today. These rules and regulations need to be revived and enforced in our home-life.

Most Effective Safeguard

It is an admitted fact that the Divine Law is the most effective safeguard against immorality and debauchery. After the commandments relating to grown up and adolescent boys in the

Holy Quran the Ahadith have also explained that the children too have the capability to think. So far as *ghair-mahrams* are concerned, it has already been explained that it is necessary to observe strict purdah from them. It is, however, allowed to expose the face and palms of hands in need; but if there is any fear of evil or mischief, these parts should also not be exposed. From mahrams purdah is for the whole body except face, palms of hands, arms, head and shanks, etc., which remain ordinarily exposed but it is not allowed to expose these parts unnecessarily. The servant is also a ghair-mahram and it is necessary to observe purdah from him. An infidel maid-servant also comes under the definition of a mahram.

What we want to tell you is that the young boys and maid servants who fall under the category of mahrams should also ask permission to enter at special times as during these times men and women do not generally exercise proper care and vigilance in observing purdah. Allah the Exalted has said:

> O ye who believe! let your slaves and those of you who have not come to puberty ask leave of you at three times (before they come into your presence): Before the prayer of dawn and when ye lay aside your raiment for the heat of noon; and after the prayer of night. Three times are of privacy for you. It is no sin for them or for you at other times, when some of you go round attendant upon others (if they come into your presence without leave). Thus Allah maketh clear the revelation for you. Allah is Knower, Wise. (24:58)

In the above verse, three special times have been mentioned. The one is that of the morning prayer. That time is fresh and pleasant and the time to wake after enjoying a sound sleep during which one cannot take proper care of purdah. The second time is that of noon when almost every one has a nap and rest after lunch. On hot days the people generally take rest at noon and during sleep it is not possible to observe purdah. The third is the time after 'Isha'. This is also the time for rest. After the daily hard labour one feels tired and goes to sleep. As all are asleep, one does not care to observe purdah. Moreover, the husband and wife generally make love during these times. It has, therefore, been ordained that even maid-servants and children should ask permission before entering their apartment. If they are busy in kissing and embracing or sexual intercourse, this scene would have a very adverse effect on their minds. They would have nothing but shame and remorse. There is, however, no restriction to enter during the other times. Moreover, it is difficult to forbid the children from coming in as they are used to come and go. The same is the case of a maid-servant. She has to enter so frequently for household work that you cannot put restriction on her.

Some commentators have written that the instructions of Istidhan in the first verses are applicable to the other people and strangers and those contained in this verse pertain to the relatives, that is to say, to the mahrams. According to some scholars the instructions contained in the verse are for the common men and for all times and those contained in the above verse are for specific persons and for specific times and this view is correct.

The word *malik* used in the above verse means a maidservant as Abd which stands for servant is according to the Shari'ah a *ghair-mahram*. A servant is permitted to come among men; but he is not allowed to go among women. The mahram on whom there is ordinarily no restriction to come are also not permitted to come during the special times, the detail of which has been given above. These preventive measures are based on prudence and wisdom. Maulana. Ashraf Ali Thanvi has given the following comments:

> O believers! your maid-servants and those who have not attained the age of puberty should seek permission to come to you at three times. Firstly, before the morning prayer and secondly at noon when you take off some of your clothes in order to take rest or sleep

and thirdly, after the 'Isha prayer. During these three times you should not come in. In other words, these three times are for rest and sleep and privacy and one is not very serious in observing purdah therein in the strict sense. So instruct your maid-servants and immature children not to come to you at these times without asking permission. At other times, however, there is no restriction on coming and going as they come to you so frequently. The servants fall under the definition of ghair mahrams and are not allowed to go in the company of women. Maid-servants and immature children are, however, free to come in and go without asking permission except at the three specific times. The other times are not for taking rest and sleeping and it is not difficult to observe *satr*. Man should cover his body from navel to the knee before his servants and a woman should observe purdah from an infidel maid-servant except her decoration. A man is not required to conceal any part of his body from the maid-servant who is lawful for him and if she is not lawful for him he should cover his body from navel to the knee. A woman is required to cover her body from navel to the knee from a Muslim maid-servant; so the latter is allowed to come in without asking permission. A man should cover his body from navel to the knee from a child and woman should observe purdah from him, except that of her decoration so he is also allowed to come in without asking permission except at the specific three times or because of some special reason. Allah, the Exalted has

> revealed, clear verses for you and He is all-knowing, All Aware. (Bayanul Quran)

The immature children are also required to ask permission to come on reaching puberty. Previously they were required to seek permission if they wanted to come in at specific times. The practice which is in vogue in India and Pakistan that those children who come in without restriction during childhood and before puberty come without asking permission even after attaining puberty and the women do not observe purdah from them is absolutely wrong and against the Shariah and should be put to an end. There is no ambiguity about this rule that the children when they come to puberty must also ask permission as the concession enjoyed by them in childhood now no longer exists. It is mentioned in the Holy Quran:

> And when the children among you come to puberty then let them ask leave even as those before them used to ask it. Thus Allah maketh clear this revelation for you. Allah is Knower, Wise. (24:59)

Uptil now the children were required to ask permission at three specific hours; but on attaining the age of puberty they are also required to ask permission at all times like the other people as in childhood and in the adolescence period they were neither aware of the implications of purdah nor women had any attraction for them and vice versa; but now there has occurred a change in them; their feelings and sentiments have awakened raging a tumult in them. Women might also feel attracted towards them. Now the rule which is applicable to the grown-up persons is to be applied to them. Maulana Ashraf Ali Thanvi has added the following comments:

> And when the children among you reach the age of competency or be nearing this age, they should also ask permission like the grown-up persons. Allah, the Exalted has revealed clear verses. He is all-knowing, All-Aware. The above commandment has been repeated

> to emphasize the advantages of the rules of seeking permission.

Observing Purdah

It has been explained above that for women it is necessary to observe purdah of the whole body except her face and the palms of her hands as is evident from the above verse so that no one should have any misconception about the implication of these words. It may be pointed out that although there is no *satr* of face and hands, yet they should not be exposed to a stranger if there is fear of evil and mischief. The aged women may, however, not cover their faces and hands although it is better for them to do so.

> As for women past child-bearing, who have no hope of marriage, it is no sin for them if they discard their (outer) clothing in such a way as not to show adornment. But to refrain is better for them and Allah is Hearer, Knower. (24:60)

It has been ordained even for the aged women not to display their decoration. It is evident that Islam does not allow the parts of the body which come under the given definition be remained uncovered without any reason. Maulana Ashraf Ali Thanvi has written:

> One thing we must understand. Although there is no satr of face and hands in the strict sense of the word, but it is not permissible that women should freely display their faces and hands to strangers as there is fear of evil and mischief. The satr of these parts of the body also becomes incumbent except upon the aged women who have lost attraction for men and have no hope for marriage, only such women are permitted to expose their face and hands and according to some their feet but they are not permitted to display their decoration. So

> far as a young lady is concerned, it is necessary for her to observe satr of these parts if there is fear of evil and mischief, but it is permitted to expose these parts in case of necessity or genuine excuse. It is, however, better that purdah should be observed.

Ibn Al-'Arabi says:

> The aged women are specifically exempted from it and the rest have been disallowed (this concession) as the heart has no attraction towards the aged women. But if they observe full satr it is better than discarding the veil. (Ahkamul Quran)

According to the Fuqaha (Jurists) although face does not come under the definition of satr, it is better that the women should be asked not to expose their face so that there should occur no mischief. Nature has created such an irresistible attraction and fascination in the face of a woman that man is automatically drawn towards it and his natural sexual instinct is excited. Allama Ibn 'Abidin writes:

> A woman should be forbidden to expose her face lest man should see her face as sometimes when the face is exposed the eyes look towards it with lewdness. (Dur Mukhtar)

In the above verse, particular words have been used which means that the women should not put on such thin clothes as do not help to maintain their satr; but reflect the outlines of their bodies and display their beauty. Ibn Al-'Arabi writes:

> It is also displaying one's decoration and charms that a woman should wear such a thin dress as reflects her body.(Ahkamul Quran)

He has mentioned the following Hadith in support of the above view. The Holy Prophet (peace and blessings of Allah be upon him) observed:

> Most of the dressed women are practically naked. They attract others or are drawn towards them. Such women should neither enter Paradise nor have its smell.

We have already mentioned the following verse of the Holy Quran:

> And stay in your houses. Bedizen not yourself with the bedizenment of the time of ignorance. (33:33)

Umm 'Alqama has reported that Hadrat Hafsa bint 'Abdur Rahman came to Hadrat 'A'isha (Allah be pleased with her) Hadrat Hafsa was wearing a thin dopatta. When Hadrat 'A'isha saw this, she tore it and threw it out and gave her a thick one. Hadrat Hafsa was the niece of Hadrat 'A'isha.

Hadrat 'A'isha has narrated another incident: Asma bint Abu Bakr (her sister) went to the Holy Prophet (peace and blessings of Allah be upon him). She was wearing thin clothes. The Holy Prophet (peace and blessings of Allah be upon him) turned away his face and said:

> O Asma! It is not permissible to look at a grown up woman except her face and the palms of her hand. (Mishkat)

There is a Hadith in Sahih Muslim. The Holy Prophet (peace and blessings of Allah be upon him) observed:

> Don thy garment and you should not walk naked. (Mishkat)

The above and many other Ahadith on this subject reveal that both man and woman should wear such garments as do not reflect their bodies. Thus their grace and beauty would remain immune from the wicked eyes and there would be no danger to their modesty and chastity.

If you ponder over what we have said about purdah, you would find that there are many advantages of this institution. The wisdom behind this institution becomes all the more manifest when we see the moral turpitude of the West.

Islam attaches utmost importance to chastity and morality and righteous conduct and behaviour. If the rules and regulations governing the moral conduct and behaviour of society are not perfect and right and do not impose any restrictions on adultery and prostitution and on the action and behaviour leading to these vices, the morality is bound to be cast to the forewinds.

Study the chapter on "Ethics" of the History of the World and see what is the basic cause of spoiling the morals and what are the reasons of the downfall of a country and a nation? In our view the root-cause of all the evils was that there existed no balanced rules and regulations for guarding the chastity and morality of the people.

Islam has given no concession in the rules and regulations pertaining to chastity and morality. You have already read the attitude of Islam about unlawful sex. Now we would tell you about the punishment prescribed by Islam for those who level false accusation against pious and chaste men and women in order to disgrace them.

Islam condemns that person who is guilty of spreading false rumours against a pious man or woman. It has been mentioned in the Holy Quran:

> Lo! as for those who traduce virtuous believing woman (who) know not. Cursed are they in the world and the Hereafter. Theirs will be aweful doom. On the day Allah will pay them their just due and they will know that Allah, He is the Manifest Truth. (24:23-25)

Study the above verse deeply. A very stern warning has been

administered for this offence. A person guilty of this sin is doomed in this world and in the Hereafter.

If any person brings a false accusation of adultery/fornication against a chaste and pious lady and fails to produce four eyewitnesses, he would be liable to beating with eighty stripes. He would be deprived of giving evidence against any person in future it has been mentioned in the Holy Quran:

> And those who accuse honourable woman but bring not four witnesses, scourge (with) eighty stripes and never (afterward) accept their testimony - they indeed are evil doers.
> (24:4)

The above verse throws a light on the significance of morality and chastity in Islam. A person who is guilty of levelling a false charge of immorality against a pious man or woman and fails to bring four witnesses in support thereof will be liable to the following punishments: 1. He should be beaten with eighty stripes. 2. In future his witnesses should not be accepted, being the biggest liar. 3. There is no doubt in his wickedness.

Part - Five

Practical Life

Eleven

Professional Role

Islam stands for merit. It wants woman to be able and efficient, so that she may perform good deeds and serve mankind. Hence, she is allowed to go out for the attainment of good cause. The study of history shows that women went for shopping and farm-work during the early period of Islam. Hazrat Ayeshah (R.A.A.) relates an incident which took place just after the revelation of Commandments of veil. She says, "When Hazrat 'Umar Farooq (R.A.A.) once saw Hazrat Sauda (R.A.A.) outside her house, and expressed his displeasure on this. She came away quietly and related the matter to the Holy Prophet (S.A.W.). Soon after there was revelation upon him (S.A.W.). When it was over, the Holy Prophet (S.A.W.) told her :

> "Of course, Allah has permitted you to go out of your home for your needs." (Bukhari)

There are such other instances which show that Islamic Society never prevented women from going out of their homes for the right cause and necessary requirements.

"But Islam has laid down certain limitations on the movements of woman. Whenever she leaves home and goes out, she has to remain within the protective bounds of her modesty and chastity. She is not permitted to move so freely and mingle with men in social gatherings.

Woman is allowed to visit mosque for the purpose of offering her prayers. However, this permission is not without conditions. The Holy Prophet (S.A.W.) has said :

> "When a wife of one of you asks for permission to go to mosque, she should not be refused." (Muslim, and Bukhari)

> But men were not directed, either to send women or bring them along to mosque. Hazrat 'Umar Farooq (R.A.A.) did not like his wife Aliqah going to mosque for offering her prayers. Whenever she asked for the permission, he kept quiet. And she herself would reply, "By Allah, I shall go to mosque to offer my prayers unless I am prohibited in clear terms." (Mu'atta)

The woman who went to mosque to offer her prayers, was neither allowed to mix with men in the congregation nor stand in the front rows. There is a clear direction of the Holy Prophet (S.A.W.) in this respect.

> "The best place for women is at the rear."

> Whether Woman is Allowed to Join Funeral Procession and Visit Graves. Hazrat Umme Atiyah (R.A.A.) relates, "We were prohibited, though not strictly, from accompanying funeral processions." (Bukhari)

Once a woman, who happened to be the close relative of the deceased, accompanied his funeral procession owing to the grief beyond her control. Hazrat 'Umar Farooq (R.A.A.) reproved her but the Holy Prophet (S.A.W.) remarked, "O 'Umar ! leave her alone."

> Similarly, the Holy Prophet (S.A.W.) prohibited the frequenting of the graves by woman. Hazrat Anas Bin Malik (R.A.A.) relates, "When the Holy Prophet (S.A.W.) saw a woman crying over a grave, he (S.A.W.) did not prevent her, but advised her, "O woman ! Fear Allah and have patience." (Bukhari)

A Muslim woman, whether spinster, married or widow, can not travel alone. She can travel only in the company of a mahram (a relative with whom her marriage is prohibited).

> "It is unlawful for a woman who believes in Allah and the Day of Judgment to travel for three days or more without accompanying either her father, brother or husband or son or any other male mahram."

Further, Hazrat Abu Hurairah (R.A.A.) relates that the Holy Prophet (S.A.W.) has said :

> "A woman should not travel for a day and night unless she is accompanied by a male mahram." (Abu Dawood)

Woman can carry on any lawful business or trade, without restriction of any kind. According to Islamic Shariah The conception of a state is of a welfare state, in which woman also plays an important role. We have various examples.

> A Sahabia named Qeela (R.A.A.) said to the Holy Prophet (S.A.W.), "I am a woman who buys and sells different commodities and wants to know the principles of trade." (Tabaqat Ibn Sa`d)

During the Caliphate of Hazrat 'Umar Farooq, Abdullah bin Abi Rabiya used to send 'Itr' (scent) to his mother Asma from Yaman and she carried on its business.

Umrah bint Tabeekh says, "Once I went to the market alongwith a maid and bought fish and put it in the bag. As the bag was small, its head and tail were visible. Hazrat Ali (R.A.A.) who was passing from there, saw the fish and asked, 'How much did you pay for it? It's very big and nice. All members of the family would eat with satisfaction." (Tabaqat Ibn Sa'd)

Women in Agriculture

Woman is also free to go on her farm and work there. Jabir bin Abdullah (R.A.A.) says that his aunt was divorced by her husband. She decided to cut and sell a few trees during the period of her Iddat (waiting period). A gentleman told her that she was not allowed to leave her home during the period of her Iddat. So she went to the Holy Prophet (S.A.W.) to seek his advice. The Holy Prophet (S.A.W.) said :

> "Go on to your field, cut your date trees and sell. You may give the earned money in charity or use it for some other good purpose and thus you may be rewarded in the Hereafter." (Abu Dawood)
>
> Sohail bin Sa'd (R.A.A.) relates the story of another woman who had her own farm where she cultivated beetroots. When he alongwith other companions visited her, on Fridays, she would entertain them with a sweet dish made from beet-root and flour. (Bukhari)

Hazrat Abu Bakr Siddiq's daughter Asma (R.A.A.) says: "The Holy Prophet (S.A.W.) had given a piece of land for cultivation to Hazrat Zubair (her husband) which was at a distance of two miles from my house. I used to bring dates stones from that farm. Once when I was carrying a basket, full of date stones on my head, I met the Holy Prophet (S.A.W.) on the way. He (S.A.W.) called me and offered a place at the back of his mount. But as there were some Ansar males with him so I felt shy to travel with them. I also thought of my husband, Hazrat Zubair (R.A.A.) who was a very self respecting man and would have never liked it. Realizing my hesitation, the Holy Prophet (S.A.W.) proceeded on."

Women in Industry

Woman participated in industrial activities also. Hazrat Abdullah bin Mas'ood's wife ran an industry very successfully and supported her husband and children through its income.

> Similarly, Khaula Bint Sa'lba (R.A.A.) earned through the industrial work and maintained her husband also.(Tabaqat Ibn Sa'd, Vol. 8)

Right of Freedom

Islam provides full protection to the rights of woman. The rights granted to her by Islamic Shariah cannot be taken away by any man. Whenever their rights were encroached upon by anyone, they defended it to their best.

Once a man married his daughter to a rich man. The girl did not like him so she complained to the Holy Prophet (S.A.W.), and said, "My father has married me to his wealthy nephew so that he may get some benefits."

> The Holy Prophet (S.A.W.) replied, "If you do not like this marriage, then you are free." She submitted, "I uphold my father's decision. By this complaint I intended to tell my fellow women that their fathers have no right to marry them against their will." (Musnad Ahmad)

A slave maid, Barera (R.A.A.) was married to a slave man named Mughees (R.A.A.). After sometime, she became free then she refused to live with Mughees (R.A.A.) as a free woman was not legally bound to remain in the wedlock of a slave man. But Mughees (R.A.A.) loved Barera (R.A.A.) so much that he became desperate and used to follow her weeping. Seeing his miserable state the Holy Prophet (S.A.W.) said to her :

"Barerah! Fear Allah and think of the love and anxiety of Mughees. He has been your husband so long, and you have borne his children as well."

Barerah (R.A.A.) asked, "Are you (S.A.W.) ordering me to remain his wife ?"

> The Holy Prophet (S.A.W.) replied, "No, how can I order you? I am just recommending his case to you."
>
> She said, "Then I do not need him." (Bukhari)

During the time of the Holy Prophet (S.A.W.), women offered prayers in mosque. Due to some reasons Hazrat 'Umar Farooq (R.A.A.) felt that it was not advisable for women to leave their homes and move out. As they had been permitted by the Holy Prophet (S.A.W.), he did not like to restrict them by force of law.

Hazrat 'Umar Farooq's own wife, 'Ateka (R.A.A.) availed the advantage of the permission and offered her prayers in congregation. Once he told her, "By Allah, you know I don't like this practice of yours, and yet you do not desist." She replied: "By Allah, I shall continue to offer my prayers in mosque unless you prevent me by law." Thus, she did not stop praying in the mosque during the lifetime of Hazrat 'Umar Farooq (R.A.A.), so much so that she was present in the mosque when the murderous attack was made on him. (Bukhari). This event proves that women's rights are fully safeguarded in the Islamic society.

Once the Holy wives of the Holy Prophet (S.A.W.) demanded from him some amenities of life. As such demand was below their dignity and status and also did not conform to the way of life he (S.A.W.) liked, hence he was very much displeased and he decided not to talk to them for one month. When Hazrat Abu Bakr Siddiq (R.A.A.) and Hazarat 'Umar Farooq (R.A.A.) came to know, they felt it very much. They told their daughters, Hazrat Ayesha (R.A.A.) and Hazrat Hafsa (R.A.A.) that their demand was not fair. Likewise, they endeavoured to explain their views to other wives of the Holy Prophet (S.A.W.). Finally they went to Hazrat Umme Salama (R.A.A.) who told them:

> "Gentlemen! What is your business here? The Holy Prophet (S.A.W.) is well aware of our position. If he (S.A.W.) wants, he may prevent

> us, then we shall not claim anything. To whom should we approach except him? Does anybody interfere in the affairs between you and-your wives? You may leave, we have not invited you."
>
> (Tabaqat Ibn Sa'd Vol. 8)

It is crystal clear that Hazrat Umme Salama (R.A.A.) would not like even such important personalities to interfere in her domestic affairs. She wanted that the dispute between wife and husband should be settled between them only and nobody else should be allowed to interfere.

Women's Duties

'Holy Prophet, Muhammad (S.A.W.) has said:

> "Woman is the care-taker of all the members of her husband's family and his children. And for this she will be questioned on the Day of Judgment." (Bukhari)

This Hadis shows that woman's primary duty is to look after her home. She has been made responsible for her domestic duties. The external affairs are looked after by the husband. However, she has been allowed to leave home when any necessity arises. But Islam does not make her responsible for any duty outside her home.

As a wife she has to look after the affairs of her husband. She has to protect and safeguard the welfare and rights of the members who are under her care. She is also responsible for the protection of her husband's wealth and property. Holy Prophet (S.A.W.) has described the characteristics of a pious and faithful wife thus:

> "When her husband is out of sight, she guards her chastity and wealth and property of her husband." (Ibn Majah)
>
> Holy Prophet (S.A.W.) had assigned the domestic duties to Hazrat Fatimah (R.A.A.)

and Hazrat Ali (R.A.A.) was to look after the matters outside the house. But this does not mean that woman has been confined to home only. Islamic Shariah has provided full freedom to woman in respect of her rights as enjoined by the Holy Qur'an. Once Hind bint Utba (R.A.A.) complained to the Holy Prophet (S.A.W.) that her husband does not give her the money required for the domestic expenses, hence, there is no other way except that she takes his money without his knowledge. The Holy Prophet (S.A.W.) replied, "You may take money required for the maintenance of yourself and your children." (Bukhari)

The wife also has the right to give alms from some portion of her husband's wealth. The Holy Prophet (S.A.W.) said, "When wife spends from the wealth of her husband within the limits of Shariah, she gets its reward and the husband gets the reward for his earning." (Bukhari)

According to the Islamic Shariah, woman is the most suitable person for nursing and bringing up children. A companion of the Holy Prophet (S.A.W.) divorced his wife. He had a child from her, whom he wanted to keep with him. But the divorcee complained to the Holy Prophet (S.A.W.) who said:

> "Your right (of the custody of the child) is superior until you re-marry."(Abu Dawood)

Explaining this hadis, Allama Shaukani (R.A.) says : "This hadis proves that the mother has greater right over her child than the father, unless she re-marries." All jurists unanimously agree on this point of law. Allama Badruddin Kashani (R.A.) says:

> "The right of custody (Hizanat) belongs to the, wives because they are more loving and

> kind and can look after the minors more carefully and diligently." (Badai-wal-Sanai)

Women's Organization

Women are allowed to play an effective and helpful role in the Islamic society. Shariah allows them to form their own organization for the uplift of the society. Though such organization did not exist during the time of the Holy Prophet (S.A.W.) and Khulafa-e-Rashideen (Pious Caliphs). (R.A.A.) because the circumstances were different and no such need arose then. But the fact cannot be denied that women used to get together during those days also and put before the Holy Prophet (S.A.W.) the problems which they faced and the Holy Prophet (S.A.W.) listened to them. Now the circumstances are different. The Muslim women have to face various difficulties all over the. world. Therefore, they can form their own organisations to solve the problems concerning women and children and they can do a lot for their upliftment.

Once a woman approached the Holy Prophet (S.A.W.) and said :

> "Men are benefited by your sermons and advises, but we have no such opportunity. Therefore, we request you to give us also some time so that we may also come to You for acquiring knowledge that you receive from Allah."
>
> The Holy Prophet (S.A.W.) said : "Well, assemble all of you on such and such day." When they all assembled at a place on the fixed day, the Holy Prophet (S.A.W.) went there and taught them the principles of Islamic (Shariah). (Bukhari)
>
> Once, the Muslim women of Madina selected a very wise woman, Asma bint Zaid, as their representative and deputed her to the Holy

> Prophet (S.A.W.) for the solution of their problems. She said to the Holy Prophet (S.A.W.), "I am a representative of the Muslim women. I have to say what they have to say and they have the same opinion as I have, that Allah has sent His Prophet and Messenger (S.A.W.) for men and women both. So we have faith in you and follow your teachings regarding the commands of Allah. But we, the women who observe Purdah (Veil), who remain confined to our homes to become the focus point of our men, who bear the children for our husbands, cannot equal the men who attend Friday congregations, funeral prayers and participate in Jihad and thus earn honourable status in the sight of Allah." The Holy Prophet (S.A.W.) turned to his companions and said, "Have you ever seen a better woman who enquired about her religion so eloquently ?" The companions replied, "By Allah, we have not heard such (a good talk)." The Holy Prophet (S.A.W.) said to Asma (R.A.A.), "Asma, go and tell women whom you represent that should they obey their husbands and behave well with them, it will equalize them with the men regarding the services of men you related."
>
> (At Targhib-wat-Tarhib)

Thus, the Muslim women have represented on many occasions to the Holy Prophet (S.A.W.) for the solution of their problems. Abu Dawood relates, "When the Holy Prophet (S.A.W.) took the Oath of Allegiance from women, an elderly woman, perhaps from the clan of Muzir stood up and said, "O Messenger of Allah (S.A.W.), we are already burden on our parents and husbands and children, so have we any right to spend from their wealth ?" The Holy Prophet

(S.A.W.) replied, "Yes, the things like dates which you can eat and present to others also."

The study of history shows that Shariah is not against the formation of separate organizations of women. The best proof is that women can form, their own rows for offering their prayers in the mosques. Sahabiyat have offered their prayers in congregations led by women. It is related by Refah al Hanafiya that Hazrat Ayeshah (R.A.A.) led the obligatory prayers, (Farz Salat) for women and stood in their midst (i.e. she did not stand like a man in front of the rows). (Dar Qutni)

Tamimah bint Salma relates, "Hazrat Ayeshah (R.A.A.) led the Maghrib prayers and stood in the middle of the women and recited the verses of the Holy Qur'an loudly."

(All Muhalla)

Hajirah bint Haseen says, Umme Salamah (R.A.A.) led the Asr (Afternoon) prayer and stood in our midst." (Dar Qutni)

'Ata says that Hazrat Ayeshah (R.A.A.) used to give call (Azan) for the prayers and say Iqamat (call for preparing rows for prayer) also. And she used to lead the prayers and stand in the middle of the women.

Hazrat Ayeshah relates that she used to lead the optional Night prayers (Taraveeh) during the month of Ramazan and stand in the middle of the row.(Kitab al Asaar-Imam Abu Yousuf)

Khairah relates that Hazrat Umm Salamah (R.A.A.) used to lead their (Women's) prayers

> during the month of Ramazan and stand in the middle of the row. (Muhalla- Vol. II)

In fact, Salat (Prayers) is a sort of mini-organization of the Ummah, therefore, the leading of prayers is called the Imamate-Sughra. When the Holy Prophet (S.A.W.) passed away from this world, the question of his successor arose. The Muhajireen (Immigrants) proposed the name of Hazrat Abu Bakr Siddiq (R.A.A.) and to support his suitability they cited that Holy Prophet (S.A.W.) had selected him to lead the prayers during his lifetime. On the basis of this (Hadis) it can be rightly said that women can form their own organization within the framework of the Islamic Shariah for the purpose of solving their own problems. And they can be allowed by law to perform various duties of the society for the welfare of the mankind.

Women and Leadership

It is a fact that Islam does not permit a woman to lead the Muslim Nation (Ummah) because she does not possess the qualities of leadership, and it shall be against her nature to entrust a woman with the task for which site is not capable. This kind of step will lead the Ummah to nothing else but destruction. The Holy Prophet (S.A.W.) has said :

> "Men were destroyed when they obeyed women." (Bukhari)
>
> "A nation which has entrusted its leadership to a woman cannot be successful." (Mustadrak Hakim)
>
> Imam Shaukani, explaining this Hadis, says, "This is a fact that woman is not capable of patronising and ruling. And it is not proper for any nation to assign leadership to a woman, because it is necessary to abstain from the act which is harmful." (Nail-al-Autar)

The consensus of the Ummah against the leadership of woman is not based on hatred or contempt. But the Islamic Shariah does not want to burden her with such heavy and onerous responsibilities, considering her weak physique and delicate temperament. The scholars and the jurists maintain that the leader (Imam) of the Muslims must be well versed in Islamic law and intellectually far sighted and thoughtful. He must be able to take right and prompt decision at the crucial times like war and peace and have firm determination to enforce it otherwise he will surely fail to lead the Muslim Ummah. These qualities are found only in men and lack in women. Therefore, they cannot be assigned heavy responsibilities which are beyond their capacity.

Suitable Responsibilities

Though women cannot be assigned the leadership of the Ummah, she can be made responsible for certain social services which she can render according to her capabilities. Allama Ibn Ilham Hanafi (R.A.) says:

> "The Shariah says that her intellect is faulty but every body knows that it is not so to the extent that she may not hold any responsibility. You should know that she can be the manager and trustee of trust and the guardian of the orphans."

Likewise, there are many other responsibilities that can be assigned to a woman for the welfare of the Muslim society and uplift of women and children. The main consideration should be that she must be able to perform the duties assigned to her. She has to abide by certain rules and principles of Shariah while taking up any task in the social set-up.

Collective Responsibilities

Islam does not lay any restriction on spiritual, social, economic or political activities of women. The Holy Qur'an provides clear cut proof that a woman is completely equal to a man in terms of her rights and responsibilities.

The Qur'an says:

> "Every soul will be (held) in pledge for its deeds." (74 : 38)

It also states :

> "....So their Lord accepted their prayers, (saying). I will not suffer to be lost the work of any of you whether male or female. You proceed one from another. (3 : 195)
>
> Woman according to the Qur'an is not blamed for Adam's first mistake. Both were jointly wrong in their disobedience to Allah; both repented and both were forgiven.(2 : 35; 7 : 20-24)

In one verse (20 : 121), Hazrat Adam was specifically blamed.

In terms of religious obligations, such as the daily prayers, fasting, payment of Zakat (Poor-due) and pilgrimage, woman has certain advantages over man.'

The pre-Islam Arabs ill-treated the women-folk. They hated the birth of girls and buried them alive. The Qur'an forbade this practice. They gave no rights to their wives and married themselves indiscriminately any number of wives; divorcing them at their will without giving them any compensation.

The Qur'an clearly states that the marriage is sharing between the two halves of the society; its objectives, besides perpetuating human race, are emotional well-being and spiritual harmony. Its bases are love and mercy. According to Islamic Law, a woman cannot be forced to marry against her will. Besides all other provisions for her protection at the time of marriage, it has been specifically decreed that a woman has full right to Mehr or dower money. It is not the price for a woman, as was the case in certain cultures but rather it is a gift symbolizing love and affection.

The Holy Qur'an has decreed that one should be kind to his parents. The Holy Book has specially recommended for the good treatment of mothers. The Holy Prophet (S.A.W.) has declared that "Paradise lies at the feet of mothers."

Islam granted the right of independent ownership of economic rights to the women, which was denied to them before Islam and after it (even as late as this century in some countries).

A fair investigation of the teachings of Islam will prove woman's equality with man in what we call today "Political Rights". This includes the right of election as well as the nomination to political offices.

Intellectual Capabilities

The responsibilities of woman in Islamic society are not limited. Its scope is vast and varied. Her responsibilities depend upon her mental faculties and capabilities. The Holy Prophet (S.A.W.) has said about women, "They are mentally and physically weaker." The jurists have said, "(in capabilities) man is superior to woman."

Not only that, Islamic Shariah has accepted woman's weakness but also provided various facilities and concessions to her: (1) She has been exempted from offering her prayers (Salat) during the period of menses as she remains unclean and feels weaker during that period. (2) The period of delivery is more difficult for her. Therefore, she has been exempted from prayers during this delicate period. (3) If her menses or pregnancy falls during the Holy month of Ramazan, she may complete her days of missed fast during some other months. (4) She has been exempted from participating in Jihad. (5) While performing Hajj, she has been allowed to leave for Mina early in the morning without passing the night of Ninth of Zil Hijja at Muzdalfa. The concession relieves her from the trouble of walking in the heavy crowd. She has been also permitted to complete her Rami Jumrat before reaching of other persons in Mina.

Evidence

Woman is weaker than man in many aspects. Therefore, in case of woman's evidence, her reliability has been lessened. The Holy Prophet (S.A.W.) has said :

> "The evidence of woman is half of the man's."
> (Bukhari)

The law of evidence has been mentioned in five places in the Holy Qur'an. Out of which only one discusses about the evidence of woman. The Holy Qur'an says:

> "O ye who believe ! When contract a debt for a fixed term, record it in writing. Let scribe record it in writing between you in (terms of) equity. No scribe should refuse to write as Allah hath taught him, so let him write, and let him who incurreth the debt dictate, and let him observe his duty to Allah, his Lord, and diminish not thereof. But if he who oweth the debt is of low understanding, or weak, or unable himself to dictate in (terms of) equity. And call witness from among your men, two witnesses. And if two men be not (at hand) then a man and two women, of such as you approve as witness so that if the one erreth (owing to forgetfulness) the other will, remember. And the, witnesses must not refuse when they are summoned. Be not averse to writing down (the contract) whether it be small or great, with (record of) the term thereof. That is more equitable in the sight of Allah and more sure for testimony, and the best way of avoiding doubts between you; save only in the case when it is actual merchandise which, ye transfer among yourselves from hand to hand. In that case it

> is no sin for you if ye write it not. And have witnesses when ye sell one to another, and let no harm be done to scribe or witness. If ye do (harm to them) lo! it is a sin in you. Observe your duty to Allah. Allah is teaching you. And Allah is Knower of all things."(2 : 282)

The law of evidence is clearly laid down in Islamic jurisprudence, specially in 'Hidayah' and "Durrul Mukhtar." The law of evidence as propounded by the Sunni School in Islam and is explained in Hidayah (Vol. III, p. 664) is in many respects the same as the law of Moses. In the Pentateuch two witnesses at least were required to establish any charge (Num. xxxv. 30) and the witness who withheld the truth was censured a (LEV. V-1.) whilst slanderous statements and officious witnesses were discouraged (ex. xxviii. 1; Lev. xix-16) and false witnesses were punished with the punishment due to the offence they sought to establish (DEUT. xix 16). According to Josephus, women and slaves were not allowed to give evidence (Ant. iv. c. 8. S. 15).

It is the duty of the witnesses to bear testimony, and it is not lawful for them to conceal it, when the party concerned demand it from them. Because it is laid down in the Qur'an (Surah 2 : 282 cited above), "Let not witnesses withheld their evidence when it is demanded from them." And again, "Conceal not your testimony for whoever conceals his testimony is an offender."

On account of woman's physical constitution, social, economic and general conditions, certain limitations have been placed on her capacity to give evidence. A woman is generally confined to her domestic chores and is rarely concerned with affairs relating to trade and commerce or matters requiring agreements and undertakings necessitating testimony.

In cases inducing corporal punishments, a woman is least expected to be a good witness. Moreover on account of her frail constitution, shyness and her inability to stand the vigour and rigour of standing in a court of law to evidence and to withstand cross examination, a woman is not a proper person.

Almost all the jurists agree that evidence of only women is enough in the matters relating to females only and of which the males are not expected to have any knowledge. Imam Shafie (R.A.) says:

> "I have not come across any scholar who has opposed the evidence of only women in the matters of birth and physical defects in the private organs of women."

Imam Zahri states:

> "It is in accordance with the Sunnah that as all matters relating to women are known to them only, the evidence of women is legal."

Hazrat Abdullah Bin 'Umar (R.A.A.) has also supported this view.

Hind Bint Talaq relates:

> "I along with some women was at a place. There lay a child covered with cloth. A woman, while passing there, crushed it. The mother of the child accused her of the childs' death. Ten women, including myself, gave the evidence before Hazrat Ali (R.A.A.) which he accepted."

Hazrat 'Umar Farooq (R.A.A.) did not consider the evidence, of women right in the case of marriage (Nikah), divorce, Hodood. (Capital punishments prescribed by Allah) and murder, but it is related that four women gave their evidence before him that such and such man had divorced his wife in the state of intoxication. Hazrat 'Umar separated the wife from her husband.

Allama Ibn Hazam (R.A.), after accepting the evidence of two women equal to one man, considers the evidence of women reliable in all matters and rights. Justice Shuraih also agrees with this view. Once a case about the household goods was brought before him. The husband and the wife were the parties to it. The husband claimed that the goods belonged to him. But four women gave their evidence in favour of the wife and maintained that the goods belonged to the wife. The wife gave him the dower money and he gave her those goods instead, justice Shuraih accepted the evidence of the women and gave his judgement in favour of the wife.

Ayas-bin-Muavia (R.A.) has accepted the evidence of two women in respect of divorce.

It is related that Hazrat Muavia settled the dispute of a house only on the evidence of Hazrat Umm Salama (R.A.A.).

Joint Evidence

There are certain matters that relate to women and only women have their knowledge. In such cases the evidence of only women is admissible. But there are other matters for which only women's evidence is not considered reliable by certain jurists. According to them the joint evidence of man and woman is essential.

Imam Malik and Imam Shafie (R.A.) maintain that only in financial matters joint evidence is admissible. All Hanafi jurists and Usman Batti (R.A.) accept the joint evidence as the basis for the judgment in respect of all matters other than Hudood (Capital Punishments) and Qisas (Murder). Imam Sufiyan Sauri also supports this view. Even in the case of Qisas, the joint evidence is acceptable to him. For Tawoos (R.A.) the joint evidence of man and woman is admissible in all cases except adultery. But Ata Bin Abee Ribah (R.A.) maintains that if three men and two women give evidence in a case of an adultery, it is acceptable.

Ata-Bin-Abee Ribah (R.A.) says that Hazraf 'Umar Farooq (R.A.A.) has allowed the evidence of two women and one man in the matters of marriage (Nikah). Justice Shuraih has allowed the joint evidence in the matter of slavery.

These arguments show that the joint evidence should be accepted in all matters except Hudood and Qisas.' Imam Zuhri relates that Holy Prophet (S.A.W.), Hazrat Abu Bakr Siddiq (R.A.A.) and Hazrat 'Umar Farooq (R.A.A.) did not approve the evidence of women in the case of Hudood and Qisas.

Credibility in Narrating Hadith

The Ahadis related by women are treated as much reliable as related by men. Men and women are given equal importance in the matter of relating Ahadis.

Once few camels of the husband of Hazrat Abu Saeed Khudri's sister, Faria (R.A.A.) disappeared. He went in search of those camels and finally found them. But the camels attacked him suddenly, consequently he died. Faria (R.A.A.) related this matter to the Holy Prophet (S.A.W.) and said, "My husband has expired. Neither he has left food for us to eat nor any house to live in. Therefore, I want your permission to live with my brother." The Holy Prophet (S.A.W.) replied, "You should complete the period of your Iddat in the house where you received the information of your husband's death."

A similar case was presented to Hazrat Usman Ghani (R.A.A.) during his Caliphate. Some people told him that a similar case of Hazrat Faria (R.A.A.) was decided by the Holy Prophet (S.A.W.). Hazrat Usman Ghani (R.A.A.) summoned her. She came and related the decision of the Holy Prophet (S.A.W.). Hazrat Usman Ghani (R.A.A.) decided the case according to the decision of the Holy Prophet (S.A.W.) and ordered that woman to complete the period of her Iddat in the house where her husband had died.

The instance and rulings cited above would show that the majority of the Muslim Jurists and Ulema have decided that in all cases the testimony of women witnesses is admissible. However, according to them there may, be an exception in the matters which concern the practical life of males and which are outside the sphere of a female's daily routine. In such cases the testimony of male is preferable over a female.

Real Field of Activity

Addressing the Holy wives of the Holy Prophet of Islam (S.A.W.), the Holy Quran has said :

> And stay in your houses. Do not exhibit your decorations as in the Days of Ignorance. Be regular in prayer and pay the poor-due and obey Allah and His Messenger, Allah's Will Is but to remove uncleanliness far from you, O Folk of the household and cleans you with a thorough cleansing. (33 : 33)

After the Hijrat (Migration from Mecca to Madina), the Holy Prophet (S.A.W.) and his companions were struggling to make Madina a model of Islamic virtues. What they could not establish in Mecca, they wished to do in Madina. But the evil forces were adversely creating hindrance in their way. As soon as the Holy Prophet (S.A.W.) launched his movement to establish Islamic way of life in Madina, the evil forces also raised their heads against him. Within the period of six years, the opposition grew so strong that they felt as if the truth will vanish and evil forces will rule forever.

The disturbance created by the hypocrites engulfed the whole city of Madina. The opponents were striving to uproot the plants of morality, and righteousness from the surface of Madina. They wanted total annihilation of piety and virtue therefrom. Their main targets were the honour of men and chastity of women. They knew that without toppling this basic principle, they would not be able to satisfy their carnal desires.

Under the circumstances, Islam formulated new laws for the protection of the country and the nation. It ordered Muslim men to fight face to face and crush the evil forces. It also allowed women to participate in the battle but within the limits of their houses. Hence, it is crystal clear that Islam has assigned the task of protecting the state and the society to men and confined the struggle of women to their own houses.

If a woman leaves her actual place home, it creates a gap which cannot be filled by anyone else. Therefore, Islam has not made incumbent upon women to participate in congregational prayers and such other prescribed duties of life.

It is incumbent upon man to offer his prayers in congregation. Prayer is also incumbent upon woman but not necessarily in congregation. If man tries to avoid congregation without any valid reason, he is subjected to warning and chastisement. Whereas, woman is encouraged to offer her prayers at home. The Holy Prophet (S.A.W.) has said :

> "The best mosques for women are the inner parts of their houses." (Musnad Ahmad).

Once the wife of a well known companion of the Holy Prophet, (S.A.W.) Abu Humaid Saa'di (R.A.A.) came to the Holy Prophet (S.A.W.) and said, "O Messenger of Allah (S.A.W.). I wish to offer my prayers alongwith you in the mosque. What is your opinion?" The Holy Prophet (S.A.W.) replied, "I know that it is your desire, but remember, it is better for you to offer your prayers in the inner room of your house rather than to offer your prayers in the outer room of your house. The prayer which you offer in your room is better than the prayer which you offer in the courtyard of your house, and the prayer which you offer in the courtyard of your house is better than the prayer which you offer in the mosque of your locality. Similarly, the prayer which you offer in the mosque of your locality, is better than your prayer which you offer in my mosque." (Musad Ahmad)

The wife of Abu Humaid Saaidi (R.A.A.) was so much impressed by the order of the Holy Prophet (S.A.W.) that she selected a corner of her room and prayed there until the end of her life.

Friday is the manifestation of congregation and the unity of the Muslim nation. But the woman has been exempted from offering Friday prayers in the mosque. The Holy Prophet (S.A.W.) has said:

> "Friday prayer is incumbent upon every

> Muslim except slave, woman, child and the sick." (Abu Dawood)

Holy Prophet Muhammad (S.A.W.) has also disapproved the participation of woman in the funeral. In this respect Umme Atiya (R.A.A.) relates : "We were prevented from taking part in the funeral procession but the Holy Prophet (S.A.W.) was not so strict with us." This Hadis shows that the Holy Prophet (S.A.W.) was not so strict but another Hadis shows that he (S.A.W.) was strict in a sense.

> Hazrat Anas (R.A.A.) relates, "Once we were accompanying the Holy Prophet (S.A.W.) in a funeral procession. He (S.A.W.) saw some women following and asked angrily, "Are you carrying the dead body?" They replied, No. The Holy Prophet again asked : "Will you participate in the burial?" They replied, "No." The Holy Prophet (S.A.W.) said, "When you have nothing to do here, why have you come? You will get nothing in return, so go home." (Fath-ul-Bari)
>
> It is also not incumbent upon women to take part in Jihad (Holy War) and come to the battle field. In such delicate situations also, they have been advised to remain within the four walls of their houses and serve the cause of Islam in the best possible way. Hazrat Ayesha (R.A.A.) relates that the Holy Prophet (S.A.W.) has said, "You (women) should remain within the four walls of your homes (i.e. look after domestic chores) and this is your Jihad." (Musnad Ahmad)

Once a Sahabia (Female Companion) asked the Holy Prophet (S.A.W.), "Allah has made Jihad incumbent upon men, so when they return victorious, they share the booty and if they are martyred, they live eternally and Allah provides them with their livelihood. But which action of ours will be equivalent to theirs

> The Holy Prophet (S.A.W.) replied, "Obedience to your husbands and the recognition of their rights." (Al Targheeb wal Tarheeb)

> Thus we see that in Islam duties of man and woman are different but the reward is the same. In no case the equal right of woman is lost. She can come out but for the welfare of her home and not for its destruction. Hazrat Ayesha (R.A.A.) asked the Holy Prophet (S.A.W.), "Is Jihad incumbent upon women ?" The Holy Prophet (S.A.W.) replied, "Yes, Jihad is obligatory for them but in that Jihad, there is no war and that is Hajj and Umra." (Ibn Majah)

> In reply to another question he (S.A.W.) remarked, "Hajj is the best Jihad for you (women)." (Bukhari)

Women are allowed to offer their prayers, in the mosque on the condition that they do not mingle with men and keep their rows separate. Hazrat Abu Hurairah relates that the Holy Prophet (S.A.W.) has said :

> "The best row of men is the first row and the worst is their last row. And the best row of women is the last and the worst is their first row." (Muslim)

Apparently we see the functioning of different organizations differently but in fact these organizations and institutions are the parts of the one single social set-up. A body of government runs the affairs of the country; the judiciary deals with justice, the municipalities look after the civic affairs of the cities; schools, colleges, and universities impart education, and commercial organizations manage the trade and industries of the country. But all these organizations are governed by one social set-up.

Though Islam has confined the place of woman to her home, she has not been deprived of her right to participate in other organizational activities. On the contrary, Islamic society makes her a useful member of the society. She can acquire education and become specialist in her own field. She can become a doctor and treat women and children. She can become a teacher and impart education to women folk. In short, she can participate in all activities of the society and choose her career within the limits of the Islamic Laws.

Islam builds human character and aims at the establishment of a society free from all vices and immoralities, Hence woman is prevented from indulging in such activities which become the cause of social degeneration. Umme Atiya relates, the Holy Prophet (S.A.W.) has said :

> "The minor and the major women and those women who are pregnant may go to Idgah (Place of Eid prayers). But those women who are in menses will be kept away from the place of prayer and participate only in supplications."

Business Pursuits

It is said that in Islam women do not enjoy freedom of economic effort whereas it is her natural and basic right to endeavour freely in earning her livelihood and take part just like men in industry, trade, agriculture, in short, whichever economic field she likes. Without it she cannot succeed in stabilising her economic position, remaining helplessly dependent on man she can find no respectable position in society. This philosophy brought together the two separate fields of man and woman in the economic efforts making them joint ventures and the one time secluded woman joined hands with man for economic endeavours. The east, hesitant and sluggish earlier, is now not far behind in the race. This brought on disastrous consequences. The West which has been in the race long enough is feeling the pinch to some extent but its oriental counterpart in the enthusiasm of novices is not conscious of it to any appreciable extent.

Here it has been overlooked that the woman belongs to the weaker and the fair sex. She cannot take to hard and labour-consuming work, and to cast on her the burden of that type of work for which she is not physically and mentally fit would be an excess. So long as she is young, she has to put up with menses, pregnancy, delivery, breast feeding the suckling and other attendant jobs. These natural processes tax her health and her working capacity is mitigated. These various stages of reproductive activity take care of her youth and soon she enters old age. Her energies are now at a low ebb (having spent them in the sacred mission of continuity of the race entrusted to her). The modern age behaves in a peculiar contradictory manner in dealing with her. It declares her fit for every job on a par with men. But when it comes to the brass tacks it is a different story. There, in practical life she is treated on the basis of turnover and the amount of solid work calculated in terms of man hours—the weaker sex getting wages proportionate to the amount of labour put in — discrimination pure and simple, isn't it? She is usually employed for lighter jobs, not being considered fit for complicated and difficult ones. Most of the shops have sales girls (to attract a larger number of customers), clerks, typists, secretaries, receptionists are also girls (both for work and embellishment). A little higher in scale, there are lady teachers, social workers, air hostesses (mostly for the amusement of the air-bone passengers), nurses, doctors and engineers. Administrative jobs are seldom offered to them. Until lately they were scarcely to be found in the capacity of police officers, in the defence forces, land, air and navy (amateur pilots an exception). Heavy machinery is never entrusted to them. Heavy vehicles are never driven by them (railway engines, heavy trucks and bus driving are exclusively men's jobs, because her nerves go jittery in handling them, particularly in a critical situation). Even for delicate surgical operations as also those fraught with danger when handled by lady surgeons, there is a senior male surgeon standing by to take over in a critical situation like excessive bleeding or threatened respiratory and cardiac failure. It is really disgraceful that the private concerns pay women at a lower rate of remuneration due to poor working capacity in face of the legal restrictions on them in those countries where discrimination in wages on the basis of sex is a crime.

A Strong Contender

Woman's entry in the field of economic effort created sort of a struggle (due to jealousy) with man. There was no love lost between them. Instead, being in the opposite camps and behaving no more as allies but as adversaries. They competed in every field, trade, agriculture, industry and services as rivals, each one in turn trying to push out the other. But this was after all a tug of war between the strong and the weaker sex, the man due to his superiority in so many ways, was advanced in the competition against her and she had to give way. So the leadership of the nation is today in the hands of man as of old. High ranks and positions of great power and influence is her domain. He pervades all the departments of life almost exclusively. Surpassing him apart, she could not claim to be on the same footing with man. Rare examples cannot contradict the rule. Such examples have presented themselves in every period. They are not peculiar to the present age.

It can be asserted that the economic condition of woman is much better than before and she is advancing towards self-sufficiency and economic stability. This is true, but it cannot be overlooked either that for the sake of her economic upliftment she is making the greatest sacrifice — that of her faith and morality and she has been compelled by circumstance to present herself to every customer as an unsaleable commodity. For a paltry gain she has had to lower her dignified position, and at the cost of her honour and prestige has to become a source of earning wealth. Today man holds the keys to trade, industry, factories and mills, markets, big five star hotels, picture halls (the entire cinema industry) and great clubs including the notorious night ones, are all under his sway. In this way all the financial resources are in his possession and the woman is just one factor to promote this wide range of his widespread business. Man is using her to develop and promote his trade and for the roaring publicity of his manufactures. It has come to this deplorable state of affairs that every article of trade, any manufacture, high-priced or lowly, must have an alluring picture of woman, half-clad or nude, must appear on it to lure the intending customers, even when it has nothing to do with her. Shop windows, placards and the huge notice boards and city walls, particularly cinema hall-fronts are all radiant, it appears, only with her saleable charms !

And it did not remain limited to the posters and labels. She was brought in person, with all her charms, natural, artificial make-up, clinging, revealing dresses and embellishments to help sell the manufacturers' articles like hot cakes. She is there to welcome his customers at the hotels and clubs and to bribe and entertain them with her ready similes and other beguiling arts. In his cinema halls, cabarets and discotheques, she dances to his tune with expressive actions and gestures to expose the body curves and at his bidding in times of need strips herself partially and then totally also, since it brings money to the master man. The fact is that perhaps never in known history she had degraded herself like this.

To justify economic endeavours it is said that lately our necessities of life, our monetary needs, have gone up to an extent where man, through his own efforts alone cannot meet them squarely and woman's participation, therefore, becomes necessary. Through their joint efforts alone can a family, however, limited, solve its problems.

In this connection certain considerations must be kept in view:

1. At the moment almost every one keeps before himself the fictitious standard of the life of this world. It is that height which he impatiently strives to attain through frantic efforts. And it is with this end in view that he thinks of adding to the fairly large income of his own through woman's efforts also. But we should not forget that women are not, one and all, usefully employed to enlarge the family income. At the most forty percent of

them may be in this happy position. And the majority of even this minority (40%) finds itself compelled to take the most ordinary jobs due to a hard competition with the job-seeking men (since the "blessing of unemployment" is becoming a glaring feature of their "ideal economy" also). So those purposely employed women also can do little credit to the family in raising its standard of living. Here a question arises whether only those families, with earning female members, can meet their needs and those "not so advantageously placed" are faced with financial difficulties. Truth to tell, it is no hard and fast general rule that only with the additional earnings of the woman the family budget can become non-deficit.

2. In the present age there is no small list of necessities. It is an expanding one with an equal number of luxury articles, if not exceeding the barely essential items, and is even awaiting completion. In a society dominated by consumerism it is constantly swelling, thanks to T.V., Radio and business magazines advertising the latest and the loveliest. And governed by this swelling list, in his quest for the latest magically advertised luxuries, he is practically running about, at his wits end. Man's greed for more and more can end only with his life.

3. The modern age has created such an unsatiable craving for economic competition that can stop nowhere. The remedy does not, however, lie in dragging the lady of the household into the streets, markets and business offices in quest of work to supplement the family income somehow. The true and effective remedy lies in a drastic change of man's mind in relation to this world and its paraphernalia, thus ridding himself of the all consuming and never satisfied hell of greed and desire for more and more. Until there is such a healthy change in his mode of thought, this problem cannot be solved even if every member of the family, including children, works for the promotion of the family income.

4. The economic effort of the woman may add to the family income, to some degree, but her attention is diverted from the family affairs and domestic responsibilities, and she cannot attend to them in the natural way. Careful and considerate housewives through their beautiful planning can bring down the domestic budget to an appreciable extent. Switching off her attention to any,other direction, makes it topsy - turvy (due to lack of proper supervision and waste and thefts by the servants) and her earnings in the world outside cannot help in the improvement of family finances in the face of this constant waste at home.

5. Owing to the economic activity of the woman the peace of the household is disturbed. Differences crop up between the husband and the wife, and the children are left uncared for, resulting in lack of their proper training. The experience and observations of the Western society tell us that the entire system goes out of gear. The very pertinent question that arises, is whether the woman's earnings are so valuable that for their sake she herself, the householders, and the society in general may put up with such a heavy loss?

Household Prime

Islam acknowledges the importance of man's livelihood and economic activity. And along with that it is also its earnest demand that the woman goes on performing her household duties undisturbed, and any occupation with her work outside may not compel her to neglect them. With this end in view it has imposed the responsibility of earning the family's bread on man, thus leaving the woman free to look after her family and household affairs with undivided attention. This division of labour on a reasonable basis is sure to guarantee greater cooperation between them as well as the perfect and peaceful running of the home.

Owing to her single-minded devotion to household

responsibilities Islam did not allow her economic position to weaken. Rather, it was made more stable than that of man.

For this purpose it has undertaken two legal steps :

1. No economic responsibilities were imposed on her. She is not responsible for the support of her own children, her father or any other close relation. In fact, she does not have to support even herself. In childhood and early youth the father looks after her upkeep and after marriage the husband has to bear her burden. If the offspring is not in a position to look after her, father or any other internally prohibited relative has to bear her burden.

2. She has been allowed a share in inheritance. She must get her share in the inheritance of the father, husband and offspring. In certain situations she also becomes entitled to a share in the property left by the brother and sister. Similarly, she gets her dower from the husband. She is also the undisputed owner of all those ornaments and other gifts, usually given on the auspicious occasion of marriage, particularly that of girls. All these are her safe assets.

In the absence of any burden on her, the income from these sources goes on accumulating with her, whereas the heavy responsibilities to which he is liable take away most of man's earnings, leaving little or nothing by way of savings with him.

In this way in the Islamic order relating to familial laws woman is not under any compulsion to leave her home, leaving its affairs to take care of themselves. And she is also spared the evil consequences in the form of social and moral ills resulting from her joint economic ventures with man. Staying in the safest asylum she is not exposed to hungry glances and evil intentions of the lascivious and the dissolute.

No Restrictions

It does not, however, mean that Islam imposes restrictions on woman's efforts outright amounting to total ban and commands her to rest contented with what little she gets as her share of maintenance from her husband, however, meagre and inadequate. Rather, what is really needed to be impressed in this behalf is that the responsibilities of her own maintenance and those of others have not been thrown on her shoulders. However, if in spite of that freedom (from responsibilities), she insists on such a venture she is free to do so. But Islam has laid down certain conditions as a code of conduct for her to be strictly observed in every economic effort, she undertakes. She is totally free in the field of her striving and the instructions to that effect are as under :

1. A woman is basically and essentially responsible for the management of her household. She is the protector of her husband's property and the caretaker of the children. Therefore, it will not be permissible for her to take to any trade which will obstruct or totally prevent performance of her prime duties and meeting her responsibilities.

2. In the familial system of discipline she is subordinate to her husband and can undertake any economic effort only in consultation will her husband or with his express permission. For, if she devotes her time and energy to anything outside the normal sphere of activity, her household programme must receive a jolt, a setback, in one way or the other due to lack of proper attention. In extreme cases the home may be ruined.

3. She is not allowed to enter any business or trade where free-mixing with men is unavoidable, since the damage caused to her by moral lapses and other much more serious evils resulting from such contacts, is of much greater concern to a pious Muslim woman than the expected monetary gains accruing to her from this hazardous business or trade. Material gains cannot atone for the moral losses!

With due regard to these restrictions, rather we should say, the safety limits, she can enter any permitted business or earning proposition, depending, of course, on her age, state of health, circumstances as also the opportunities that offer themselves. Islam does not obstruct her path here. Similarly, she can invest, all the capital at her command in any gainful business within the Islamic limits. The gains accruing from such investment are hers exclusively. No one can put forth any claim to her honestly earned wealth.

In the present day world with these Islamic safety limits imposed on her, economic efforts on the part of a Muslim woman are not likely to suit her. As is well known, the entire economic order is in the hands of those who regard free mixing of sexes not only a necessity but the most elegant feature of modern business. And they are putting up with the ruination of the families, though willy-nilly. The weak point and a great drawback of Muslim society is that it has, to date, no economic set-up offering opportunities of economic effort for women, being at the same time free from the hazards of moral evils inherent in the existing social order.

Twelve

Political Role

Like man, the Muslim woman, has a broad political responsibility and an important role to play in public life, a role that was put at the service of the nascent Islamic community in Medina and for a while thereafter in the early period of Islam. For women, especially during the Prophet's time, were very active socially and politically. They were allowed and even encouraged to participate in the process of building up the Medinan society and they proved to be up to the task.

With the establishment of the Islamic state, the role of women in the political affairs of the new society gained momentum. They became part of the nation and effective members of the community, fully involved in public affairs . For instance, right from the beginning, women, like men, gave support and allegiance to the political system which was set up under the leadership of Muhammad. This was done through the so-called *bay'a.* Bay'a in Islam is an important political institution by which the nation or the Umma grants or ensures legitimacy for the political system. It includes a pledge by the nation to be loyal to the system and its leader as long as this leader upholds Islamic principles. Hence it is a covenant (mithaq) entered into by three parties: the leader (who is to be given the pledge or recognition; the nation or Umma (which is to give its allegiance and loyalty); and the Sharia (which is to be respected and upheld by both the leader as well as the nation). Bay'a moreover, is divided into *bay'a 'ayniya*, related to the political commitment (iltizam) to the system, and is compulsory on every Muslim man and woman, and *bay'a kayfiyya* related to particular duties and is obligatory on a particular group of men and women.

During Muhammad's(PBUH) leadership, "allegiance and loyalty" were given to him by both men and women without any difference in content or responsibility. For he took a pledge from women, as from men, to support the state and obey him in enjoining good and forbidding evil (bay'a 'ayniya). Also, he received bay'a kayfiyya from some prominent women; among them was Nusaiba bint Kab, who gave her word to participate in Jihad and indeed she did take part in many battles alongside men. This illustrates her determination to fulfil the bay'a despite the fact that it was bay' a kayfiyya; for this kind of bay'a is mandatory on those men and women with special talents. As she thought herself to be one of them, she decided to go ahead and fulfil it. This indicates that women (like men) are under an obligation to realise their individual capabilities to the full, and thus to take up the specific duties related to these capabilities, whether these duties be individual or collective.

In addition to bay'a, women also participated in Shura (mutual consultation) which is one of the foundations of the Islamic political system. The practice of Shura is obligatory on both the leader as well as the Umma. The Quran says, 'Take counsel with them in the conduct of affairs; and when you are resolved, put your trust in Allah'. We also have the verse which praises those 'who obey their Lord, attend to their prayers and conduct their affairs by mutual consent'. In these verses, it is clear that the ruler is required to consult with the ruled, while the Umma is bound in its turn to offer counsel to the ruler. Shura or mutual consultation is a tool by which the nation can achieve the objectives of the Sharia. Therefore, it is the responsibility of the nation to uphold it, protect it and under no circumstances allow it to be abandoned.

Exercise of Shura

The exercise of Shura can take place at different levels; hence the commitment to practise it by the individual members of the community varies according to the subject under consultation on the one hand, and on individual ability, on the other. For example, regarding legislative matters concerning Sharia, consultation is required with scholars or the Mama; regarding technical issues, consultation is mandatory with experts in these fields; for general issues concerning the whole nation, some form of consultation with every member of the community would be ideal. This could take the shape of a referendum or general elections. Within this context, women can take part in consultation at various levels depending on the subject matter and on individual capability.

For instance, they can participate in consultation at the legislative level, experts' level, or at the general public level as ordinary members of the community. Women were consulted at all levels during the period of the Prophet's rule and that of his companions. They used to seek their advice (mashwara) before most important decisions were made. For example, the Prophet used to receive delegations of women presenting their cases to him. Among them was Asma bint Yazid al-Ansari, who was an outspoken woman. She used to speak and argue on behalf of her fellow Muslim women, and the Prophet used to encourage her and expressed his admiration for her strong personality. His wives, especially Umm Salama and Aisha, never hesitated to ask searching questions and speak their minds when they felt it necessary; and the Prophet admired this questioning attitude. In fact, on one occasion, he had to rely on the advice (mashwara) of one of his wives, Umm Salama, to solve a problem that bewildered the Muslims at a crucial time of the Islamic history. Umm Salama with her wisdom, prudence and good judgement helped the Prophet to solve the predicament, thus avoiding a situation that could have divided the community and weakened Muhammad's mission.

Hazrat Aisha, renowned for her wit and intelligence, was trained by the Prophet to question, discuss, argue and correct, to the extent that he recommended that the Muslims should learn from her knowledge and wisdom, especially in religious matters: take half of your religion from Aisha he said. By the time the Prophet passed away she had already become a great scholar and attained the position of a religious judge. She was accepted as a religious authority during the caliphate of Abu Bakr, Umar and Uthman. Very often they used to consult her and seek her advice if they were faced with difficult issues. If they disagreed with her, the judgement she recommended- turned out to be the correct one and then it was gladly accepted. Also, she gave a verdict in favour of one companion against another and at a certain stage she criticised and corrected them.

Hazrat Hafsa, the daughter of the second caliph Umar, and one of the wives of the Prophet, was also active in public affairs. Her insight and guidance were very often sought by the companions. For example, on one occasion her father had to consult her before he could take a decision regarding the time limit for a husband to be away from his wife. (Also, based on his consultation with other women, he either amended or cancelled decisions, which he thought would run contrary to the interests of women.) Hafsa, moreover, expressed her concern about the political situation following the assassination of her father. While he was on his death bed she urged her brother Abdullah to discuss the issue with her father and ensure a smooth and peaceful transition of power. Also, she played a crucial role in persuading her brother, who was unwilling to get involved in the conflict that erupted between Ali and Muawiyah, to attend the arbitration which was set up to discuss the conflict and solve the problem peacefully and amicably.

Contrary to the traditional image of women being secluded and suppressed, women in early Islam participated in armed conflict either by organising food and water and taking care of the wounded or through playing a crucial part in the actual fighting when it was needed. Among the many examples of women who took active part in the battles was Safiyya, an aunt of the Prophet, who defended a fortress in Medina at the time of the Battle of the Trench. She noticed an intruder who had penetrated the defences of the fortress; she managed to manoeuvre and kill him before he was able to do any harm to the women and children.

Women also reached positions of high responsibility as was the case with al-Shafa' who was appointed by the second Caliph Umar as a market inspector in Medina. Their involvement in politics, furthermore, manifested itself by the fact that they were alert and actively opposed to any rulers who they thought were deviating from implementing Islamic principles and maintaining a just society. Two examples can be cited in this context. First, there is the case of the woman who publicly opposed Umar for passing a law restricting the dowries of women. He was forced, after admitting his mistake to repeal his decision. The second case was that of Aisha who genuinely believed that it was within her right to oppose the fourth Caliph Ali and fight him for failing to find the murderers of Uthman. She led an army which included prominent companions such as Talha and Zubayr and fought a battle that was to be named the Battle of the Camel, because of the camel she was riding.

Women's influence in public affairs reached its climax when their action to protect or give immunity from punishment were sanctioned by the Prophet. He approved and accepted all the Ijara (protection) cases licensed by women, this being a clear indication by the Prophet and the early community, of the ability and capacity of women to judge wisely and act responsibly even in matters of great concern to the stability and security of the Islamic state. There are many examples in which women accorded protection or asylum (Ijara) and the Prophet gladly supported them. It has been reported that the Prophet never opposed or rejected any Ijara extended to enemies by women. It must be stressed that the high level of political (as well as social) activities performed by women in early Islam could not have been achieved without the realisation of three important and interrelated factors: first, the recognition of the political ability or competence of women.

Women were regarded as full-fledged citizens capable of participating in all political activities (including bay'a, shura, granting asylums, taking part in Jihad and holding prominent positions) and indeed they were allowed to do so; second, this recognition or acknowledgement gained momentum when women became politically conscious or aware of their responsibilities in society. An awareness which Muhammad (PBUH) undertook to raise and promote among all women. This was accomplished through instructing women to gain knowledge and education and encouraging them to attend public gatherings (especially Eid celebrations, which often took place in mosques) even when they were menstruating this being an illustration that although women were at certain times relieved from the obligations of their daily worshipping, this did not lead to an automatic reduction in their duty to participate in annual public meetings. On the contrary, they were urged to attend Eid festivals and the congregational Jumah (i.e. Friday) prayers, which were regarded as general political meetings during which important issues concerning the whole nation were discussed and debated. This provided the minimum level of political (as well as social) awareness needed for the majority of them, especially those whose domestic responsibilities prevented them from attending congregational prayers such as Friday prayers. To achieve maximum benefit for them, the Prophet, moreover, used to give them advice and guidance, especially when he learnt that they could not hear him properly during one of his Eid sermons.

The Prophet actively supported those women with special abilities and a higher level of awareness and whose circumstances allowed them to attend the regular congregational prayers. In fact, he instructed men (their husbands or relatives) not to prevent them from doing so even if they wanted to attend the dawn and night prayers, during which time the Quran used to be recited, explained and interpreted. Such sessions formed the basis for their religious education as well as their social and political awareness.

Intellectual Needs

In order to satisfy their intellectual needs, the Prophet designated a special day for this group of women in which he used to teach them the principles of Islam and other related issues. This raised the self awareness of Muslim women and increased their understanding of their responsibility in society, leading, consequently, to greater public participation; and third, the broad political participation of women which was conditioned by their abilities and their degree of self-awareness was practised in a favourable social setting that gave it its stimulus and momentum. This supportive environment was the result of determined efforts, by the Prophet, to eradicate any practices and habits that would hinder or resist the progress towards wider political engagement of women in society.

Hence, he pushed ahead the process of social change and ensured that the community would accept and regard women's activity in the political sphere as an asset and a valuable contribution to a healthy society. This was fulfilled: firstly, through the Quranic injunctions and Hadith regulations, both of which encourage women to be energetic and creative, while at the same time, exhort men to help them fulfil their roles as active and equal members of the community; secondly, the example set by the Prophet in dealing with his family in particular and the companions (women) in general. He constantly encouraged them to take part in all aspects of life: social, political, economic and religious. This support found its echo when women, especially the Ansari women, demonstrated their interest and eagerness to participate in all activities, thus, setting a role model for other women to follow. In doing so, they pioneered the way for radical social change that allowed more space and greater mobility for women in society.

Despite the clear-cut Quranic and Hadith instructions encouraging women to play an effective role in public life (alongside their private one), the general tendency, among Muslims, has been one which opposes women's involvement in politics. Most scholars prefer an interpretation that enjoins women to stay at home and not to 'interfere' in public life. They argue that women are incapable of handling public affairs; therefore, it is better for them to perform the work they are good at that is, to be mothers and wives only. According to them, women never participated in the politics of the Muslims throughout their history. And, it is argued that despite the fact that Islam gave women rights equal to those of men, Islam deems it necessary that women should stay at home and concentrate on their domestic affairs, in the interest both of women themselves and of society as a whole.

The scholars then respond by insisting that those were mere individual cases which cannot be cited to legitimise the participation of women in political affairs' Anyone who thinks to the contrary is mistaken, they say, and does not comprehend history. As for Aishah who played a prominent role in politics, they argue that although she fought a famous battle, in the end she regretted her act (for she should not have left her home and taken part in that battle) and asked for forgiveness.

Consequently, it cannot be claimed that her act is a proof for the participation of Muslim women in politics, for it was an individual act which proved to be a complete failure. It is important to stress that those who oppose women's involvement in politics differ among themselves regarding the level or degree of women's exercise of power. For example, while some are prepared to tolerate the idea that women can have limited access to politics (such as the right to vote and nominate persons for certain public offices), others deny them any political rights. However, they all agree that women cannot be allowed to hold ministerial positions or become prime minister or president of a state. They base their prohibition on the following:

Quran: They maintain that Chapter 4, verse 34 of the Quran which reads thus: 'Men have authority over women because Allah has made the one superior to the other, and because they spend their wealth to maintain them', has virtually closed the door to women's advancement to higher positions. For them, this verse has sanctioned men's authority over women and made the domain of politics or power an exclusively male preserve. This is because men have strong leadership characteristics which entitle them to rule over women who tend to be weak and more emotional. According to them, the verse is clear in entrusting men (not women) with the Qiwama or guardianship. It follows that since men are the caretakers (Qawwamun) of women, it is not possible for them to hold positions of authority which would allow them to exercise power over men.

Moreover, they argue that even if they have to accept the view which states that this verse deals specifically with family affairs and cannot be generalised to include male-female relations in public life, the proof (hujja) still stands: women cannot rule over men. For if they are unqualified to manage their family undertakings, by the same token, they are unfit to handle public matters. However, we are of the strong opinion that this verse (4: 34) deals exclusively with family affairs and has nothing to do with the relationships between men and women in public life. This is because the verse is mentioned solely within the context of married life, in which one party—the husband is charged with the responsibility of being the head and caretaker of the family, bearing in mind that relieving the wife from such a responsibility is by no means an indication of her inability to do the job properly; on the contrary, she can easily replace him if he is absent (for whatever reason) or unfit to fulfil his duty. Therefore, it is not right to generalise the ruling of this verse (which handles only marital matters) to encompass the relationships between men and women in society, so as to deny women the opportunity to hold public offices.

Hadith: Two Hadiths are of particular importance in this issue. The Prophet is reported to have said 'O women! Give alms, as I have seen that the majority of the dwellers of Hell-fire were you (women). They asked, is it so, O Allah's Messenger? He replied, you curse frequently and are ungrateful to your husbands. I have not seen anyone more deficient in intelligence and religion than you. A cautious, sensible man could be led astray by some of you. The women asked, O Allah's Messenger! What is deficient in our intelligence and religion? He said, is not the evidence of two women equal to the witness of one man? They replied in the affirmative. He said, this is the deficiency in her intelligence. Isn't it true that a woman can neither pray nor fast during her menses? The women replied in the affirmative. He said, this is the deficiency in her religion. This Hadith is used, by the opponents of women's rights in politics, to prove their point in saying that women cannot be trusted with handling public matters.

They stress that the above Hadith makes it clear that women cannot have power over men because they are spiritually as well as cognitively deficient. They thus associate deficiency with womanhood and insist that women, by nature, are less prepared (rationally and emotionally) than men to cope with the pressure of public life. Therefore, God, according to them, has relieved them from certain duties (such as attending Jumah prayers and participating in Jihad) which are compulsory for men. However, there are those who see the Hadith differently: some do not accept it and consider it as fabricated or at best a weak Hadith, which ought to be abandoned because weak Hadiths usually do not carry any legal effects; others acknowledge the Hadith as authentic, but stress that it has been grossly misinterpreted.

They argue that the deficiency mentioned in the Hadith does not refer to natural but rather specific deficiency. In other words, there are two forms of deficiencies: (a) natural or innate deficiency (naqs fitri), a form of natural defect which hampers the human intellect—at various levels, the extreme one being madness. This does not include women categorically because they are regarded (from the Quranic viewpoint) as accountable and responsible human beings capable of fulfilling their duties; (b) specific deficiency (naqs naw'i) of two types: (i) casual defect (aradi), which can temporarily upset the natural disposition of a person, especially during menstruation and pregnancy. This form of frailty does not weaken or impair women's natural abilities; (ii) incidental defect of long-term effects which results usually from living in special conditions (such as confinement to four walls, constant engagement in pregnancy and childbirth, etc.) that are not conducive to contacts and interactions with outside world. This, in time, lessens women's social, political and economic awareness of their surroundings and reduces them to their private circle-of ladies, with devastating consequences on their potential for playing an active role in public life. It must be stressed, however, that this form of deficiency can be remedied by altering the circumstances that lead to its existence.

Testimony in Law

As for the link made in the Hadith between women's intellectual deficiency and their testimony in law, we might point out that the connection occurs only in one case, namely, the evidence which requires the testimony of one man and two women. This testimony is mentioned in the Quran in Chapter 2, verse 282, which deals solely with financial matters. And this is the only testimony in which the issue of gender is a dominant factor; in other testimonies the Quran stipulates justice rather than gender.

Therefore, it is not right to use this verse in order to accuse women of being intellectually deficient. For it is no more than a guiding verse aiming at promoting justice when dealing with complicated financial issues. In other words, the verse is meant to give advice that if, under certain circumstances, men are not available to testify, the alternative is to accept the testimony of two women (who could be ordinary members of the public, having little or no experience with financial matters, or who could be undergoing temporary disturbances resulting from menstruation or postnatal conditions) as being equal to that of man; the aim here being to ensure that precautionary measures are in place when dealing with an area where women are less likely to be experts.

The deficiency referred to in the Hadith, therefore, is not natural but rather contingent or casual and does not necessarily contradict the fact that there are women who possess high qualities and enjoy special capacities in comparison with ordinary men and women. Indeed, in some cases there are those who are wiser, well-advised, and more intelligent than men. The second Hadith which is reported in Bukhari and reads as thus: Abu Bakra said 'when Allah's Messenger was informed that the Persians had crowned the daughter of Kisra (Khosrau) as their ruler, he said, such people as ruled by a lady will never be successful. This Hadith has been widely cited to block' any attempts to give women the opportunity to wield power in society.

The opponents argue that the Prophet in this Hadith advises Muslims not to follow in the footsteps of the Persians who appointed a woman as their leader and consequently led them to a disastrous end. For them, the Hadith contains a clear-cut warning (for Muslims) to be vigilant and not to allow women to overstep the line and enter into politics; otherwise, their fate would be the same as that of Persia before Islam: defeat and humiliation. However, one has to disagree with this view for two reasons: first, the Hadith deals mainly with a specific case, ' namely, the situation of Persia at the time of the Prophet. Indeed, it is no more than a prophesy (bishara) in which the Prophet predicted the fate of the Persian empire. As such, it has no legal ruling and therefore it cannot be generalised to include all women at all times; second, if the Hadith is to be accepted as general, it would surely contradict the Quran, and this cannot happen.

The Quran, in Chapter 27, speaks highly of the Queen of Sheba, Bilqis, who ruled over her people with wisdom and insight and led them to success and prosperity: 'I found a woman reigning over the people. She is possessed of every virtue and has a splendid throne'. The only fault found with her, was not her position and authority as a woman, but her false faith 'she and her subjects worship the sun instead of Allah'. Later, the wise woman met Solomon, admitted her sin (for not worshipping God) and, along with her people, accepted Islam: 'Lord', she said, 'I have wronged my own soul. Now I submit with Sulayman to Allah, Lord of the creation'. From the above, we can deduce that the Hadith is not general, but rather specific and is related to the episode of the people of Persia.

The opponents point out that there is no precedent in early Islam which indicates that women were appointed to high positions, despite the fact that there were ample opportunities for such appointments. Neither the Prophet nor any of his companions invited women to take part in the administration of the state. Moreover, women themselves, and although there were many who excelled men in their abilities, did not show any interest in holding public office. In response, one can mention the example of the second Caliph Umar, who appointed a woman (al-Shafa') as superintendent in a market in Medina. This position was, at the time, more of a political than a business office, as the market was not only a centre for trading but also a focal point for political activities.

The fact that few women were at the top of the administration does not reflect badly on the abilities of women to run public offices.

Moreover, one has to bear in mind the nature of the social setting prevailing at the time, in which pre-Islamic customs were still competing and resisting any changes brought about by Islam. So, although the social environment was favourable (due to the changes brought about by Islam) and allowed women greater mobility in society; yet it was still less willing and less amenable to the idea of entrusting women with governmental positions.

Social practices (Adat) should not be allowed to take precedence over Divine instructions. Most importantly, they should not be used as a pretext to continue to neglect or even (in some cases) abandon the Islamic principles, which oblige women to have their shares in public life and be active and effective in society. For social customs are subject to change; they change with time and place, while Divine principles are meant for all times and all places. As such, the emphasis should be on the Divine tenets not social customs.

The Consensus

The Consensus (ijma) that there are those who stress regarding an agreement among scholars on the so-called 'unsuitability' of women to hold public office. However, invoking the issue of consensus is no more than a fallacy since there is hardly any unity among them on this subject. For example, the position of Judge is regarded by some to be suitable for men only. Abu Hanifa, however, disagrees and allows a woman to be appointed as Judge and gives her the right to deal with all matters except those under the penal code. Ibn Jarir al-Tabari, on the other hand, qualifies a woman for the post of judge without any restrictions. This renders the whole issue of the existing consensus among scholars suspicious and, in fact, a mere sham. Moreover, it is essential to bear in mind whether the ijma (on a particular question, and, in this case, the issue of women) takes into consideration the overall interest of the community. For if it runs counter to the social interest, then there is no use in accepting it in the first place.

The opponents argue that permitting women to occupy public positions would be detrimental to both society as well as family.

According to them, top jobs require courage, wisdom and strength, and women, in general, lack these characteristics; they are feeble and can be easily misled. As such, they cannot be trusted with executive roles, especially leadership roles. For instance, a president or a ruler in an Islamic state needs to perform important and not merely ceremonial duties such as: conducting war, signing peace treaties, defending the country, delivering sermons, and leading people in prayers-all of which women cannot cope with, because of their fragilities and emotional vulnerabilities.

Furthermore, they state that woman's advancement to executive power goes against her social function: that is to be a good wife and mother. They argue that if she is to assume an executive role—which is a full-time commitment—this would inevitably force her to neglect her household duties, with devastating consequences on the stability of the family in society. They point out that even if there are some women who can handle both roles, they are, in reality, exceptions; therefore, it is unwise to set up and accept rules on rare cases. It must be stressed, however, that those who think that female leadership would damage state-interest base their view on the assumption that women are, by nature, incapable of coping with public responsibilities. But this is not the case as we explained earlier; women, like men, are qualified to run state affairs.

The opponents view public positions, especially state leadership as a one-person responsibility, thus neglecting the shura principle, which makes state affairs a collective responsibility. Moreover, they regard the state system as more or less similar to that of the Medinan or tribal system with limited scope and structure, hence, confining the Islamic concept of state within a particular historical context. In doing so, they contradict the universal vision of the Islamic state. As for the welfare of the family, the assumption is that only those women whose domestic responsibilities permit them to engage in public duties should do so. Having said that, domestic responsibility should not be taken as pretext (by both men and women) to discourage or prevent women, especially able ones, from involvement in public activities.